OCS Study
MMS 2002-054

Coastal Marine Institute

Socioeconomic Baseline Study for the Gulf of Mexico

Final Report: Description of the Dataset, 1930-1990

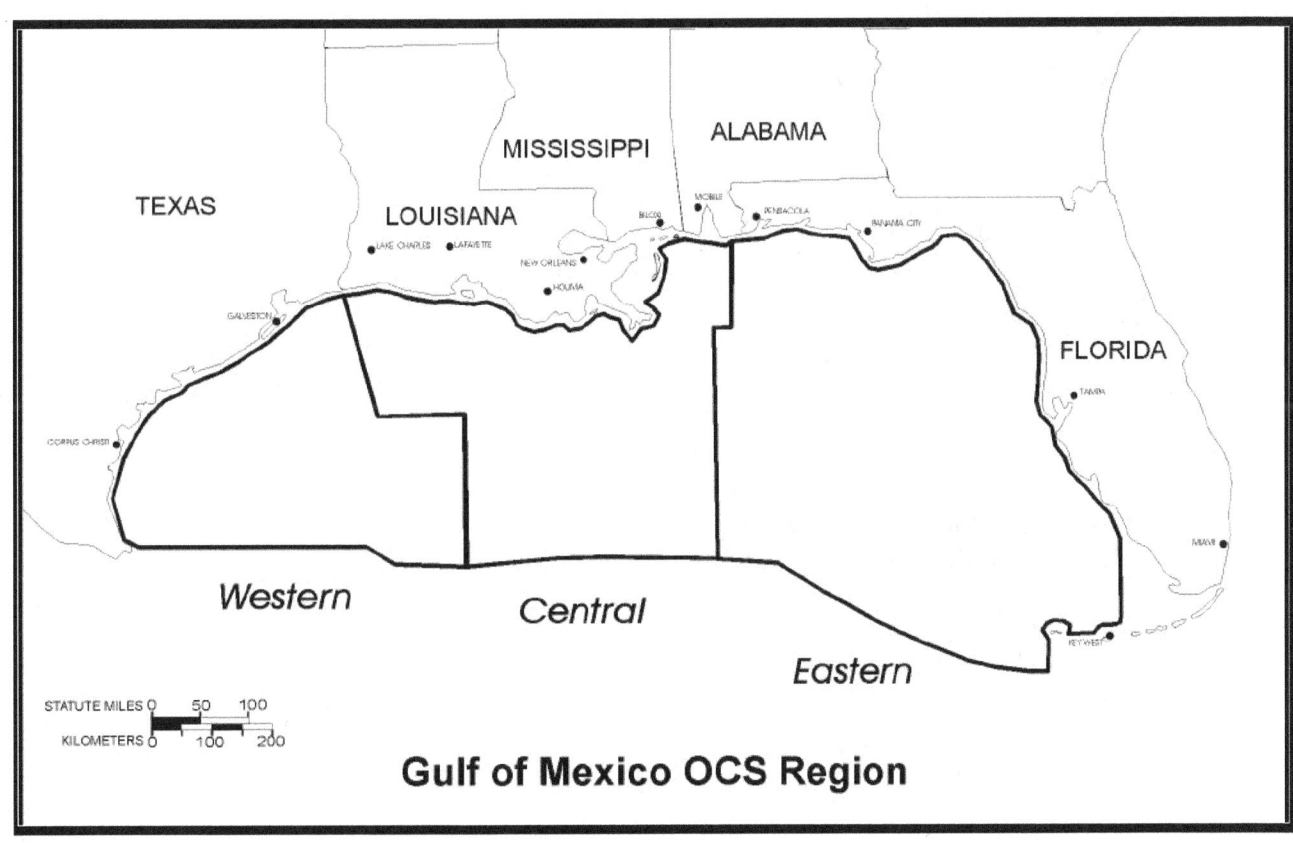

TEXAS

MISSISSIPPI

ALABAMA

LOUISIANA

MOBILE

PENSACOLA

PANAMA CITY

BILOXI

LAKE CHARLES

LAFAYETTE

NEW ORLEANS

HOUMA

FLORIDA

GALVESTON

TAMPA

CORPUS CHRISTI

Western

Central

MIAMI

Eastern

KEY WEST

STATUTE MILES 0   50   100

KILOMETERS 0   100   200

Gulf of Mexico OCS Region

U.S. Department of the Interior
Minerals Management Service
Gulf of Mexico OCS Region

Cooperative Agreement
Coastal Marine Institute
Louisiana State University

OCS Study
MMS 2002-054

Coastal Marine Institute

Socioeconomic Baseline Study for the Gulf of Mexico

Final Report: Description of the Dataset, 1930-1990

Authors

Natsumi Aratame
Joachim Singelmann

September 2002

Prepared under MMS Contract
14-35-0001-30660-19913
by
Louisiana State University
Departments of Sociology and Rural Sociology
Baton Rouge, Louisiana 70803

Published by

U.S. Department of the Interior
Minerals Management Service
Gulf of Mexico OCS Region

Cooperative Agreement
Coastal Marine Institute
Louisiana State University

DISCLAIMER

This research was supported by the Minerals Management Service (MMS) under MMS Cooperative Agreement No. 14-35-0001-30660. This report has been technically reviewed by MMS and approved for publication. Approval does not signify that the contents necessarily reflect the views and policies of the Service, nor does mention of trade names or commercial products constitute endorsement or recommendation for use. It is, however, exempt from review and compliance with MMS editorial standards.

REPORT AVAILABILITY

Extra copies of the report may be obtained from the Public Information Office (Mail Stop 5034) at the following address:

U.S. Department of the Interior
Minerals Management Service
Gulf of Mexico OCS Region
Attention: Public Information Office (MS 5034)
1201 Elmwood Park Boulevard
New Orleans, Louisiana 70123-2394
Telephone Number: 1-504-736-2519
                       1-800-200-GULF

CITATION

Suggested citation:

Aratame, N. and J. Singelmann. 2002. Socioeconomic Baseline Study for the Gulf of Mexico. Final Report: A Description of the Dataset, 1930-1990. U.S. Dept. of the Interior, Minerals Management Service, Gulf of Mexico OCS Region, New Orleans, LA. OCS Study MMS 2002-054. 146 pp.

ABSTRACT

This database is constructed as part of "A Socioeconomic Baseline Study for the Gulf of Mexico (Phase I)." It contains over 3,000 variables that include information about population, employment, income, establishments, and government finance for counties (or parishes) in Alabama, Florida, Louisiana, Mississippi, and Texas for the period 1930-90. The data assembled include extracts from machine readable datasets as well as data entered manually. Information on oil/gas dependency is also added based on an industry-occupation matrix specially obtained from the U.S. Bureau of the Census.

TABLE OF CONTENTS

1. OVERVIEW

1.1. The Purpose of the Database

Despite the long history of offshore oil and gas activities in the Gulf of Mexico (GOM) region, little information exists on the socioeconomic impact of offshore drilling in the GOM region in general, and its coastal areas in particular. The purpose of this database, therefore, is to provide a consolidated source of information for the five states in the GOM region (Alabama, Florida, Louisiana, Mississippi, and Texas), which will enable the researchers to

1.   identify counties/parishes whose employment structures were strongly affected by oil/natural gas extraction activities,

2.   examine how this impact has changed over the period 1930-90,

3.   analyze the socio-economic impact of oil/natural gas extraction for the period 1930-90.

This database has a number of unique features as well as potential pitfalls, because the information is extracted from various datasets collected under different survey designs. In the following, the characteristics of the database are briefly described. More detailed descriptions and explanations will be provided in Sections 3 and 4.

1.2. Universe Description

The universe varies depending on the data sources. For example, the universe of demographic information obtained from the decennial censuses is either the entire population or every housing unit. The universe of data on government finance and employment is all governmental units including states, counties, municipalities, townships, special districts and school districts. The universe of the establishment data is all establishments.

The accuracy of data depends on the size of sample, the method of sampling as well as the method of data collection, such as field interview or mail canvass. For example, the data on government finance and employment and on establishment are based on comprehensive surveys. Therefore, they are not subject to sampling errors. However, the government censuses are generally based on mail canvass, which gives rise to reporting errors.

The demographic data, in comparison, may be based on either the 100% count or a sample of a relevant universe. The demographic data based on a sample are subject to sampling errors, the magnitude of which depends on the size and method of selecting a sample, which varies from one census year to the next.

More information on the definition of sample and survey design of each survey from which data are extracted is provided later (Section 3). Regarding the accuracy of the data, please consult the reference materials mentioned below (Section 2.7.)

1.3. Organization of the Database

1.3.1. Subject Matter

The data in this dataset are classified and organized in terms of the following modules: demography (except vital statistics), vital statistics, civilian employment, establishments, income and poverty status, and government finance and employment. For more detail on each module, refer to the Variable Names and Type (Section 1.3.2), Guide to Subject Category (Section 3.) a nd Data Dictionary (Section 4.)

The demographic data include information on age, sex, marital status, race, educational attainment, place of birth, and migration experience. Many of these data are cross-tabulated by race and sex. The data on vital statistics (live birth, deaths, marriage, and divorce) are collected separately to supplement the demographic data. The data on civilian employment include information on labor force status, class of worker, industry and occupation. These data are also cross-tabulated by race and sex whenever data are available. The employment information on mining for 1940-70, oil/natural gas for 1980-90, and the location quotient for employment in the mining industry for 1940-90 are also added to facilitate the analysis on oil dependency.

The data on government revenue include the sources of revenue (inter-governmental and own sources). Expenditure data are collected in terms of major functions such as education, highways, and public welfare that comprise the direct general expenditure. The data on debt and assets are added whenever available. The government employment data include "full-time employment equivalent" workers by major function. The data on establishment include the number, size and employment for manufacturing, retail, wholesale, service establishments and farms. Lastly, the income data include personal and family (household) income as well as poverty status.

1.3.2. Variable Names and Types

In general, variable names are defined in terms of subject prefixes, followed by two digit numbers showing the reference year, and the sequential number of the variable in a particular reference year. The subject prefixes used in this dataset are,

D	Demography
EM	Civilian employment
ES	Establishments
GF	Government finance
GE	Government employment
IN	Income (from the decennial censuses)
PIN	Personal income (from the Bureau of Economic Analysis estimates)
VS	Vital statistics.

E.g.   D400081   Demographic information for 1940, #81 in that year

GF87035   Government finance data for 1987, #35 in that year

The variable names for vital statistics and establishment statistics are organized differently. For vital statistics, the variable names consist of a prefix showing the subject category (digit 1-2), table number (digit 3-5), and reference year (last two digits).

E.g.   VS00148   Vital statistics table 1 (live birth) for 1948

VS00150   Vital statistics table 1 (live birth) for 1950

For establishment statistics, the variable names consist of subject category (digit 1-2), table number (digit 3-4), and reference year (remaining digits).

ES0182 Establishment statistics, table 1 (the number of manufacturing establishments) for 1982.

ES0187 Establishment statistics, table 1 (the number of manufacturing establishments) for 1987.

1.3.3. Data Files

This dataset is available in the following formats, which are all included on the CD-ROM:

ASCII raw data file	1 file
SAS/Windows system file	1 file
SAS transport file	2 file
SAS program to read ASCII data	1 file
SAS program to read SAS transport file	1 file
SPSS/Windows system file	1 file
SPSS export file	1 file
SPSS program to read ASCII data	1 file
SPSS program to read SAS transport file	1 file
Lotus 123 (.wk1) files	27 files

The most original datasets on the CD-ROM are the SAS/Windows and SAS/transport files (lpdcsas.ssd and lpdcsas.exp). All other files are derived from these two files including the ASCII dataset.

1.4. Geographic Coverage

All data in this dataset are presented by county (or parish in Louisiana) in the five GOM states. The values of most variables are simply the sum of <u>single</u> sampling units, such as person, household, establishment, etc. For government finance and employment data, however, they are the summation of all financial (or employment) data of all local governments (such as county government, school, fire, police districts) within the geographic boundary of respective county area (or parish).

All counties and states are assigned a unique geographic identification code based on the Federal Information Processing System (FIPS) (See Appendix B).

1.5. Reference Periods

The exact reference periods covered vary from subject to subject. While every effort was made to collect data for the period between 1930 and 1990, the data for earlier periods are either not available or only partially available. For example, while demographic and employment data are generally available from decennial censuses conducted every 10 years, government finance and employment data include only those from the 1957, 1962, 1972, 1977, 1982, and 1987 Census of Government. Data on vital statistics, establishments and personal income are available for some other years.

1.6. Data Suppression

1.6.1. 1970 Census

Variables taken from the 1970 Census may include suppression flags. According to the 1970 Census User's Guide, there are two types of suppression represented by -1 and -2, respectively. For type one (-1) suppression, both total and breakdown of the relevant table are suppressed, represented by a blank (or a single dot in SAS dataset).

E.g.   Aggregate income of population 14 Years old and over by sex:

var 1   var 2   var 3

Total pop   males   females

-1   .   .

Minus one above indicates the presence of suppression that applies to total population as well as males and females.

With type two (-2) suppression, the suppression code will appear in the first item, a total count of the universe is supposed to appear in the second item, and all further items will be blank (or represented by a single dot in SAS dataset).

E.g.   Counts of persons by age:

var 1   var 2   var 3   var 4

total pop   psns 0-1   psns 1-5   psns 5-9

-2   25   .   .

However, the inspection of the original data tape (Summary Tape File 4C) from which the 1970 data were extracted revealed that the total frequency in the second item is also not suppressed. For that reason, the present dataset cannot distinguish between type 1 and type 2 suppression.

Unlike the 1980 and 1990 Censuses, there is no explanation in the 1970 Census documentation as to the criteria for the decision to apply one of these types of suppression to a given table, strata, or cell. Thus, with the suppression information available, all we know for the 1970 Census is that more than zero frequency exists, presumably a small one, though the exact quantity cannot be determined. It is recommended that negative values for 1970 Census variables be replaced with zero.

The investigation by another researcher suggests that there was very little suppression at the county (parish) level other than on the ethnicity variable. For more details, see the documentation to the "Census of Population and Housing, 1970 United States: Extract Data" by Terry K. Adams (ICPSR 9694).[1]

1.6.2. 1980 Census

The data suppression is represented by zero. Thus, unlike the 1970 Census, it cannot be determined if zero is due to suppression or due to zero frequency. The data tables that include breakdowns such as frequency by sex, race and age groups are often subject to suppression.

The following variables are never suppressed: total persons (D80001), total white persons (D80011), total black persons (D80012) and total hispanic origin persons (D80013). Totals for white, black, hispanic persons are provided separately (D80016, D8019, D80022, D80025), which are derived by summing the components categories given by age and sex. These totals are subject to suppression that applies to component categories. The comparison of two kinds of totals (totals with and without suppression) will reveal the presence and extent of suppression in this census year.

1.6.3. 1990 Census

The suppression is more undetectable in the 1990 Census. Since there are no flags as in the 1970 Census or discrepancies as in the 1980 Census between the totals of some variables given as a separate

---

[1]The ICPSR (Inter-university Consortium for Politcal and Social Research) located at the University of Michigan is a central repository for machine-readable social science data. The ICPSR number identifies the dataset in their archive. The information on data availability may be obtained from http://www.icpsr.umich.edu.

variable and the corresponding totals derived by summing the component categories such as age breakdowns, there is no way to know the presence of suppression. Consequently, only one set of totals are given for this census year.

In general, the 1990 Census underwent a confidentiality edit in the following manner. First, a small subset of individual households was selected and the data items on these households were blanked. Responses to those data items were then imputed using the same imputation procedures that were used for nonresponse. A large subset of households is selected for the confidentiality edit for small areas to provide greater protection for these areas (for more information, see the 1990 Census Appendix C "Accuracy of the Data").

The following variables taken from Co-Stata 4 and USA Counties 1994 include character strings for numeric variables that indicate missing values for various reasons:

ES2178

ES2182

ES2187

ES2278

ES2282

ES2287

ES2482

ES2487

VS01082

VS01182

VS01270

VS01278

VS01279

VS01280

VS01282

VS01284

VS01370

VS01378

VS01379

VS01380

VS01382

VS01384

The meaning of the missing value codes are:

NA(N)	Not available
D	Suppressed to avoid disclosure of confidential information
X	Not applicable
S	Suppressed; does not meet publication standards
Z	Value greater than zero but less than half unit of measure shown.

1.6.4. Missing Values and Software

In general, all missing values in the ASCII dataset are replaced with blanks. However, partly because the data are extracted from various data sources with different coding schemes for representing missing values, some numeric fields may contain character strings as described above.

SAS and SPSS, when encountering such data, convert them into the system-missing value and exclude them from subsequent statistical computation unless told otherwise explicitly. However, whereas SAS converts all such data into the system-missing values, SPSS by default issues up to 80 warnings and stops processing further. For SPSS to continue to read all data (because there are more than 80 such cases), include the following statement at the top of the data definition program:

set mxwarnings = 500.

This statement is not necessary when reading the SPSS export file or system file.

However, if one wants to retain missing value codes rather than automatically convert them into the system-missing value, one must define the variable as character rather than as numeric. This is done in the following manners:

SAS: D30001 $ 33-40

SPSS: D30001 33-40 (A).

The dollar ($) sign in SAS and (A) in SPSS indicate that the variable is a character variable, rather than numeric variable.

In the Loutus 123 version of this dataset, every missing value is replaced with blank cells.

1.7. Reference Materials

The major data sources utilized for building this dataset include the following:

Data on population, civilian employment and income:

1930-1960

- Historical demographic, economic and social data. The United States, 1790-1970 (ICPSR 0003)
- Census of Population 1960: General Social and Economic Characteristics (Bureau of the Census)

1970

- Census of Population and Housing 1970: Summary Statistics File 4C (ICPSR 8107)

1980

- Census of Population and Housing 1980: Summary Tape File 3C (ICPSR 80380)

1990

- Census of Population and Housing 1990: Summary Tape File 3 (ICPSR 6054)

In addition, the following datasets were consulted:

County and City Data Book Consolidated File (ICPSR 7736)

County Statistics File (Co-Stat 4) (ICPSR 9806)

USA Counties 1994 (Bureau of the Census, CD94-CTY02)

Data on government employment:

Census of Government 1962, 1972, 1977, 1982, 1988 (ICPSR 0017, 0069, 8117, 8395, 6069)

Data on government finance:

Census of Government 1962, 1972, 1977, 1982, 1988 (ICPSR 0017, 0069, 8118, 8394, 9484)

Data on establishment:

County and City Data Book Consolidated File (ICPSR 7736)

County Statistics File (Co-Stat 4) (ICPSR 9806)

USA Counties 1994 (Bureau of the Census, CD94-CTY02)

County Business Patterns 1980 and 1990 (ICPSR 8142, 6030)

2. GUIDE TO MAJOR SUBJECT CATEGORIES

The following chart illustrates the variables included in the dataset together with their availability by year. The purpose of this chart is to give users a quick overview regarding the range of information available from this dataset. It differs from the "real" dataset (see Data Dictionary in detail) in the following ways:

1. Many variables, although not shown explicitly in this chart, may be available by race and sex.

2. Some variables are available for more detailed categories than presented in the chart. For example, the educational attainment variables for 1940 are available for grades 1-4, grades 5-6 and grades 7-8 separately. However, to make it more comparable with other years which do not have any breakdown (for instance, the 1990 Census), and to make viewing easier, the availability information is presented just in terms of grades 1-8 combined.

It is important to recognize that data availability across several periods does not guarantee comparability because of possible changes in the definition of variables. Detailed information on the definition of variables is provided in Section 4.

3. DEFINITIONS AND EXPLANATION OF SELECTED TERMS

Terms presented in this section are primarily compiled from the latest censuses, supplemented by earlier censuses and surveys listed in Section 2.7. Each section below consists of two parts: the description of data sources wherever appropriate and a brief definition/explanation of selected terms relevant to this dataset.

3.1. Census Geography

3.1.1. Government Units and Types of Governments

3.1.1.1. Government Units

A government is an organized entity whose governmental character is evidenced by popular election of the officials or their appointment by public officials, a high degree of public accountability, and the power to raise revenue to provide authorized services. In addition, a governmental unit must have sufficient discretion in the management of its own affairs to distinguish it from the administrative structure of any other governmental unit.

3.1.1.2. Local Governments

The Census Bureau classifies local governments by five major types as described below: county (or parish in Louisiana), municipality which includes cities, towns and villages, township, school system and special district.

3.1.1.3. County Area

Geographic areas corresponding to the boundaries of county or county-type areas. The "county area" statistics are derived from the aggregation of all local governments (county, municipal, township, school district, and special district) in these county or county-type geographic areas.

3.1.2. Urban, Rural, Extended City, and Urbanized Area

3.1.2.1. Urban and Rural

The Census Bureau defines "urban" for the 1990 Census as comprising all territory, population, and housing units in urbanized areas and in places of 2,500 or more persons outside urbanized areas. More specifically, "urban" consists of territory, persons, and housing units in:

1.   Places of 2,500 or more persons incorporated as cities, villages, boroughs (except in Alaska and New York), and towns (except in the six New England States, New York, and Wisconsin), but excluding the rural portions of "extended cities (see below)."

2.   Census designated places of 2,500 or more persons.

3.   Other territory, incorporated or unincorporated, included in urbanized areas.

Territory, population, and housing units not classified as urban constitute "rural." In this dataset (which is based on the sample data), rural population and housing units are subdivided into "rural farm" and "rural nonfarm." "Rural farm" comprises all rural households and housing units on farms (places from which $1,000 or more of agricultural products were sold in 1989); "rural nonfarm" comprises the remaining rural.

The urban and rural classification cuts across the other hierarchies; for example, there is generally both urban and rural territory within both metropolitan and nonmetropolitan areas.

In censuses prior to 1950, "urban" comprised all territory, persons, and housing units in incorporated places of 2,500 or more persons, and in areas (usually minor civil divisions) classified as urban under special rules relating to population size and density. This definition of urban excluded many large, densely settled areas merely because they were not incorporated. Prior to the 1950 Census, the Census Bureau attempted to avoid some of the more obvious omissions by classifying selected areas as "urban under special rules." Even with these rules, however, many large, closely built-up areas were excluded from the urban category.

To improve its measure of urban territory, population, and housing units, the Census Bureau adopted the concept of urbanized area and delineated boundaries for unincorporated places (now, census designated places) for the 1950 Census. Urban was defined as territory, persons, and housing units in urbanized areas and, outside urbanized areas, in all places, incorporated or unincorporated, that had 2,500 or more persons. With minor changes, the 1950 census definition of urban has continued essentially unchanged.

The data for the 1960 urban and rural-farm population were taken from the City and County Data Book. Unlike other years, the figures were provided in percentage with one decimal place. To maintain consistency with other census years, the urban-rural population were derived by multiplying the total population by these percentages. Consequently, the urban-rural population for this year in this dataset, albeit with small margin of errors, may not agree with the published statistics.

Documentation of the urbanized area and extended city criteria is available from the Chief, Geography Division, U.S. Bureau of the Census, Washington, DC 20233.

3.1.2.2. Extended City

Since the 1960 Census, there has been a trend in some States toward the extension of city boundaries to include territory that is essentially rural in character. The classification of all the population and living quarters of such places as urban would include in the urban designation territory, persons, and housing units whose environment is primarily rural. For the 1970, 1980, and 1990 censuses, the Census Bureau identified as rural such territory and its population and housing units for each extended city whose closely settled area was located in an urbanized area. For the 1990 Census, this classification also has been applied to certain places outside urbanized areas.

3.1.2.3. Urbanized Areas (UA)

The Census Bureau delineates urbanized areas (UA's) to provide a better separation of urban and rural territory, population, and housing in the vicinity of large places. A UA comprises one or more places ("central place") and the adjacent densely settled surrounding territory ("urban fringe") that together have a minimum of 50,000 persons. The urban fringe generally consists of contiguous territory having a density of at least 1,000 persons per square mile. The urban fringe also includes outlying territory of such density if it was connected to the core of the contiguous area by road and is within 1 1/2 road miles of that core, or within 5 road miles of the core but separated by water or other undevelopable territory. Other territory with a population density of fewer than 1,000 people per square mile is included in the urban fringe if it eliminates an enclave or closes an indentation in the boundary of the urbanized area.

The population density is determined by (1) outside of a place, one or more contiguous census blocks with a population density of at least 1,000 persons per square mile or (2) inclusion of a place containing census blocks that have at least 50 percent of the population of the place and a density of at least 1,000 persons per square mile. The complete criteria are available from the Chief, Geography Division, U.S. Bureau of the Census, Washington, DC 20233.

3.2. Population Characteristics

3.2.1. Data Sources

3.2.1.1. Decennial Censuses

Most population (and employment) statistics for the period 1930-1990 are based on results from Censuses of Population and Housing conducted by the Bureau of the Census as of April 1 in each of those years. Data from the decennial censuses are based on tabulations of 100-percent, or complete, counts (i.e., information obtained for all persons and housing units) and sample estimates (i.e., additional information asked of a sample of persons). The sampling rates and sampling methods are different in each census year. Consequently, the accuracy of data varies from table to table depending on the sampling rates and sampling methods. For more detail on accuracy, please refer to the technical note in Census publications in each census year.

3.2.1.2. Vital Statistics

The registration of births, deaths, fetal deaths, and other vital events in the United States is primarily a state and local function. The civil laws of every state provide for a continuous and permanent birth- and death-registration system. Through the National Vital Statistics System, the National Center for Health Statistics (NCHS) collects and publishes data on births and deaths for the country as a whole. The Division of Vital Statistics at NCHS obtains information on births and deaths from the registration offices of all States, New York City, and the District of Columbia.

In the United States today, practically all births and deaths are registered. The most recent test of the completeness of birth registration, conducted on a sample of births from 1964 to 1968, showed that 99.3 percent of all births in the United States during that period were registered.

State requirements for reporting fetal deaths vary. Most states require reporting of fetal deaths of gestations of 20 weeks or more. There is substantial evidence that not all fetal deaths for which reporting is required are indeed reported.

Since most data items on demography including vital statistics, employment, and establishments in this dataset come from the Census of Population and Housing, the terminologies related to them will be described together below. In general, the definitions adapted in the 1990 Census will be described first, followed by a comparison with those of earlier censuses.

3.2.2. Selected Terms

3.2.2.1. Age

The data on age for the 1990 Census are based on the age of the person in complete years as of April 1, 1990. However, when the age response was unacceptable or unavailable, a person's age was derived from an acceptable year-of-birth response.

Age data have been collected in every census. In each census since 1940, the age of a person was assigned when it was not reported. In censuses before 1940, with the exception of 1880, persons of unknown age were shown as a separate category. Since 1960, assignment of unknown age has been performed by a general procedure described as "imputation." The specific procedures for imputing age have been different in each census.

Median age. This measure divides the age distribution into two equal parts: one-half of the cases falling below the median value and one-half above that value. Generally, median age is computed on the basis of more detailed age intervals than are shown in this dataset; thus, a median based on a less detailed distribution (generally 5-year interval in this dataset) may differ slightly from a corresponding median for the same population based on a more detailed distribution.

3.2.2.2. Birth

Birth represents the number of births during the year. The data are by place of residence and excludes events occurring to nonresidents of the United States. Birth rates represent the number of births per

1,000 resident population enumerated as of April 1 for decennial census years and estimated as of July 1 for other years.

3.2.2.3. Citizenship

The data on citizenship for the 1990 Census were asked of a sample of persons. Citizens are persons who indicated that they were native-born, or foreign-born persons who indicated that they have become naturalized. (For more information on native and foreign born, see the discussion under "Place of Birth.") There are four categories of citizenship: (1) born in the United States, (2) born in Puerto Rico, Guam, the Virgin Islands of the United States, or the Commonwealth of the Northern Mariana Islands, (3) born abroad of American parents, and (4) citizen by naturalization.

Similar questions on citizenship were asked in the censuses of 1820, 1830, 1870, 1890 through 1950, 1970, and 1980. The 1980 question was asked of a sample of the foreign-born population. In 1990, both native and foreign-born persons who received the long-form questionnaire were asked to respond to the citizenship question.

3.2.2.4. Death

Death represents the number of deaths during the year. The data are by place of residence and exclude events occurring to nonresidents of the United States. Death rates represent the number of deaths per 1,000 resident population enumerated as of April 1 for decennial census years and estimated as of July 1 for other years.

Figures for infant deaths include deaths of children under 1 year of age; they exclude fetal deaths. The infant death rate represents the number of infant deaths per 1,000 live births.

3.2.2.5. Divorce (See Marital Status, Section 3.2.3.4; Marriage and Divorce, Section 3.2.3.5)

3.2.2.6. Educational Attainment

Data on educational attainment for the 1990 Census were asked of a sample of persons. Data are tabulated as attainment for persons 15 years old and over. Persons are classified according to the highest level of school completed or the highest degree received. The question included instructions to report the level of the previous grade attended or the highest degree received for persons currently enrolled in school. The question included response categories which allowed persons to report completing the 12th grade without receiving a high school diploma, and which instructed respondents to report as "high school graduate(s)"-persons who received either a high school diploma or the equivalent, for example, passed the Test of General Educational Development (G.E.D.), and did not attend college. (On the Military Census Report questionnaire, the lowest response category was "Less than 9th grade.")

From 1840 to 1930, the Census measured educational attainment by means of a basic literacy question. In 1940, a single question was asked on highest grade of school completed. In the Censuses of 1950 through 1980, a two-part question was used to construct highest grade or year of school completed: (1) highest grade of school attended, and (2) whether that grade was completed. For persons who have not attended college, the response categories in the 1990 educational attainment question should produce data which are comparable to data on highest grade completed from earlier censuses.

The response categories for persons who have attended college were modified from earlier censuses because there was some ambiguity in interpreting responses in terms of the number of years of college completed. For instance, it was not clear whether "completed the fourth year of college," "completed the senior year of college," and "college graduate" were synonomous. Research conducted shortly before the census suggests that these terms were more distinct in 1990 than in earlier decades, and this change may have threatened the ability to estimate the number of "College graduates" from the number of persons reported as having completed the fourth or a higher year of college. It was even more difficult to make inferences about post-baccalaureate degrees and "Associate" degrees from highest year of college completed. Thus, comparisons of post-secondary educational attainment in this and earlier censuses should be made with great caution.

In the 1960 and subsequent censuses, persons for whom educational attainment was not reported were assigned the same attainment level as similar persons whose residence was in the same or a nearby area. In the 1940 and 1950 censuses, persons for whom educational attainment was not reported were not allocated.

In prior censuses, "Median school years completed" was used as a summary measure of educational attainment. In 1990, the median can only be calculated for groups of which less than half the members have attended college. "Percent high school graduate or higher" and "Percent bachelors degree or higher" are summary measures which can be calculated from the present data and offer measures of differences between population subgroups that are quite readily interpretable. To make comparisons over time, "Percent high school graduate or higher" can be calculated and "Percent bachelor's degree or higher" can be approximated with data from previous censuses.

3.2.2.7. Hispanic Origin

Information about Spanish/Hispanic origin for the 1990 Census was asked of all persons. Persons of Hispanic origin are those who classified themselves in one of the specific Hispanic- origin categories listed on the questionnaire-"Mexican," "Puerto Rican," or "Cuban"-as well as those who indicated that they were of "other Spanish/Hispanic" origin. Persons of "Other Spanish/Hispanic" origin are those whose origins are from Spain, the Spanish-speaking countries of Central or South America, or the Dominican Republic, or they are persons of Hispanic origin identifying themselves generally as Spanish, Spanish-American, Hispanic, Hispano, Latino, and so on. Write-in responses to the "other Spanish/Hispanic" category were coded only for sample data.

Origin can be viewed as the ancestry, nationality group, lineage, or country of birth of the person or the person's parents or ancestors before their arrival in the United States. Persons of Hispanic origin may be of any race.

Some tabulations are shown by the Hispanic origin of the householder. In all cases where households, families, or occupied housing units are classified by Hispanic origin, the Hispanic origin of the householder is used. (See the discussion of householder under "Household Type and Relationship.")

During direct interviews conducted by enumerators, if a person could not provide a single origin response, he or she was asked to select, based on self-identification, the group which best described his or her origin or descent. If a person could not provide a single group, the origin of the person's mother was used. If a single group could not be provided for the person's mother, the first origin reported by the person was used.

If any household member failed to respond to the Spanish/Hispanic origin question, a response was assigned by the computer according to the reported entries of other household members by using specific rules of precedence of household relationship. In the processing of sample questionnaires, responses to other questions on the questionnaire, such as ancestry and place of birth, were used to assign an origin before any reference was made to the origin reported by other household members. If an origin was not entered for any household member, an origin was assigned from another household according to the race of the householder.

There may be differences between the total Hispanic origin population based on 100-percent tabulations and sample tabulations. Such differences are the result of sampling variability, nonsampling error, and more extensive edit procedures for the Spanish/ Hispanic origin item on the sample questionnaires.

The 1990 data on Hispanic origin are generally comparable with those for the 1980 census. However, there are some differences in the format of the Hispanic origin question between the two censuses.

For 1990, the word "descent" was deleted from the 1980 wording. In addition, the term "Mexican-Amer." used in 1980 was shortened further to "Mexican-Am. " to reduce misreporting (of "American") in this category detected in the 1980 Census. Finally, the 1990 question allowed those who reported as "other Spanish/ Hispanic" to write in their specific Hispanic origin group.

Misreporting in the "Mexican-Amer." category of the 1980 Census item on Spanish/Hispanic origin may affect the comparability of 1980 and 1990 Census data for persons of Hispanic origin for certain areas of the country. An evaluation of the 1980 Census item on Spanish/ Hispanic origin indicated that there was misreporting in the Mexican origin category by White and Black persons in certain areas. That study results showed evidence that the misreporting occurred in the South (excluding Texas), the Northeast (excluding the New York City area), and a few States in the Midwest Region. Also, results based on available data suggest that the impact of possible misreporting of Mexican origin in the 1980 Census was severe in those portions of the above-mentioned regions where the Hispanic origin population was generally sparse. However, national 1980 Census data on the Mexican origin population or total Hispanic origin population at the national level were not seriously affected by the reporting problem. (For a more detailed discussion of the evaluation of the 1980 Census Spanish/Hispanic origin item, see the 1980 Census Supplementary Reports.)

The 1990 and 1980 Census data on the Hispanic population are not directly comparable with 1970 Spanish origin data because of a number of factors: (1) overall improvements in the 1980 and 1990 censuses, (2) better coverage of the population, (3) improved question designs, and (4) an effective public relations campaign by the Census Bureau with the assistance of national and community ethnic groups.

Specific changes in question design between the 1980 and 1970 Censuses included the placement of the category "No, not Spanish/ Hispanic" as the first category in that question (The corresponding category appeared last in the 1970 question.) Also, the 1970 category "Central or South American" was deleted because in 1970 some respondents misinterpreted the category; furthermore, the designations "Mexican-American" and "Chicano" were added to the Spanish/Hispanic origin question in 1980. In the 1970 Census, the question on Spanish origin was asked of only a 5-percent sample of the population.

3.2.3. Household Type and Relationship

3.2.3.1. Household

A household includes all the persons who occupy a housing unit. A housing unit is a house, an apartment, a mobile home, a group of rooms, or a single room that is occupied (or if vacant, is intended for occupancy) as separate living quarters. Separate living quarters are those in which the occupants live and eat separately from any other persons in the building and which have direct access from the outside of the building or through a common hall. The occupants may be a single family, one person living alone, two or more families living together, or any other group of related or unrelated persons who share living arrangements.

The 1990 definition of a household is the same as that used in 1980. The 1980 relationship category "Son/daughter" has been replaced by two categories, "Natural-born or adopted son/daughter" and "Stepson/stepdaughter." "Grandchild" has been added as a separate category. The 1980 nonrelative categories: "Roomer, boarder and "Partner, roommate" have been replaced by the categories "Roomer, boarder, or foster child ... .. Housemate, roommate," and "Unmarried partner." The 1980 non-relative category "Paid employee" has been dropped.

3.2.3.2. Family Type

A family consists of a householder and one or more other persons living in the same household who are related to the householder by birth, marriage, or adoption. All persons in a household who are related to the householder are regarded as members of his or her family. A household can contain only one family for purposes of census tabulations. Not all households contain families since a household may comprise a group of unrelated persons or one person living alone.

Families are classified by type as either a "married-couple family" or "other family" according to the sex of the householder and the presence of relatives. The data on family type are based on answers to questions on sex and relationship which were asked on a 100 percent basis.

Married-couple family. A family in which the house-holder and his or her spouse are enumerated as members of the same household.

Other family. Male Householder, No Wife Present: A family with a male householder and no spouse of householder present. Female Householder, No Husband Present: A family with a female householder and no spouse of householder present.

3.2.3.3. Subfamily

A subfamily is a married couple (husband and wife enumerated as members of the same household) with or without never-married children under 18 years old, or one parent with one or more never-married children under 18 years old, living in a household and related to, but not including, either the householder or the householder's spouse. The number of subfamilies is not included in the count of families, since subfamily members are counted as part of the householder's family.

3.2.3.4. Marital Status

Marital status for the 1990 Census was asked of all persons. The marital status classification refers to the status at the time of enumeration. Data on marital status are tabulated only for persons 15 years old and over.

All persons were asked whether they were "now married," "widowed," "divorced," "separated," or "never married." Couples who live together (unmarried persons, persons in common-law marriages) were allowed to report the marital status they considered the most appropriate.

Never married. This term includes all persons who have never been married, including persons whose only marriage(s) was annulled.

Ever married. This term includes persons married at the time of enumeration as well as those separated, widowed, or divorced.

Now married (except separated). This term includes persons whose current marriage has not ended through widowhood, divorce, or separation (regardless of previous marital history). The category may also include couples who live together or persons in common-law marriages if they consider this category the most appropriate. In certain tabulations, currently married persons are further classified as "spouse present" or "spouse absent."

Separated. This term includes persons legally separated or otherwise absent from their spouse because of marital discord. Included are persons who have been deserted or who have parted because they no longer want to live together but who have not obtained a divorce.

Widowed. This term includes widows and widowers who have not remarried.

Divorced. This term includes persons who are legally divorced and who have not remarried.

Now married. This term refers to all persons whose current marriage has not ended by widowhood or divorce. This category includes persons defined above as separated.

Differences between the number of currently married males and the number of currently married females occur because of reporting differences and because some husbands and wives have their usual residence in different areas. In sample tabulations, these differences can also occur because different weights are applied to the individual's data. Any differences between the number of "now married, spouse present" males and females are due solely to sample weighting. By definition, the numbers would be the same.

When marital status was not reported, it was imputed according to the relationship to the householder and sex and age of the person.

The 1990 marital status definitions are the same as those used in 1980 with the exception of the term "never married" which replaces the term "single" in tabulations. A general marital status question has been asked in every census since 1880.

3.2.3.5. Marriage and Divorce

Marriage and divorce statistics are total counts of events gathered by collecting already summarized data reported by State offices of vital statistics and by county offices of registration.

Marriage and divorce statistics are limited to events occurring in the specified area during the year and include events occurring to nonresidents of the United States. Marriages or divorces occurring to U.S. residents outside the United States are excluded. Reported annulments are included in the divorce statistics.

The marriage and divorce rates are based on resident population enumerated as of April 1 for decennial census years and estimated as of July 1 for other years.

3.2.3.6. Place of Birth

The data on place of birth were asked on a sample basis. The place-of-birth question asked respondents to report the U.S. State, commonwealth or territory, or the foreign country where they were born. Persons born outside the United States were asked to report their place of birth according to current international boundaries. Since numerous changes in boundaries of foreign countries have occurred in the last century, some persons may have reported their place of birth in terms of boundaries that existed at the time of their birth or emigration, or in accordance with their own national preference.

Persons not reporting place of birth were assigned the birthplace of another family member or were allocated the response of another person with similar characteristics. Persons allocated as foreign born were not assigned a specific country of birth but were classified as "Born abroad, country not specified."

Nativity. Information on place of birth and citizenship was used to classify the population into two major categories: native and foreign born. When information on place of birth was not reported, nativity was assigned on the basis of answers to citizenship, if reported, and other characteristics.

Native. This term includes persons born in the United States, Puerto Rico, or an outlying area of the United States. The small number of persons who were born in a foreign country but have at least one American parent also are included in this category.

The native population is classified in the following groups: persons born in the State in which they resided at the time of the census; persons born in a different State, by region; persons born in Puerto Rico or an outlying area of the U.S.; and persons born abroad with at least one American parent.

Foreign born. This term includes persons not classified as "Native." Prior to the 1970 Census, persons not reporting place of birth were generally classified as native. The foreign-born population is shown by selected area, country, or region of birth: the places of birth shown in data products were selected based on the number of respondents who reported that area or country of birth.

Data on the State of birth of the native population have been collected in each census beginning with that of 1850. Similar data were shown in tabulations for the 1980 Census and other recent censuses. Non-response was allocated in a similar manner in 1980; however, prior to 1980, non-response to the place of birth question was not allocated. Prior to the 1970 Census, persons not reporting place of birth were generally classified as native.

The questionnaire instruction to report mother's State of residence instead of the person's actual State of birth (if born in a hospital in a different State) was dropped in 1990. Evaluation studies of 1970 and 1980 Census data demonstrated that this instruction was generally either ignored or misunderstood. Since the hospital and the mother's residence is in the same State for most births, this change may have a slight effect on State of birth data for States with large metropolitan areas that straddle State lines.

3.2.3.7. Race

Race was asked of all persons in the 1990 Census. The concept of race as used by the Census Bureau reflects self-identification; it does not denote any clearcut scientific definition of biological stock. The data for race represent self-classification by people according to the race with which they most closely identify. Furthermore, it is recognized that the categories of the race item include both racial and national origin or sociocultural groups.

During direct interviews conducted by enumerators, if a person could not provide a single response to the race question, he or she was asked to select, based on self-identification, the group which best described his or her racial identity. If a person could not provide a single race response, the race of the mother was used. If a single race response could not be provided for the person's mother, the first race reported by the person was used. In all cases where occupied housing units, households, or families are classified by race, the race of the householder was used.

The racial classification used by the Census Bureau generally adheres to the guidelines in Federal Statistical Directive No. 15, issued by the Office of Management and Budget, which provides standards on ethnic and racial categories for statistical reporting to be used by all Federal agencies.

White: Includes persons who indicated their race as "White" or reported entries such as Canadian, German, Italian, Lebanese, Near Easterner, Arab, or Polish.

Black: Includes persons who indicated their race as "Black or Negro", or reported entries such as African American, Afro-American, Black Puerto Rican, Jamaican, Nigerian, West Indian, or Haitian.

If the race entry for a member of a household was missing on the questionnaire, race was assigned based upon the reported entries of race by other household members using specific rules of precedence of household relationship. For example, if race was missing for the daughter of the householder, then the race of her mother (as female householder or female spouse) would be assigned. If there were no female householder or spouse in the household, the daughter would be assigned her father's (male householder) race. If race were not reported for anyone in the household, the race of a householder in a previously processed household was assigned. This procedure is a variation of the general imputation procedures described in Appendix C, Accuracy of the Data.

In the 1990 Census, respondents sometimes did not fill in a circle or filled the "Other race" circle and wrote in a response, such as Arab, Polish, or African American in the shared write-in box for "Other race" and "Other API" responses. During the automated coding process, these responses were edited and assigned to the appropriate racial designation. Also, some Hispanic origin persons did not fill in a circle, but provided entries such as Mexican or Puerto Rican. These persons were classified in the "Other race" category during the coding and editing process.

Differences between the 1990 Census and earlier censuses affect the comparability of data for certain racial groups and American Indian tribes. The 1990 Census was the first census to undertake, on a 100-percent basis, an automated review, edit, and coding operation for written responses to the race item. The automated coding system used in the 1990 Census greatly reduced the potential for error associated with a clerical review. Specialists with a thorough knowledge of the race subject matter reviewed, edited, coded, and resolved inconsistent or incomplete responses. In the 1980 Census, there was only a limited clerical review of the race responses on the 100-percent forms with a full clerical review conducted only on the sample questionnaires.

Another difference between 1990 and preceding censuses is the approach taken when persons of Spanish/Hispanic origin did not report in a specific race category but reported as "Other race" or "Other." These persons commonly provided a write-in entry such as Mexican, Venezuelan, or Latino. In the 1990 and 1980 censuses, these entries remained in the "Other race" or "Other' category, respectively. In the 1970 Census, most of these persons were included in the "White" category.

3.2.3.8. Residence in 1985

The 1990 Census asked for the State (or foreign country), county, and place of residence on April 1, 1985 for those persons reporting that on that date they lived in a different house than their current residence. Residence in 1985 is used in conjunction with location of current residence to determine the extent of residential mobility of the population and the resulting redistribution of the population across the various States, metropolitan areas, and regions of the country.

When no information on residence in 1985 was reported for a person, information for other family members, if available, was used to assign a location of residence in 1985. All cases of nonresponse or incomplete response that were not assigned a previous residence based on information from other family members were allocated the previous residence of another person with similar characteristics who provided complete information.

The tabulation category, "Same house," includes all persons 5 years old and over who did not move during the 5 years as well as those who had moved but by 1990 had returned to their 1985 residence. The category, "Different house in the United States," includes persons who lived in the United States in 1985 but in a different house or apartment from the one they occupied on April 1, 1990. These movers are then further subdivided according to the type of move.

In most tabulations, movers are divided into three groups according to their 1985 residence: "Different house, same county," "Different county, same State," and "Different State." The last group may be further subdivided into region of residence in 1985. The category, "Abroad," includes those persons who were residing in a foreign country, Puerto Rico, or an outlying area of the U.S. in 1985, including members of the Armed Forces and their dependents. Some tabulations show movers who were residing in Puerto Rico or an outlying area in 1985 separately from those residing in other countries.

In tabulations for metropolitan areas, movers are categorized according to the metropolitan status of their current and previous residences, resulting in such groups as movers within an Metropolitan Statistical Area (MSA)/Primary Metropolitan Statistical Area (PMSA), movers between MSA/PMSA's, movers from nonmetropolitan areas to MSA/PMSA, and movers from central cities to the remainder of an MSA/ PMSA. In some tabulations, these categories are further subdivided by size of MSA/ PMSA, region of current or previous residence, or movers within or between central cities and the remainder of the same or a different MSA/ PMSA.

The number of persons who were living in a different house in 1985 is somewhat less than the total number of moves during the 5-year period. Some persons in the same house at the two dates had moved during the 5-year period but by the time of the census had returned to their 1985 residence. Other persons who were living in a different house had made one or more intermediate moves. For similar reasons, the number of persons living in a different county, MSA/PMSA, or State or moving between nonmetropolitan areas may be understated.

Similar questions were asked on all previous censuses beginning in 1940, except the questions in 1950 referred to residence 1 year earlier rather than 5 years earlier. Although the questions in the 1940 Census covered a 5-year period, comparability with that census was reduced somewhat because of different definitions and categories of tabulation. Comparability with the 1960 and 1970 census is also somewhat reduced because non-response was not allocated in those earlier censuses. For the 1980 Census, nonresponse was allocated in a manner similar to the 1990 allocation scheme.

3.2.3.9. Year of Entry

Information on year of entry came from a sample of persons. The question, "When did this person come to the United States to stay?" was asked of persons who indicated in the question on citizenship that they were not born in the United States. (For more information, see the discussion under "Citizenship.")

The 1990 Census questions, tabulations, and census data products about citizenship and year of entry include no reference to immigration. All persons who were born and resided outside the United States before becoming residents of the United States have a date of entry. Some of these persons are U.S. citizens by birth (e.g., persons born in Puerto Rico or born abroad of American parents). To avoid any possible confusion concerning the date of entry of persons who are U.S. citizens by birth, the term, "year of entry" is used in this report instead of the term "year of immigration."

The census questions on nativity, citizenship, and year of entry were not designed to measure the degree of permanence of residence in the United States. The phrase, "to stay" was used to obtain the year in which the person became a resident of the United States. Although the respondent was directed to indicate the year he or she entered the country "to stay," it was difficult to ensure that respondents interpreted the phrase correctly.

A question on year of entry, (alternately called "year of immigration") was asked in each decennial census from 1890 to 1930, 1970, and 1980. In 1980, the question on year of entry included six arrival time intervals. The number of arrival intervals was expanded to ten in 1990. In 1980, the question on year of entry was asked only of the foreign-born population. In 1990, all persons who responded to the long-form questionnaire and were not born in the United States were to complete the question on year of entry.

3.3. Civilian Employment

3.3.1. Data Sources

See decennial censuses in Section 3.2.above.

3.3.2. Selected Terms

3.3.2.1. Employment Status

Information on employment status for the 1990 Census is based on a sample of persons. The series of questions on employment status was asked of all persons 15 years old and over and was designed to identify, in this sequence: (1) persons who worked at any time during the reference week; (2) persons who did not work during the reference week but who had jobs or businesses from which they were temporarily absent (excluding layoff); (3) persons on layoff; and (4) persons who did not work during the reference week, but who were looking for work during the last four weeks and were available for work during the reference week. (For more information, see the discussion under "Reference Week.")

The data on employment status data in this and other 1990 Census tabulations relate to persons 16 years old and over. Some tabulations showing employment status, however, include persons 15 years old. By definition, these persons are classified as "Not in Labor Force." In the 1940, 1950, and 1960 censuses, employment status data were collected for persons 14 years old and over. The change in the universe was made in 1970 to agree with the official measurement of the labor force as revised in January 1967 by the U.S. Department of Labor. The 1970 Census was the last to show employment data for persons 14 and 15 years old. This dataset, therefore, includes, for the 1970 Census, employment status data for persons 16 years and over as well as persons 15 and 16 years. The definition of employment status for the 1990 Census is as follows:

Employed: All civilians 16 years old and over who were either (1) "at work"-those who did any work at all during the reference week as paid employees, worked in their own business or profession, worked on their own farm, or worked 15 hours or more as unpaid workers on a family farm or in a family business; or (2) were "with a job but not at work" -those who did not work during the reference week but had jobs or businesses from which they were temporarily absent due to illness, bad weather, industrial dispute, vacation, or other personal reasons. Excluded from the employed are persons whose only activity consisted of work around the house or unpaid volunteer work for religious, charitable, and similar organizations; also excluded are persons on active duty in the United States Armed Forces.

Unemployed: All civilians 16 years old and over are classified as unemployed if they (1) were neither "at work" nor "with a job but not at work" during the reference week, and (2) were looking for work during the last 4 weeks, and (3) were available to accept a job. Also included as unemployed are civilians who did not work at all during the reference week and were waiting to be called back to a job from which they had been laid off. Examples of job seeking activities are:

*   Registering at a public or private employment office

*   Meeting with prospective employers

*   Investigating possibilities for starting a professional practice or opening a business

*   Placing or answering advertisements

*   Writing letters of application

*   Being on a union or professional register

Civilian labor force: Persons classified as employed or unemployed in accordance with the criteria described above.

Experienced unemployed: Unemployed persons who have worked at any time in the past.

Experienced civilian labor force: The employed and the experienced unemployed.

Labor force: All persons classified in the civilian labor force plus members of the U. S. Armed Forces (persons on active duty with the United States Army, Air Force, Navy, Marine Corps, or Coast Guard).

Not in labor force: All persons 16 years old and over who are not classified as members of the labor force. This category consists mainly of students, housewives, retired workers, seasonal workers enumerated in an off season who were not looking for work, institutionalized persons, and persons doing only incidental unpaid family work (less than 15 hours during the reference week).

Worker. This term appears in connection with several subjects: journey-to-work items, class of worker, weeks worked in 1989, and number of workers in family in 1989. Its meaning varies and, therefore, should be determined in each case by referring to the definition of the subject in which it appears.

The census could understate the number of employed persons because persons who have irregular, casual, or unstructured jobs sometimes report themselves as not working. The number of employed persons "at work" is probably overstated in the census (and conversely, the number of employed "with a job, but not at work" is understated), since some persons on vacation or sick leave erroneously reported themselves as working. This problem has no effect on the total number of employed persons. The reference week for the employment data is not the same for all persons. Since persons can change their employment status from one week to another, the lack of a uniform reference week may mean that the employment data do not reflect the reality of the employment situation of any given week. (For more information, see the discussion under "Reference Week.")

The questionnaire items and employment status concepts for the 1990 Census are essentially the same as those used in the 1980 and 1970 censuses. However, these concepts differ in many respects from those associated with the 1940, 1950 and 1960 censuses. As mentioned above, employment data in the 1940-60 censuses were collected for persons 14 years old and over, whereas later censuses collected data for persons 16 years old and over. Significant changes also took place between the 1940 Census and the 1950 Census. Three points merit special attention:

First, in the 1940 Census, the classification of the labor force is not available in terms of civilian and non-civilian (armed forces), whereas beginning with the 1950 Census, such classification became available. The number of employed persons between 1940 and 1950, therefore, is not comparable, for the 1940 figures include those employed by the armed forces.

Second, the 1940 Census definition of persons in the labor force included three categories: (1) persons actually at work, (2) with a job (not at work but with jobs, businesses, or professional enterprises from which they were temporarily absent, and (3) persons on public emergency work. In the original 1940 Census tables as well as in this dataset for 1940, "employed" comprises only the first two categories.

Lastly, in 1940, unemployed was defined as persons (1) seeking work and without any form of public or private employment and (2) on public emergency work programs established to provide jobs for the unemployed. However, considerable number of public emergency workers were reported as "at work" rather than "on public emergency work." The number of unemployed persons, for this reason, is understated, the extent of which varies from State to State.

Since employment data from the census are obtained from respondents in households, they differ from statistics based on reports from individual business establishments, farm enterprises, and certain government programs. Persons employed at more than one job are counted only once in the census and are classified according to the job at which they worked the greatest number of hours during the reference week. In statistics based on reports from business and farm establishments, persons who work for more than one establishment may be counted more than once. Moreover, some tabulations may exclude private household workers, unpaid family workers, and self-employed persons, but may include workers less than 16 years of age.

An additional difference in the data arises from the fact that persons who had a job but were not at work are included with the employed in the census statistics, whereas many of these persons are likely to be excluded from employment figures based on establishment payroll reports. Furthermore, the employment status data in census tabulations include persons on the basis of place of residence regardless of where they work, whereas establishment data report persons at their place of work regardless of where they live. This latter consideration is particularly significant when comparing data for workers who commute between areas.

For several reasons, the unemployment figures of the Census Bureau are not comparable with published figures on unemployment compensation claims. For example, figures on unemployment compensation claims exclude persons who have exhausted their benefit rights, new workers who have not earned rights to unemployment insurance, and persons losing jobs not covered by unemployment insurance systems (including some workers in agriculture, domestic services, and religious organizations, and self-employed and unpaid family workers). In addition, the qualifications for drawing unemployment compensation differ from the definition of unemployment used by the Census Bureau. Persons working only a few hours during the week and persons with a job but not at work are sometimes eligible for unemployment compensation but are classified as "Employed" in the census. Differences in the geographical distribution of unemployment data arise because the place where claims are filed may not necessarily be the same as the place of residence of the unemployed worker.

The figures on employment status from the decennial census are generally comparable with similar data collected in the Current Population Survey. However, some difference may exist because of variations in enumeration and processing techniques.

3.3.3. Industry, Occupation, and Class of Worker

Information on data on industry, occupation, and class of worker for the 1990 Census was asked of a sample of persons. Information on industry relates to the kind of business conducted by a person's employing organization; occupation describes the kind of work the person does on the job; class of worker provides information about the employment status of a person.

For employed persons, the data refer to the person's job during the reference week. For those who worked at two or more jobs, the data refer to the job at which the person worked the greatest number of hours. For unemployed persons, the data refer to their last job. The industry and occupation statistics are derived from the detailed classification systems developed for the 1990 Census as described below. The Classified Index of Industries and Occupations provided additional information on the industry and occupation classification systems.

3.3.3.1. Industry

The industry classification system developed for the 1990 Census consists of 235 categories for employed persons, classified into 13 major industry groups. Since 1940, the industrial classification has been based on the Standard Industrial Classification Manual (SIC). The 1990 Census classification was developed from the 1987 SIC published by the Office of Management and Budget Executive Office of the President.

The SIC was designed primarily to classify establishments by the type of industrial activity in which they were engaged. However, census data, which were collected from households, differ in detail and nature from those obtained from establishment surveys. Therefore, the census classification systems, while defined in SIC terms, cannot reflect the full detail in all categories. There are several levels of industrial classification found in census products. For example, the 1990 CP-2 (Social and Economic Characteristics) report includes 41 unique industrial categories, while the 1990 Summary Tape File 4 (STF 4) presents 72 categories.

3.3.3.2. Occupation

The occupational classification system developed for the 1990 Census consists of 500 specific occupational categories for employed persons arranged into 6 summary and 13 major occupational groups. This classification was developed to be consistent with the Standard Occupational Classification (SOC) Manual: 1980, published by the Office of Federal Statistical Policy and Standards, U.S. Department of Commerce. Tabulations with occupation as the primary characteristic present several levels of occupational detail. The most detailed tabulations are shown in a special 1990 subject report and tape files on occupation. These products contain all 500 occupational categories plus industry or class of worker subgroupings of occupational categories.

Some occupation groups are related closely to certain industries. Operators of transportation equipment, farm operators and workers, and private household workers account for major portions of their respective industries of transportation, agriculture, and private households. However, the industry categories include persons in other occupations. For example, persons employed in agriculture include truck drivers and bookkeepers; persons employed in the transportation industry include mechanics, freight handlers, and payroll clerks; and persons employed in the private household industry include occupations such as chauffeur, gardener, and secretary.

New occupations emerge with the change in technologies which gave rise to the change in the occupational and industrial classifications. However, this change makes the across-time comparision difficult. For example, before the 1970 Census, some technical occupations such as health technicians, electrical engineers, lab technicians, and air plane pilots were considered "professionals." Beginning with the 1980 Census, these occupations are called "technicians and related support occupations" and are treated as part of sales and clerical occupations. Thus, to compare the number of professionals over time, it is necessary to combine "professionals" and "technicians and related support occupations" for 1980 and 1990. The matrix chart (Section 3) presents the most comparable categories across time.

3.3.3.3. Class of Worker

The information on class of worker refers to the same job as a respondent's industry and occupation and categorizes persons according to the type of ownership of the employing organization. The class of worker categories are defined as follows:

Private wage and salary workers: Includes persons who worked for wages, salary, commission, tips, pay-in-kind, or piece rates for a private for profit employer or a private not-for-profit, tax-exempt or charitable organization. Self-employed persons whose business was incorporated are included with private wage and salary workers because they are paid employees of their own companies. Some tabulations present data separately for these subcategories: "For profit," "Not for profit," and "Own business incorporated." Employees of foreign governments, the United Nations, or other formal international organizations were classified as Private-not-for-profit.

Government workers: Includes persons who were employees of any local, State, or Federal governmental unit, regardless of the activity of the particular agency. For some tabulations, the data were presented separately for the three levels of government.

Self-employed workers: Includes persons who worked for profit or fees in their own unincorporated business, profession, or trade, or who operated a farm.

Unpaid family workers: Includes persons who worked 15 hours or more without pay in a business or on a farm operated by a relative.

Salaried/self-employed. In tabulations that categorize persons as either salaried or self-employed, the salaried category includes private and government wage and salary workers; self-employed includes self-employed persons and unpaid family workers.

The industry category, "Public administration," is limited to regular government functions such as legislative, judicial, administrative, and regulatory activities of governments. Other government organizations such as schools, hospitals, liquor stores, and bus lines are classified by industry according to the activity in which they are engaged. On the other hand, the class of worker category "government" includes all government workers.

Comparability of industry and occupation data is affected by a number of factors, primarily by the systems used to classify the questionnaire responses. For both the industry and occupation classification systems, the basic structures were generally the same from 1940 to 1970, but changes in the individual categories limited comparability of the data from one census to another. These changes were needed to recognize the "birth" of new industries and occupations, the "death" of others, and the growth and decline in existing industries and occupations, as well as the desire of analysts and other users for more detail in the presentation of the data. Probably the greatest cause of incomparability is the transfer of a segment of a category to a different category in the next census. Changes in the nature of jobs and respondent terminology and refinement of category composition made these movements necessary.

In the 1990 Census, the industry classification underwent minor revisions to reflect recent changes to the SIC. The 1990 occupational classification system is essentially the same as that for the 1980 Census. However, the conversion of the census classification to the SIC in 1980 meant that the 1990 classification system was less comparable to the classifications used prior to the 1980 Census.

Other factors that affect data comparability include the universe to which the data referred (in 1970, the age cutoff for labor force was changed from 14 years to 16 years); how the industry and occupation questions were worded on the questionnaire (for example, important changes were made in 1970); improvements in the coding procedures (the Employer Name List technique was introduced in 1960); and how the "not reported" cases are handled. Prior to 1970, they were placed in the residual categories, "Industry not reported" and "Occupation not reported." In 1970, an allocation process was introduced that assigned these cases to major groups. In 1990, as in 1980, the "Not reported" cases were assigned to individual categories. Therefore, the 1980 and 1990 data for individual categories included some persons who were tabulated in a "Not reported" category in previous censuses.

The following publications contain information on the various factors affecting comparability and are particularly useful for understanding differences in the occupation and industry information from earlier censuses: U.S. Bureau of the Census, Changes Between the 1950 and 1960 Occupation and Industry Classifications With Detailed Adjustments of 1950 Data to the 1960 Classifications, Technical Paper No. 18, 1968; U.S. Bureau of the Census, 1970 Occupation and Industry Classification Systems in Terms of their 1960 Occupation and Industry Elements, Technical Paper No. 26, 1972; and U.S. Bureau of the Census, The Relationship Between the 1970 and 1980 Industry and Occupation Classification Systems, Technical Paper No. 59, 1988. For citations for earlier census years, see the 1980 Census of Population report, PC80-1-D, Detailed Population Characteristics.

The 1990 Census introduced an additional class of worker category for "private not-for-profit" employers. This category is a subset of the 1980 category "employee of private employer." Also in 1990, employees of foreign governments, the United Nations, etc., are classified as "private not-for-profit," rather than Federal Government as in 1970 and 1980. While this change in theory represents a change in comparability, the small number of U.S. residents working for foreign governments makes this change negligible for the counties included in the present database.

Comparability between the statistics on industry and occupation from the 1990 Census and statistics from other sources is affected by many of the factors described in the section on "Employment Status." These factors are primarily geographic differences between residence and place of work, different dates of reference, and differences in counts because of dual job holding. Industry data from population censuses cover all industries and all kinds of workers, whereas data from establishments often excluded private household workers, government workers, and the self-employed. Also, the replies from household respondents may have differed in detail and nature from those obtained from establishments.

Occupation data from the census and data from government licensing agencies, professional associations, trade unions, etc., may not be as comparable as expected. Organizational listings often include persons not in the labor force or persons devoting all or most of their time to another occupation; or the same person may be included in two or more different listings. In addition, relatively few organizations, except for those requiring licensing, attained complete coverage of membership in a particular occupational field.

3.3.3.4. Oil Dependency

For the period 1940-90, the data on employment in mining are available from published decennial censuses included in this database. For 1980 and 1990, breakdowns of mining employment are available from the special tabulation obtained from the census office that provides employment data in oil/natural gas, metal, coal and other mining.

The data extracted from the special tabulation are different from the data in the published decennial censuses. Employment data in decennial censuses are based on <u>employed persons</u> 14 years (or 16 years) and over who are civilians at work or with a job but not at work at the data of census, whereas the special tabulation data refer to persons 16 years and over ever worked between 1975-80 for the 1980 data, and 1985-90 for the 1990 data. Consequently, the special tabulation data include unemployed and retired persons at the data of census.

Based on the data on employment in mining (for the period 1940-90) and oil/gas employment (for the period 1980-90), we have derived two measures of mining (or oil/gas) dependency for each county: (1) the percentage of workers employed in mining (or oil/gas) industry, and (2) location quotient. Location quotient in mining (oil/gas) of county A is defined as,

$$\text{LQ (mining)} = \frac{\%\text{mining (or oil/gas) in county A}}{\%\text{mining (or oil/gas) of the state in which county A is located.}}$$

3.3.3.5. Reference Week

The data on labor force status work were related to a reference week; the reference week refers to the calendar week preceding the date on which respondents completed their questionnaires or were interviewed by enumerators. This week is not the same for all respondents since the enumeration was not completed in one week. The occurrence of holidays during the enumeration period could affect the data on actual hours worked during the reference week, but probably had no effect on overall measurement of employment status (see the discussion below on "Comparability").

The reference weeks for the 1990 and 1980 Censuses differ in that Passover and Good Friday occurred in the first week of April 1980, but in the second week of April 1990. Many workers presumably took time off for those observances. The differing occurrence of these holidays could affect the comparability of the 1990 and 1980 data on actual hours worked for some areas if the respective weeks were the reference weeks for a significant number of persons. The holidays probably did not affect the overall measurement of employment status since this information was based on work activity during the entire reference week.

3.4. Income and Poverty Status

3.4.1. Data Sources

Two types of income statistics are included in this dataset: money income and personal income. The former, money income, is obtained from the Census, whereas the latter, personal income, is obtained from the Bureau of Economic Analysis (BEA). Unless specifically mentioned as personal income, the variables on income refer to money income. For the definitions of money and personal income, see Money Income and Per Capita Personal Income below.

The data on income in 1989 were requested from persons 15 years old and over. "Total income" is the algebraic sum of the amounts reported separately for

- wage or salary income

- net non-farm self-employment income

- net farm self-employment income

- interest, dividend, or net rental or royalty income

- Social Security or railroad retirement income

- public assistance or welfare income

- retirement or disability income

- and all other income.

"Earnings" is defined as the algebraic sum of wage or salary income and net income from farm and nonfarm self-employment. "Earnings" represent the amount of income received regularly before deductions for personal income taxes, Social Security, bond purchases, union dues, medicare deductions, etc.

Receipts from the following sources are not included as income: money received from the sale of property (unless the recipient was engaged in the business of selling such property); the value of income "in kind" from food stamps, public housing subsidies, medical care, employer contributions for persons, etc.; withdrawal of bank deposits; money borrowed; tax refunds; exchange of money between relatives living in the same household; gifts and lump-sum inheritances, insurance payments, and other types of lump-sum receipts.

The income data collected in the 1980 and 1970 censuses are similar to the 1990 Census data, but there are variations in the detail of the questions. In 1980, income information for 1979 was collected from persons in approximately 19 percent of all housing units and group quarters. Each person was required to report:

- Wage or salary income

- Net nonfarm self-employment income

- Net farm self-employment income

- Interest, dividend, or net rental or royalty income

- Social Security income

- Public assistance income

- Income from all other sources

In 1970, information on income in 1969 was obtained from all members in every fifth housing unit and small group quarters (less than 15 persons) and every fifth person in all other group quarters. Each person was required to report:

- Wage or salary income

- Net nonfarm self-employment income

- Net farm self-employment income

- Social Security or Railroad Retirement

- Public assistance or welfare payments

- Income from all other sources

In 1960, data on income were obtained from all members in every fourth housing unit and from every fourth person 14 years old and over living in group quarters. Each person was required to report:

- wage or salary income

- net self-employment income

- income other than earnings received in 1959.

An assumption was made in the editing process that no other type of income was received by a person who reported the receipt of either wage and salary income or self-employment but who had failed to report the receipt of other money income.

For several reasons, the income data shown in census tabulations are not directly comparable with those that may be obtained from statistical summaries of income tax returns. Income, as defined for Federal tax purposes, differs somewhat from the Census Bureau concept. Moreover, the coverage of income tax statistics is different because of the exemptions of persons having small amounts of income and the inclusion of net capital gains in tax returns. Furthermore, members of some families file separate returns and others file joint returns; consequently, the income reporting unit is not consistently either a family or a person.

The earnings data shown in census tabulations are not directly comparable with **earnings records** of the Social Security Administration. The earnings record data for 1989 excluded the earnings of most civilian government employees, some employees of nonprofit organizations, workers covered by the Railroad Retirement Act, and persons not covered by the program because of insufficient earnings. Furthermore, earnings received from any one employer in excess of $48,000 in 1989 are not covered by earnings records. Finally, because census data are obtained from household questionnaires, they may differ from Social Security Administration earnings record data, which are based upon employers' reports and the Federal income tax returns of self-employed persons.

The Bureau of Economic Analysis (BEA) of the Department of Commerce publishes annual data on aggregate and per-capita personal income received by the population for States, metropolitan areas, and selected counties. Aggregate income estimates based on the income statistics shown in census products usually would be less than those shown in the BEA income series for several reasons. The Census Bureau data are obtained directly from households, whereas the BEA income series is estimated largely on the basis of data from administrative records of business and governmental sources. Moreover, the definitions of income are different. The BEA income series includes some items not included in the income data shown in census publications, such as income "in kind," income received by nonprofit institutions, the value of services of banks and other financial intermediaries rendered to persons without the assessment of specific charges, Medicare payments, and the income of persons who died or emigrated prior to April 1, 1990. On the other hand the census income data include contributions for support received from persons not residing in the same household and employer contributions for social insurance.

3.4.2. Selected Terms

3.4.2.1. Income of Households

Household income includes the income of the householder and all other persons 15 years old and over in the household, whether related to the householder or not. Because many households consist of only one person, average household income is usually less than average family income.

3.4.2.2. Income of Families and Persons

In compiling statistics on family income, the incomes of all members 15 years old and over in each family are summed and treated as a single amount. However, for persons 15 years old and over, the total amounts of their own incomes are used. Although the income statistics covered the calendar year 1989, the characteristics of persons and the composition of families refer to the time of enumeration (April 1990). Thus, the income of the family does not include amounts received by persons who were members of the family during all or part of the calendar year 1989 if these persons no longer resided with the family at the time of enumeration. Yet, family income amounts reported by related persons who did not reside with the family during 1989 but who were members of the family at the time of enumeration are included. However, the composition of most families was the same during 1989 as in April 1990.

3.4.2.3. Mean Income

Mean income is the amount obtained by dividing the total income of a particular statistical universe by the number of units in that universe. Thus, mean household income is obtained by dividing total household income by the total number of households. For the various types of income the means are based on households having those types of income. "Per capita income" is the mean income computed for every man, woman, and child in a particular group. It is derived by dividing the total income of a particular group by the total population in that group.

Care should be exercised in using and interpreting mean income values for small subgroups of the population. Because the mean is influenced strongly by extreme values in the distribution, it is especially susceptible to the effects of sampling variability, misreporting, and processing errors. The median, which is not affected by extreme values, is, therefore, a better measure than the mean when the population base is small. The mean, nevertheless, is shown in some data products for most small subgroups because, when weighted according to the number of cases, the means can be added to obtain summary measures for areas and groups other than those shown in census tabulations.

3.4.2.4. Median Income

The median divides the income distribution into two equal parts, one having incomes above the median and the other having incomes below the median. For households and families, the median income is based on the distribution of the total number of units including those with no income. The median for persons is based on persons with income. The median income values for all households, families, and persons are computed on the basis of more detailed income intervals than shown in most tabulations. Median household or family income figures of $50,000 or less are calculated using linear interpolation. For persons, corresponding median values of $40,000 or less are also computed using linear interpolation. All other median income amounts are derived through Pareto interpolation. (For more information on medians and interpolation, see the discussion under "Derived Measures.")

3.4.2.5. Money Income

The income data obtained from the censuses covers money income only. The fact that many farm families receive an important part of their income in the form of "free" housing and goods produced and consumed on the farm rather than in money should be taken into consideration in comparing the income of farm and nonfarm residents. Nonmoney income such as business expense accounts, use of business transportation and facilities, or partial compensation by business for medical and educational expenses was also received by some nonfarm residents. Many low income families also receive income "in kind" from public welfare programs. In comparing income data for 1989 with earlier years, it should be noted that an increase or decrease in money income does not necessarily represent a comparable change in real income, unless adjustments for changes in prices are made.

3.4.2.6. Per Capita Personal Income

Data for personal income earnings obtained from the Bureau of Economic Analysis (BEA) are based on place of work, unlike civilian labor force data obtained from the Bureau of the Census, which are based on place of residence. Total personal income is adjusted to place of residence.

Per capita personal income is defined as the personal income of the residents of an area divided by the resident population of the area. It is based on resident population enumerated as of April 1 for decennial census years and estimated as of July 1 for other years.

Personal income differs from money income, which is prepared by the Census Bureau, in that money income is measured before deduction of personal contributions for social insurance and does not include imputed income, lump sum payments, and income received by quasi-individuals. Money income does include income from private pensions and annuities and from interpersonal transfer, such as child support.

3.4.2.7. Poverty Status

The data on poverty status were derived from answers to the same questions as the income data asked in the census. Poverty statistics presented in census publications were based on a definition originated by the Social Security Administration in 1964 and subsequently modified by Federal interagency committees in 1969 and 1980 and prescribed by the Office of Management and Budget in Directive 14 as the standard to be used by Federal agencies for statistical purposes.

At the core of this definition was the 1961 economy food plan, the least costly of four nutritionally adequate food plans designed by the U.S. Department of Agriculture (USDA). It was determined from USDA's 1955 survey of food consumption that families of three or more persons spend approximately one-third of their income on food; hence, the poverty level for these families was set at three times the cost of the economy food plan. For smaller families and persons living alone, the cost of the economy food plan was multiplied by factors that were slightly higher to compensate for the relatively larger fixed expenses for these smaller households.

The income cutoffs used by the Census Bureau to determine the poverty status of families and unrelated individuals included a set of 48 thresholds arranged in a two-dimensional matrix consisting of family size (from one person to nine or more persons) cross-classified by presence and number of family members under 18 years old (from no children present to eight or more children present). Unrelated individuals and two-person families were further differentiated by age of the householder (under 65 years old and 65 years old and over).

The total income of each family or unrelated individual in the sample was tested against the appropriate poverty threshold to determine the poverty status of that family or unrelated individual. If the total income was less than the corresponding cutoff, the family or unrelated individual was classified as "below the poverty level."

The number of persons below the poverty level was the sum of the number of persons in families with incomes below the poverty level and the number of unrelated individuals with incomes below the poverty level.

The poverty thresholds are revised annually to allow for changes in the cost of living as reflected in the Consumer Price Index. The average poverty threshold for a family of four persons was $12,674 in 1989, (For more information see Table A below.)

Poverty thresholds were applied on a national basis and were not adjusted for regional, State or local variations in the cost of living. For a detailed discussion of the poverty definitions, see U.S. Bureau of the Census, Current Population Reports, Series P-60, No. 171, Poverty in the United States: 1988 and 1989.

Table A. Poverty Thresholds in 1989 by Size of Family and Number of Related Children Under 18 Years

Size of Family Unit	Weighted average thresholds	Related children under 18 years				
		None	One	Two	Three	Four
One person (unrelated individual)	$6,310					
Under 65 years	6,451	$6,451				
65 years and over	5,947	5,947				
Two persons	8,076					
Householder under 65 years......	8,343	8,303	$8,547			
Householder 65 years and over.	7,501	7,495	8,515			
Three persons	9,885	9,699	9,981	$9,990		
Four persons	12,674	12,790	12,999	12,575	$12,619	
Five persons	14,990	15,424	15,648	15,169	14,798	$14,572
Six persons	16,921	17,740	17,811	17,444	17,092	16,569
Seven persons	19,162	20,412	20,540	20,101	19,794	19,224
Eight persons	21,328	22,830	23,031	22,617	22,253	21,738
Nine or more persons	25,480	27,463	27,596	27,229	26,921	26,415

Size of Family Unit	Related children under 18 years			
	Five	Six	Seven	Eight or more
One person (unrelated individual)				
Under 65 years				
65 years and over				
Two persons				
Householder under 65 years				
Householder 65 years and over				
Three persons				
Four persons				
Five persons				
Six persons	$16,259			
Seven persons	18,558	$17,828		
Eight persons	21,084	20,403	$20,230	
Nine or more persons	25,719	25,089	24,933	$23,973

The poverty definition used in the 1990 and 1980 censuses differed slightly from the one used in the 1970 Census. Three technical modifications were made to the definition used in the 1970 Census as described below:

1. The separate thresholds for families with a female householder with no husband present and all other families were eliminated. For the 1980 and 1990 censuses, the weighted average of the poverty thresholds for these two types of families was applied to all types of families, regardless of the sex of the householder.

2. Farm families and farm unrelated individuals no longer had a set of poverty thresholds that were lower than the thresholds applied to non-farm families and unrelated individuals. The farm thresholds were 85 percent of the corresponding levels for non-farm families in the 1970 Census. The same thresholds were applied to all families and unrelated individuals regardless of residence in 1980 and 1990.

3. The thresholds by size of family were extended from seven or more persons in 1970 to nine or more persons in 1980 and 1990.

These changes resulted in a minimal increase in the number of poor at the national level. For a complete discussion of these modifications and their impact, see **The Current Population Reports**, Series P-60, No. 133.

The population covered in the poverty statistics derived from the 1980 and 1990 censuses was essentially the same as in the 1970 Census. The only difference was that in 1980 and 1990, unrelated individuals under 15 years old were excluded from the poverty universe, while in 1970, only those under 14 years old were excluded. The poverty data from the 1960 Census excluded all persons in group quarters and included all unrelated individuals regardless of age. It is unlikely that these differences in population coverage would have had significant impact when comparing the poverty data for persons since the 1960 censuses.

Because of differences in the questionnaires and data collection procedures, estimates of the number of persons below the poverty level by various characteristics from the 1990 Census may differ from those reported in the March 1990 Current Population Survey.

3.4.2.8. Specified Poverty Levels

Because the poverty levels currently in use by the Federal Government do not meet all the needs of data user, some of the data are presented for alternate levels. These specified poverty levels are obtained by multiplying the income cutoffs at the poverty level by the appropriate factor. For example, the average income cutoff at 125 percent of poverty level was $15,843 ($12,674 x 1.25) in 1989 for a family of four persons.

3.4.2.9. Weighted Average Thresholds at the Poverty Level

The average thresholds shown in the first column of Table A are weighted by the presence and number of children. For example, the weighted average threshold for a given family size is obtained by multiplying the threshold for each presence and number-of- children category within the given family size by the number of families in that category. These products are then aggregated across the entire range of presence and number of children categories, and the aggregate is divided by the total number of families in the group to yield the weighted average threshold at the poverty level for that family size.

Since the basic thresholds used to determine the poverty status of families and unrelated individuals are applied to all families and unrelated individuals, the weighted average poverty thresholds are derived using all families and unrelated individuals rather than just those classified as being below the poverty level. To obtain the weighted poverty thresholds for families and unrelated individuals below alternate poverty levels, the weighted thresholds shown in table A may be multiplied directly by the appropriate factor. The weighted average thresholds presented in Table A are based on the March 1990 Current Population Survey. However, these thresholds would not differ significantly from those based on the 1990 Census.

3.4.2.10. Poverty Status of Households in 1989

The data on poverty status of households were derived from answers to the income questions. The income items were asked on a sample basis. Households are classified below the poverty level when the total 1989 income of the family or of the non-family householder is below the appropriate poverty threshold. The income of persons living in the household who are unrelated to the householder is not considered when determining the poverty status of a household, nor does their presence affect the household size in determining the appropriate poverty threshold. The poverty thresholds vary depending upon three criteria: size of family, number of children, and age of the family householder or unrelated individual for one and two-persons households (For more information, see the discussion Of "Poverty Status in 1989" and "Income in 1989" under Population Characteristics.)

3.5. Establishments

3.5.1. Data Sources

3.5.1.1. The Census of Agriculture

The 1987 Census of Agriculture, the latest included in this dataset, is the 23rd taken by the U.S. Bureau of the Census. The first agricultural census was taken in 1840 as part of the sixth decennial census of population. From 1840 to 1950, an agricultural census was taken as part of the decennial census. A separate mid-decade Census of Agriculture was conducted in 1925, 1935, and 1945. From 1954 to 1974, a Census of Agriculture was taken for the years ending in a 4 and 9. In 1976, Congress authorized the Census of Agriculture to be taken for 1978 and 1982 to adjust the data reference year so that it coincided with the economic censuses covering manufacturing, mining, construction, retail trade, wholesale trade, service industries, and selected transportation activities. This adjustment in timing established the Census of Agriculture on a 5-year cycle collecting data for years ending in 2 and 7. The census is conducted primarily by mail, the list of which is comprised of all individuals, businesses, and organizations that could be readily identified as being associated with agriculture.

3.5.1.2. The Census of Manufactures

Since 1947, the Census of Manufactures has covered all establishments as defined in the 1987 and earlier editions of the Standard Industrial Classification (SIC) Manual. The SIC Manual defines manufacturing as the mechanical or chemical transformation of inorganic or organic substances into new products. The assembly of component parts of products is also considered to be manufacturing if the resulting product is neither a structure nor other fixed improvement. These activities are usually carried out in plants, factories, or mills that characteristically use power-driven machines and materials-handling equipment.

The Census of Manufactures is conducted on an establishment basis. That is, a company with operations at more than one location is required to submit a report for each location. On the other hand, a company engaged in distinctly different lines of activity at one location is required to submit a separate report for activity if the plant records permit such a separation and if the activities are substantial in size. This census includes information for separately operated administrative offices, warehouses, garages, and other auxiliary units that serve manufacturing establishments of the same company.

In accordance with Federal law governing census reports, no data are published that would disclose the operations of an individual establishment or business.

3.5.1.3. The Surveys of Retail Trade

Retail (and wholesale) trade data were first collected in 1930; in 1933 information on selected service industries was added. These business censuses, as they were called, were again taken for 1935, 1939 (as part of the 1940 decennial program), 1948, 1954, 1958, 1963, and 1967. Since 1967, these censuses have been taken quinquennially (covering years ending in 2 and 7) as part of the Census Bureau's economic census program.

A significant innovation for the 1948 and succeeding censuses was that the classifications were based on the Standard Industrial Classification (SIC) Manual. In previous censuses, the Bureau had developed its own classifications after consultation with specialists in Government and the private sector.

The 1987 Census of Retail Trade covered retail trade as defined in the 1987 SIC Manual. It included all establishments primarily engaged in selling merchandise for personal or household consumption and rendering services incidental to the sale of goods. The census excluded governmental organizations classified in the covered industries except for liquor stores operated by State and local governments. Data for direct sellers with no paid employees, post exchanges, ship stores, and similar establishments operated on military posts by agencies of the Federal Government are not included. Establishments that are auxiliary (primary function is providing a service, such as warehouses) to retail establishments within the same organization are not included.

Census of Retail Trade information represents a summary of reports for individual establishments rather than companies. For cases where a census report was received, separate information was obtained for each location where business was conducted. When administrative records of other Federal agencies were used instead of a census report, no information was available on the number of locations operated. Estimates of this number were derived from a sample. Each retail establishment was tabulated according to the physical location at which business was conducted.

Establishments covered by the census were assigned kind-of-business classifications according to the industry classification defined in the 1987 SIC Manual and earlier versions. For 1982 and 1987, data are not shown by kind of business for all establishments, but only for establishments with payroll. In 1977, kind-of business data were available for both types of establishments. Retail trade covers major groups 52 through 59.

The 1977 and 1982 Censuses of Retail Trade were conducted under similar conditions and procedures except for the following:

(1)   Geographic areas

The boundaries of a number of areas for which data are shown in the 1982 Census are not the same as in the 1977 Census because of annexations, other boundary changes, redefinitions of SMSA's, and changes in qualifying criteria since 1977.

(2)   Nonemployer firms

In 1977, the census included any retail nonemployer firm which reported a sales volume of $2,500 or more, plus firms in operation for less than the full year that reported sales which, if projected to an annual basis, would have reached a total of $2,500 or more. In the 1982 Census, nonemployer firms are included if, on an annual basis, they reported a sales volume of at least $1,000. Had the 1982 criterion been applied in the 1977 Census of Retail Trade, an additional 62,000 non-employers with sales of $120.6 million would have been included.

(3)   Leased departments

In 1977 and prior censuses, data for leased departments were consolidated with the data for stores in which they were located. In the 1982 Census, each leased department was treated as a separate establishment and was classified according to the kind of business it conducted. For detailed information on 1987 Census changes, see the source (U.S. Bureau of the Census).

3.5.1.4. The Survey of Wholesale Trade

The first census of business, which included wholesale trade, was conducted in 1930. Between 1933 and 1963, seven subsequent business censuses were taken (see The Survey of Retail Trade above for specific years.) Beginning with 1967, the economic censuses have been taken at 5-year intervals covering years ending in 2 and 7.

The 1987 Census of Wholesale Trade covered wholesale trade as defined in the 1987 Standard Industrial Classification (SIC) Manual. It includes all establishments with one or more paid employees primarily engaged in selling merchandise to retailers; to industrial, commercial, institutional, farm or professional users; or to other wholesalers. Companies selling products to which they have title, as well as those acting as agents or brokers in buying merchandise for or selling merchandise to others, are included. Two major industry groups, durable goods and nondurable goods, are classified in wholesale trade. Their two-digit SIC code numbers are 50 and 51, respectively. The census included wholesale liquor warehouses operated by State and local governments. Excluded were warehouses and other units that serviced or were auxiliary to wholesale establishments within the same organization.

The 1977 and 1982 Censuses were conducted under similar conditions and procedures except for the following:

(1)   The boundaries of a number of areas for which data are shown in the 1982 Census are not the same as in the 1977 Census because of annexations, other boundary changes, redefinitions of SMSA's, and changes in qualifying criteria since 1977.

(2)   The 1977 employment item included three pay-period statistics omitted from the 1982 inquiry: The number of paid employees for the pay period including the 12th of May, August, and November. These statistics are collected and published by the Bureau of Labor Statistics.

(3)   In 1982, inventories were reported at cost or market using generally accepted accounting methods. Inventories calculated on a LIFO basis were reported before the LIFO adjustment. In 1977, inventories were reported by valuation method and summed to a total for each establishment. Method of valuation data are collected by the Bureau of the Census in the Annual Trade Survey.

3.5.1.5. The Survey of Service Industries

Information on selected service industries, which were part of the economic censuses, was first collected in 1933. Between 1933 and 1967, seven subsequent censuses were taken. Since 1967, the census of service industries, as well as the other economic censuses, have been taken at 5-year intervals for years ending in 2 and 7.

The 1987 Census of Service Industries covered service industries as defined in the 1987 Standard Industrial Classification (SIC) Manual (see LBR 300-390). For 1982 and 1987, only establishments with some payroll during the year are covered. For previous years, all establishments were covered. The data do not include establishments that are auxiliary (primary function is providing a service, such as warehouses) to

34

service establishments within the same organization. There are major revisions to the earlier structure which limit the comparability of data between 1982 and 1987 censuses.

The 1977 and 1982 Censuses of Service Industries were conducted under similar conditions and procedures except for the following:

(1)   Geographic areas

For discussion, see The Survey of Retail above.

(2)   Non-employer firms

For discussion, see The Survey of Retail above.

(3)   Scope

Some industries covered in the 1977 Census were not covered for 1982: SIC's 806 (Hospitals), 821 (Elementary and secondary schools), 822 (Colleges, universities, professional schools, and junior colleges), 863 (labor unions and similar labor organizations), and 865 (political organizations). SIC 4722 (Arrangement of passenger transportation) was covered in 1982 under the Census of Transportation, not service industries.

(4)   Federal income tax status/kind-of-business combinations

In 1977, a few kinds of business were assumed to be exempt from Federal income tax and were tabulated in the tax-exempt category. Establishments of firms that were exempt from Federal income tax, but which were in a kind of business not expected to be exempt, were tabulated in a miscellaneous kind-of-business category. For 1982, the same kinds of business are definitionally considered exempt from Federal income tax and tabulated in the tax-exempt category; the remaining kinds of business are definitionally considered subject to Federal income tax. The miscellaneous kind-of-business category has been eliminated.

3.5.2. Selected Terms

3.5.2.1. Apparel (and Accessory) (Retail)

Apparel (and accessory) stores (SIC Major Group 56) include retail stores primarily engaged in selling clothing of all kinds and related articles for personal wear and adornment. Not included are establishments that meet the criteria for department stores or miscellaneous general merchandise stores even though most of their receipts are from the sale of apparel and apparel accessories. They consist of men's and boys' clothing and furnishings stores; women's ready-to-wear stores; women's accessory and specialty stores; children's and infants' wear stores; family clothing stores; men's, women's, children's and juveniles', and family shoe stores; furriers and fur shops; and establishments primarily engaged in the retail sale of lines of apparel and accessories not elsewhere classified, such as uniforms, bathing suits, raincoats, riding apparel, sports apparel, umbrellas, wigs, and toupees. Also included are custom tailors primarily engaged in making and selling men's and women's clothing (except fur apparel) to individual order.

3.5.2.2. Automotive Dealers (Retail)

Automotive dealers excluding gasoline service stations (SIC Major Group 55 less SIC 554) are retail dealers selling new and used automobiles, boats, recreational vehicles and utility trailers, and motorcycles and mopeds, and dealers selling new automobile parts and accessories. They include establishments dealing exclusively in used automobiles, but not establishments dealing exclusively in used parts. Also included are automobile repair shops maintained by establishments engaged in the sale of new automobiles. Automotive distributors, the greater part of whose sales are to dealers or to institutional or industrial users, are classiffied in wholesale trade.

3.5.2.3. Eating and Drinking (Retail)

Eating and drinking places (SIC Major Group 58) include retail establishments selling prepared food and drinks for consumption on the premises; they also include lunch counters and refreshment stands selling prepared foods and drinks for immediate consumption. They consist of restaurants and lunchrooms, social caterers, cafeterias, refreshment places, contract feeding, ice cream and frozen custard stands, and drinking places (alcoholic beverages).

3.5.2.4. Employers (Manufacturing)

The all employees number is the average number of production workers plus the number of other employees in mid-March. Included are all persons on paid sick leave, paid holidays, and paid vacations during the pay period. Officers of corporations are included as employees; proprietors and partners of unincorporated firms are excluded.

3.5.2.5. Establishment

An establishment is a single physical location at which business is conducted. It is not necessarily identical with a company or enterprise, which may consist of one or more establishments. The count of establishments for 1987 represents the number in business at any time during the year. For prior censuses, the count represents the number of establishments in business at the end of the year.

When two or more activities were carried on at a single location under a single ownership, all activities generally were grouped together as a single establishment. The entire establishment was classified on the basis of its major activity, and all data for it were included in that classification. However, when distinct and separate economic activities (for which different industry classification codes were appropriate) were conducted under the same ownership at a single location, and when conditions prescribed by the SIC Manual for recognizing the existence of more than one establishment were met, separate establishment reports for each of the different activities were obtained in the census.

3.5.2.6. Farm

Since 1850, when minimum criteria defining a farm for census purposes first were established, the farm definition has been changed nine times. The current definition, first used for the 1974 Census, is any place from which $1,000 or more of agricultural products were produced and sold or normally would have been sold during the census year.

3.5.2.7. Food (Retail)

Food stores (SIC Major Group 54) are establishments primarily engaged in selling food for home preparation and consumption. They include grocery stores; meat and fish (seafood) markets; fruit stores and veg-etable markets; candy, nut, and confectionery stores; dairy products stores; retail bakeries; and establishments primarily engaged in the retail sale of specialized foods not elsewhere classified, such as eggs and poultry, health foods, spices, herbs, coffee, and tea.

3.5.2.8. Home Furnishings (and Furniture) (Retail)

Furniture and home furnishings stores (SIC Major Group 57) include retail stores selling goods used for furnishing the home, such as furniture, floor coverings, draperies, glass and chinaware, domestic stoves, refrigerators, and household electrical and gas appliances. Establishments selling electrical and gas appliances are included in this group only if the major part of their sales consists of articles for home use. Dealers primarily engaged in selling antique and second-hand furniture are classified in miscellaneous retail stores (SIC Major Group 59). Stores primarily engaged in selling merchandise but also providing an interior decorating service are classified according to the merchandise handled. Interior designers primarily engaged in advising clients on the selection of interior decorations are classified in service industries.

3.5.2.9. Gasoline Service (Retail)

Gasoline service stations (SIC 554) are establishments primarily engaged in selling gasoline and automotive lubricants. Usually these establishments also sell tires, batteries, and accessories, and perform minor repair work and services. Establishments called garages but deriving more than half of their receipts from the sale of gasoline and automotive lubricants are included.

3.5.1.10. General Merchandise (Retail)

General merchandise stores (SIC Major Group 53) include retail stores that sell a number of lines of merchandise, such as dry goods, apparel and accessories, furniture and home furnishings, small wares, hardware, and food. The stores included in this group are known as department stores, variety stores, general merchandise stores, general stores, etc. Establishments primarily engaged in selling used general merchandise and those selling general merchandise by mail, vending machine, or direct selling are classified in miscellaneous retail stores (SIC Major Group 59).

3.5.1.11. Land in Farms

The acreage designated as "land in farms" consists primarily of agricultural land used for crops, pasture, or grazing. It also includes woodland and wasteland not actually under cultivation or used for pasture or grazing, provided it was part of the farm operator's total operation.

Land in farms is an operating-unit concept and includes land owned and operated, as well as land rented from others. Land used rent free was to be reported as land rented from others. Land rented or assigned to a tenant was considered the tenant's farm and not the owner's. All land in Indian reservations used for growing crops or grazing livestock was to be included as land in farms.

With few exceptions, the land in each farm was tabulated as being in the operator's principal county. The principal county was defined as the one where the largest value of agricultural products were raised or produced. It was usually the county containing all or the largest proportion of the land in the farm. For a limited number of Western States, this procedure resulted in the allocation of more land in farms to a county than the total land area of the county. To minimize this distortion, separate reports were required for large farms, identified from the 1974 Census and prior special surveys as having more than one separately reportable farm unit. Other reports showing land in more than one county were separated into two or more reports if the data would significantly affect the county totals. These reports were assigned to the appropriate counties during office processing.

Farmland as a percent of total land is based on the approximate total land area of counties.

3.5.2.12. Paid Employees (Retail/Wholesale/Service)

Paid employees consist of the full-time and part-time employees, including salaried officers and executives of corporations, who were on the payroll in the pay period including March 12. Included are employees on paid sick leave, paid holidays, and paid vacations; not included are proprietors and partners of unincorporated businesses.

3.5.2.13. Unincorporated Businesses (Retail)

Figures for establishments operated by unincorporated businesses represent the number of retail establishments that were unincorporated as defined by law. In 1982, the legal form of organization for firms in the mail universe was based on the response to the organization status inquiry on the various census forms.

The legal form of organization of non-mail firms was generally based on information available from the administrative records from other Federal agencies.

3.5.2.14. Value of Farm Products Sold

The value of farm products sold by farms represents the gross market value before taxes and production expenses of an agricultural products sold or removed from the place, regardless of who received the payment. It includes sales by the operator as well as the value of any shares received by partners, landlords, contractors, and others associated with the operation. It represents the sum of all crops, including nursery products sold and livestock and poultry and their products sold. It excludes income from farm-related sources such as custom work or agricultural service, income from non-farm sources, and sales of forest products from farms and ranches. The value of agricultural products sold was collected from all operators. Where the operator failed to report a value of sales, estimates were made based on the amount of crops harvested or the number of livestock or poultry sold. Extensive estimation was required for farmers growing crops and livestock under contract.

The value of crops sold for a year does not necessarily represent the sales from crops harvested that year. The data include sales from crops produced in earlier years and exclude some crops produced that year but held in storage and not sold. For crops sold through a co-op that made payments in several installments, only the amount received that year was to be reported.

3.6. Government Finance and Employment

3.6.1. Data Sources

3.6.1.1. The Census of Governments

Data on local governments are based on results of the Census of Governments. During the period 1850 to 1942, the census was taken at approximately 10-year intervals. The Census of Governments for the year 1957 was the first census taken after 1942. Information on county areas (explained below) are not available from the 1942 Census. Therefore, this dataset includes information after the 1957 census. The data were obtained primarily by mail canvass.

Beginning with 1957, the census has been conducted by the Bureau every fifth year (for years ending in 2 and 7). For each county area, the financial data comprise amounts for all local governments; not only the county government but also any municipalities, townships, school districts, and special districts within the county. Data from governmental units located in two or more county areas are assigned to the county area containing the administrative office.

The original universe of the 1987 Census of Government consists of the Federal Government, the 50 State governments, and the 82,934 local governments in existence as of October 1987 (3,042 counties; 19,227 municipalities; 16,685 townships; 29,270 special districts; and 14,710 school districts). The universe of other government censuses is similar to that of the 1987 Census with the actual number of local government slightly varying from census to census.

The concepts, categories and terms applied in each census round from which data are assembled is reasonably comparable. However, the data on total expenditure in particular (and total direct expenditure to a lesser degree) turned out to be very problematic, and are included in this dataset only as references (for detail, see the section on expenditure below).

In addition, changes in the level or type of government providing particular services occur over time. Thus, for example, a decrease in employment for a particular function of a government does not, in and of itself, signify a diminution of services the population receives. Moreover, certain services may be "contracted out" and the contractor's employees are not counted as employees of the contracting government. Also, annexations, other boundary changes, consolidations of governmental entities, and changes in the demographic makeup of the area served may affect not only the number of persons for whom services must be provided, but also the nature and scope of the necessary services.

3.6.1.2. Comparability of Data

The data on total expenditure, total direct expenditure, intergovernmental expenditure and total direct general expenditure for the country area are all available, and believed to be accurate, for the year 1982 and 1987. Prior to 1982, the information about total expenditure and total direct expenditure becomes less reliable because:

For 1977, total direct expenditure and total expenditure are not available from the published Census of Government volume. They are derived by summing the appropriate expenditure categories in the data tape. However, the data on intergovernmental expenditure (which comprises the total expenditure) in the census publication does not agree with the result of our computations based on the data in the data tape (ICPSR 8118). Since the same method of calculation are used for computing the 1982 and 1987 data, the discrepancy suggests that either the published data have errors, or items included under intergovernmental expenditure have changed between 1977 and 1982. We were unable to identify the source of these errors. Consequently, the total expenditure, which is a sum of total direct expenditure and intergovernmental expenditure, is less reliable. It is shown here only as a reference.

For 1972, the data on intergovernmental expenditure are not available from the published Census of Government volumes. Although they are included in the data tape (ICPSR 0069), there is no way to check the accuracy of the total expenditure derived using the data in the data tape since the intergovernmental expenditure (and total expenditure) data are not published. The comparison of the difference between total expenditure and total direct general expenditure for the period 1972-1987 suggests that total expenditure for 1972 may be substantially underestimated.

For 1962, no data on intergovernmental data (and thus, total expenditure) are available either from published sources or in a data tape (ICPSR 0017). Thus it is not possible to derive data on total expenditure. Furthermore, since no information is available on utility expenditure other than water (there should be expenditure on gas, electricity and transit), government-run liquor store and insurance trust (or retirement system), we could not derive data on total direct expenditure.

The 1957 data, in comparison with the 1962, 1972, and 1977, are actually more comparable with the 1982 and 1987 dataset. Both utility expenditure from all sources and intergovernmental expenditure are available. However, since the data on government-run liquor store and insurance trust (or retirement system) are not available, total direct expenditure and total expenditure data may be underestimated.

In conclusion, the most consistently available, and probably accurate figure representing the overall spending level of the county area for the periods 1957-1987 is total direct general expenditure, which is a sum of all function (for detail, see below). Total direct general expenditure comprises about 85% of total expenditure, judging from the 1982 and 1987 datasets.

3.6.2. Selected Terms: Government Revenue

3.6.2.1. Total Revenue

Total revenue refers to all amounts received by a government from external sources, that is, total intergovernmental revenue, general revenue from own sources, utility and liquor and insurance trust revenue-net of refunds and other correcting transactions excluding revenue from issuance of debt, liquidation of investments, and as agency and private trust transactions. Note that revenue excludes noncash transactions such as receipt of services, commodities, or other "receipts in kind."

3.6.2.2. Total General Revenue

Total general revenue refers to all government revenue except utility revenue, liquor store revenue, and employee retirement and other insurance trust revenue. The basis for distinction is not the fund or administrative unit receiving particular amounts, but rather the nature of the revenue sources concerned.

3.6.2.3. Total General Revenue From Own Sources

Total general revenue from own sources includes all government revenue from taxes, charges and other miscellaneous general revenue. It excludes intergovernmental revenue, utility revenue, liquor store revenue, and employee retirement and other insurance trust revenue.

3.6.2.4. Current Charges

Current charges are the amounts received from the public for performance of specific services benefiting the person charged, and from sales of commodities and services except by government utilities and liquor stores. They include fees, assessments, and other reimbursements for current services, rents and sales derived from commodities or services furnished incident to the performance of particular functions, gross income of commercial activities, and the like. They exclude amounts received from other governments (see Intergovernmental Revenue) and interdepartmental charges and transfers. Current charges are distinguished from license taxes, which relate to privileges granted by the government or regulatory measures for the protection of the public.

3.6.2.5. Insurance Trust System

Insurance trust system is a government-administered program for employee retirement and social insurance protection relating to unemployment compensation, workmen's compensation, old age, survivors', disability, and health insurance, and the like.

3.6.2.6. Insurance Trust Revenue

Insurance trust revenue comprises amounts from contributions required of employers and employees for financing these social insurance programs and earnings on assets of such systems.

3.6.2.7. Intergovernmental Revenue

Intergovernmental revenue refers to amounts received from other governments as fiscal aid in the form of shared revenues and grants-in-aid, as reimbursements for performance of general government functions and specific services for the paying government (e.g., care of prisoners or contractual research) or in lieu of taxes. Excludes amounts received from other governments for sale of property, commodities, and utility services. All intergovernmental revenue is classified as general revenue.

Total intergovernmental revenue. This term includes intergovernmental revenue from federal and state government.

Intergovernmental revenue from federal government: Intergovernmental revenue received by a government directly from the Federal Government. For local governments excludes Federal aid channeled through state governments.

Intergovernmental revenue from state government: All intergovernmental revenue received from the state government, including amounts originally from the Federal Government but channeled through the state.

Intergovernmental revenue for general local government support: Fiscal aid revenue that allows the receiving government unrestricted use as to function or purpose.

3.6.2.8. Liquor Store Revenue

Amounts received from sale of liquor by government liquor stores and other revenues from government liquor store operations. Excludes any taxes collected by government liquor monopoly systems.

3.6.2.9. Miscellaneous Commercial Activities

Miscellaneous commercial activities are provision and operation of commercial facilities not classified under particular functions. Includes only activities owned by the government concerned. Typical examples are markets, cemeteries, and disaster insurance systems.

3.6.2.10. Taxes

Taxes are compulsory contributions exacted by a government for public purposes, except employee and employer assessments for retirement and social insurance purposes, which are classified as insurance trust revenue. All tax revenue is classified as general revenue and comprises amounts received (including interest and penalties but excluding protested amounts and refunds) from all taxes imposed by a government. Note that local government tax revenue excludes any amounts from shares of state-imposed and collected taxes which are classified as intergovernmental Revenue. The taxes included in the tabulation are:

Corporation Net Income Taxes

Death and Gift Taxes

Individual Income Taxes

License Taxes

Property Taxes

Property Tax Relief

Sales and Gross Receipts Taxes

General Sales or Gross Receipts Taxes

Selective Sales and Gross Receipts Taxes

Severance Taxes

Property taxes. Property taxes are taxes conditioned on ownership of property and measured by its value. They include general property taxes related to property as a whole, real and personal, tangible or intangible, whether taxed at a single rate or at classified rates, and taxes on selected types of property, such as motor vehicles or certain or all intangibles.

3.6.2.11. Utility

A government owned and operated water supply, electric light and power, gas supply or transit system. Government revenue, expenditure, and debt relating to utility facilities leased to other governments or persons, and other commercial type activities of governments, such as port facilities, airports, housing projects, radio stations, steam plants, ferries, abattoirs, etc., are classified as general government activities.

Electric power: Operation and maintenance of electric power system including production or acquisition and distribution of electric power.

Gas supply: Operation and maintenance of gas supply systems including acquisition and distribution of natural gas.

Water supply: Operation and maintenance of water supply system including acquisition and distribution of water to the general public or to other local governments for domestic or industrial use. Acquisition and distribution of water for irrigation of agricultural lands are classified under Natural Resources.

3.6.2.12. Utility Revenue

This refers to revenue from sale of utility commodities and services to the public and to other governments. Does not include amounts from sales to the parent government. It also excludes income from utility fund investments and from other non-operating properties (treated as general revenue). Any revenue from taxes, special assessments, and intergovernmental aid is classified as general revenue, not utility revenue.

3.6.3. Selected Terms: Government Expenditure

3.6.3.1. Cash Assistance (See Public Welfare, Sections 3.6.3.21 and 3.6.5.15)

3.6.3.2. Correction

This refers to confinement and correction of adults and minors convicted of offenses against the law, and pardon, probation, and parole activities.

3.6.3.3. Education

Education is defined as the provision or support of schools and facilities for elementary and secondary, higher, and other education. Elementary and Secondary Education includes the provision of public kindergarten through high school education by state and local governments.

It encompasses instructional, support, and auxiliary services (school lunch, student activities, and community services) offered by public school systems revenues and expenditures for enterprise activities are included on a gross basis. Higher Education consists of all state and local institutions of higher education.

It excludes agricultural experiment stations and agricultural extension services (included under Natural Resources), university-operated hospitals (included under Hospitals), and scholarship and fellowship payments (included under Other Education).

Other Education includes all federal Government educational activities with the exception of service academies (which are classified as part of national defense and international relations), state government administrative supervision of elementary and secondary and higher education, scholarship and fellowship payments, aid to private schools, and support of special schools for deaf, blind, and other handicapped persons.

3.6.3.4. Expenditure

Expenditure refers to all amounts of money paid out by a government--net of recoveries and other correcting transactions--other than for retirement of debt, investment in securities, extension of credit, or as agency transactions. Note that expenditure includes only external transactions of a government and excludes noncash transactions such as the provision of perquisites or other payments in kind.

Total expenditure: Total direct expenditure plus intergovernmental expenditure.

Total direct expenditure: Total direct general expenditure plus utility expenditure, liquor stores expenditure, and employee-retirement or other insurance trust expenditure. This item includes payments to employees, suppliers, contractors, beneficiaries and other final recipients of government payments.

Total direct general expenditure: All government expenditure other than the specially enumerated kinds of expenditure classified as utility expenditure, liquor stores expenditure, and employee-retirement or other insurance trust expenditure.

Intergovernmental expenditure: Amounts paid to other governments as fiscal aid in the form of shared revenues and grants-in-aid, as reimbursements for performance of general government activities and for specific services for the paying government, or in lieu of taxes. Excludes amounts paid to other governments for purchase of commodities, property, or utility services, any tax imposed and paid as such, and employer contributions for social insurance-e.g., contributions to the federal government for Old-Age, Survivors' Disability, and Health Insurance for government employees. All intergovernmental expenditure is classified as general expenditure.

3.6.3.5. Financial Administration

Financial administration includes officials and agencies concerned with tax assessment and collection, accounting, auditing, budgeting, purchasing, custody of funds, and other central finance activities.

3.6.3.6. Fire Protection

Fire protection consists of fire fighting organization and auxiliary services; fire inspection and investigation; support of volunteer fire forces; and other fire prevention activities. Includes cost of fire fighting facilities, such as fire hydrants and water, furnished by other agencies of the government.

3.6.3.7. Health

This term refers to out-patient health services, other than hospital care, including: public health administration; research and education; categorical health programs; treatment and immunization clinics; nursing; environmental health activities such as air and water pollution control; ambulance service if provided separately from fire protection services; and other general public health activities such as mosquito abatement, School health services provided by health agencies (rather than school agencies) are included here, Sewage treatment operations are classified under Sewerage.

3.6.3.8. Hospitals

The definition of hospitals includes financing, construction, acquisition, maintenance or operation of hospital facilities, provision of hospital care, and support of public or private hospitals. It includes expenditures by public hospitals under welfare programs for medical assistance such as medicaid. However, see Public Welfare (Section 3.6.3.21) concerning vendor payments under welfare programs

3.6.3.9. Housing and Community (Urban) Development

This category refers to construction and operation of housing and redevelopment projects, and other activities to promote or aid housing and community development.

3.6.3.10. Insurance Trust Expenditure

This term corresponds with the character and object category, insurance benefits and repayments, and comprises only cash payments to beneficiaries (including withdrawals of contributions). These categories exclude costs of administering insurance trust systems, which are classed as general expenditure. Insurance trust revenue and expenditure do not include any contributions of a government to a system it administers. Any amounts paid by a government as employer contributions to an insurance trust system administered by another government are classed as general expenditure for current operation, and as insurance trust revenue of the particular system and receiving government.

Insurance benefits and repayments: Social insurance payments to beneficiaries, employee-retirement annuities and other benefits, and withdrawals of insurance or employee-retirement contributions. Includes only amounts paid to beneficiaries; administrative expenditure for such activities are classified as Current Operation.

3.6.3.11. Interest Expenditure (Interest on General Debt)

This is the amount paid for the use of borrowed money. Interest on utility debt is included in Utility Expenditures.

3.6.3.12. Libraries

This term refers to establishment and operation of public libraries and support of privately operated libraries (excludes those operated as part of a school system, primarily for the benefit of students and teachers, and law libraries).

3.6.3.13. Liquor Store Expenditure

This is defined as expenditures for purchase of liquor for resale and provision and operation of liquor stores. It excludes expenditure for law enforcement and licensing activities carried out in conjunction with liquor store operations.

3.6.3.14. Natural Resources

Natural resources include conservation, promotion, and development of natural resources, such as soil, water, forests, minerals, and wildlife. Includes irrigation, drainage, flood control, forestry and forest fire protection, soil reclamation, soil and water conservation, fish and game programs, and agricultural fairs. For the Federal Government, includes agricultural experiment stations and extension services, farm price stabilization programs, farm insurance and credit activities, and multipurpose power and reclamation projects.

3.6.3.15. N.E.C. (Not elsewhere classified)

3.6.3.16. Other Governmental Administration

This includes the functions of judicial and legal, and general public buildings; and activities of the governing body, office of the chief executive, and central staff services and agencies concerned with personnel administration, recording, planning, zoning, and the like.

General public buildings (state-local): Provision and maintenance of public buildings not allocated to particular functions. This category is not applied in reporting federal data.

Judicial and legal: Courts and activities associated with courts including law libraries, prosecutorial and defendant programs, probate functions, and juries.

3.6.3.17. Own Hospitals (See Hospitals, Section 3.6.3.8)

3.6.3.18. Parks and Recreation

Provision and support of recreational and cultural-scientific facilities and activities including golf courses, play fields, playgrounds, public beaches, swimming pools, tennis courts, parks, auditoriums, stadiums, auto camps, recreation piers, marinas, botanical gardens, galleries, museums, and zoos. It also includes building and operation of convention centers and exhibition halls.

3.6.3.19. Police Protection

Police protection refers to preservation of law and order and traffic safety, including police patrols and communications, crime prevention activities, detention and custody of persons awaiting trial, traffic safety and vehicular inspection.

3.6.3.20. Protective Inspection and Regulation

Regulation of private enterprise for the protection of the public and inspection of hazardous activities except for major functions, such as fire prevention, health, natural resources, etc. Distinctive licensing collection activities are classified under Financial Administration.

3.6.3.21. Public Welfare

Support of, and assistance to, needy persons contingent upon their need. It excludes pensions to former employees and other benefits not contingent on need. Expenditures under this heading include cash assistance paid directly to needy persons under the federal categorical programs (Supplemental Security Income and Age Assistance Aid to Families With Dependent Children) and under any other welfare programs, Vendor Payments made directly to private purveyors for medical care, burials, and other commodities and services provided under welfare programs; and provision and operation by the government of welfare institutions. Other public welfare includes payments to other governments for welfare purposes, amounts for administration, support of private welfare agencies, and other public welfare services. Health and hospital services including those under public welfare programs like medicaid, provided directly by the government through its own hospitals and health agencies, and any payments to other governments for such purposes are classed under those functional headings rather than here.

Sanitation other than sewerage: Street cleaning, solid waste collection and disposal, and provision of sanitary landfills.

3.6.3.22. Securities

Stocks and bonds, notes, mortgages, and other formal evidences of indebtedness.

3.6.3.23. Sewerage

Provision of sanitary and storm sewers and sewage disposal facilities and services, and payments to other governments for such purposes.

3.6.3.24. Transportation

Comprises the functions of highways, air transportation, parking facilities, water transport and terminals, and transit subsidies.

Air transportation: Construction, maintenance, operation, and support of airport facilities, assistance and subsidies. Cash contributions and subsidies to persons and foreign governments, not in payment for goods or services or for claims against the government. For local governments, this object category comprises only direct Cash Assistance Payments to public welfare recipients. For states, it includes also veterans' bonuses and direct cash grants for tuition, scholarships, and aid to nonpublic educational institutions. Major federal subsidy payments are for veterans' benefits, agricultural support programs, and foreign aid.

Highways: Construction, maintenance, and operation of highways, streets, and related structures, including toll highways, bridges, tunnels, ferries, street lighting and snow and ice removal. However, highway policing and traffic control are classed under Police Protection.

Parking facilities: Construction, purchase, maintenance, and operation of public-use parking lots, garages, parking meters, and other distinctive parking facilities on a commercial basis. Applies only to local governments.

Water transport and terminals: Construction, maintenance, operation, and support of canals and other waterways, harbors, docks, wharves, and related marine terminal facilities.

Transit subsidies: Payments in support of subway, bus, surface rail and street railroad, and other passenger transportation systems, including public support of a private utility or railroad and intergovernmental subsidy payments. Excludes amounts paid by a parent government to its dependent transit utility. Also see under Utility.

3.6.3.25. Utility Expenditure

Expenditure for construction of utility facilities or equipment, for production and distribution of utility commodities and services (except those furnished to parent government), and for interest on utility debt. It does not include expenditure in connection with administration of utility debt and investments (treated as general expenditure) and the cost of providing services to the parent government (such costs, when identifiable, are treated as expenditure for the function served).

3.6.3.26. Vendor Payments (See Public Welfare, Section 3.6.3.21)

3.6.4. Selected Terms: Government Debt

3.6.4.1. Debt

All long-term credit obligations of the government and its agencies whether backed by the government's full faith and credit or nonguaranteed, and all interest-bearing short-term credit obligations. It includes judgments, mortgages, and revenue bonds as well as general obligation bonds, notes, and interest-bearing warrants. Excludes noninterest-bearing short-term obligations, interfund obligations, amounts owed in a trust or agency capacity, advances and contingent loans from other governments, and rights of individuals to benefits from government-administered employee retirement funds. Refunding of Long-Term Debt is the issuance of long-term obligations in exchange for, or to finance the retirement of, outstanding long-term debt, generally to obtain more favorable interest rates.

Long-term debt: Debt payable more than 1 year after date of issue

Short-term debt: Interest-bearing debt payable within 1 year from date of issue, such as bond anticipation notes, bank loans, and tax anticipation notes and warrants, Includes obligations having no fixed maturity date if payable from a tax levied for collection in the year of their issuance.

Utility debt: Debt originally issued specifically to finance government owned and operated water, electric, gas, or transit utility facilities.

3.6.5. Selected Terms: Government Employment

3.6.5.1. Correction

Activities pertaining to the confinement and correction of adults and minors convicted of criminal offenses. Pardon, probation, and parole activities are also included here.

3.6.5.2. Education

Elementary and secondary education: All activities associated with the operation of public elementary and secondary schools and locally operated vocational-technical schools. Special education programs operated by elementary and secondary school systems are also included as are all ancillary services associated with the operation of schools, such as pupil transportation and food service.

Higher education: State and local government degree granting institutions which provide academic training above grade 12. Instructional employees includes persons engaged in teaching and related academic research.

Instructional employees: Instructional employees includes not only classroom teachers, but also principals, supervisors of instruction, librarians, teacher aides, library aides, and guidance and psychological personnel. Other employees includes all persons not included as instructional employees (e.g., school superintendents and other administrative personnel clerical and secretarial staffs, plant operation and maintenance personnel health and recreation employees, transportation and food service personnel and any student employees).

3.6.5.3. Employment and Employers

Employment refers to all persons gainfully employed by and performing services for a government. Employees include all persons paid for personal services performed, including persons paid from federally funded programs; paid elected officials; persons in paid leave status; and persons paid on a per meeting, annual, semiannual, or quarterly basis. Unpaid officials, pensioners, persons whose work is performed on a fee basis, and contractors and their employees are excluded from the count of employees.

Full-time employment. Full-time employees are defined to include those persons whose hours of work represent full-time employment in their employer government; part-time employees are those persons who work less than the standard number of hours for full-time work in their employer government.

Full-time equivalent employment. This is a computed statistic representing the number of full-time employees that could have been employed if the reported number of hours worked by part-time employees had been worked by full-time employees. This statistic is calculated separately for each function of a government by dividing the "part-time hours paid" by the standard number of hours for full-time employees in the particular government and then adding the resulting quotient to the number of full-time employees.

3.6.5.4. Financial Administration

This includes activities concerned with tax assessment and collection, custody and disbursement of funds, debt management, administration of trust funds, budgeting, and other government wide financial management activities. This function is not applied to school district or special district governments.

3.6.5.5. Fire Protection

Fire protection applies to local government fire protection and prevention activities plus any ambulance, rescue, or other auxiliary services provided by the fire protection agency. Volunteer fire fighters, if remunerated for their services on a "per fire" or some other basis, are included as part-time employees. The subcategory of fire fighters includes personnel trained and/or engaged in fire suppression and prevention.

3.6.5.6. Health

Health includes the following services: Administration of public health programs, community and visiting nurse services, immunization programs, drug abuse rehabilitation programs, health and food inspection activities, operation of outpatient clinics, and environmental pollution control activities.

3.6.5.7. Hospitals

This category includes only government-operated medical care facilities which provide inpatient care. Employees and payrolls of private corporations which lease and/or operate government-owned hospital facilities are excluded.

3.6.5.8. Housing and Community Development (Urban Renewal)

This category refers to the operation of housing and redevelopment projects and other activities to promote or aid housing and community development.

3.6.5.9. Judicial and Legal

The judicial and legal categories includes all court and court related activities (except probation and parole activities which are included in the "Correction" category), court activities of sheriffs offices, prosecuting attorneys and public defender's offices, legal departments, and attorneys providing government wide legal service.

3.6.5.10. Libraries

This category applies only to libraries operated by local governments for use by the general public. School and law libraries are included in the "Elementary and secondary education" or "Higher education," and "Judicial and legal" categories, respectively.

3.6.5.11. Natural Resources

These are activities primarily concerned with the conservation and development of natural resources, forest fire prevention and control, flood control, irrigation, drainage, land and forest reclamation, fish and game preservation and control, soil conservation, forestry, agricultural fairs and research, agricultural development and inspection, and mineral resources activities.

3.6.5.12. Other and Unallocatable

This classification represents all activities not individually specified.

3.6.5.13. Other Government Administration

Other government administration applies to the legislative and government wide administrative agencies of governments. Included here are overall planning and zoning activities, central personnel and administrative activities. This function is not applied to school district or special district governments.

3.6.5.14. Police Protection

This category comprises all activities concerned with the enforcement of law and order, including coroner's offices, police training academies, investigation bureaus, and local jails, "lockups," or other detention facilities not intended to serve as correctional facilities. The subcategory of police officers includes only persons with the power of arrest.

3.6.5.15. Public Welfare

Included in this category are such activities as the administration of various public assistance programs for the needy, operation of homes for the elderly, indigent care institutions, and programs that provide payments for medical care and other services for the needy. Health care and hospital services provided directly by a government, however, are included in the "Health" and "Hospital" functions rather than here.

3.6.5.16. Sanitation Other than Sewerage

Refuse collection and disposal, operation of sanitary landfills, and street cleaning activities are included in this category.

3.6.5.17. Sewerage

Sewerage refers to the provision, maintenance, and operation of sanitary and storm sewer systems and sewage disposal and treatment facilities.

3.6.5.18. Social Insurance Administration

The administration and conduct of social insurance programs include unemployment compensation and worker compensation programs, work/study programs, and determination of eligibility for federal old age, survivors, disability, and health insurance (social security). Federal activities in this category are primarily those performed by the social security administration and the pension benefit Guarantee Corporation.

3.6.5.19. Transportation

Air transportation: Operation and support of publicly operated airport facilities.

Highways. Activities associated with the maintenance and operation of streets, roads, sidewalks, bridges, tunnels, toll roads, and ferries are included at this function. Snow and ice removal, street lighting, and highway and traffic engineering activities are also included here.

Parks and recreation: Government activities that include operation and maintenance of parks, playgrounds, swimming pools, public beaches, auditoriums, public golf courses, museums, marinas, botanical gardens, and zoological parks.

Water transport and terminals: Activities which are connected with the operation and support of canals and other waterways, harbors, docks, wharves, and other related marine terminal facilities.

3.6.5.20. Utilities

Electric power: Activities associated with the production or acquisition and distribution of electric power.

Gas supply: Government activities associated with the acquisition of gas supplies and distribution to individual consumers.

Water supply: Activities associated with the production or acquisition of water and distribution to the public.

APPENDIX A
DATA DICTIONARY

Data Set Name: OUT1.CMI1   Observations: 534

Member Type: DATA   Variables: 3149

Engine: V608   Indexes: 0

Created: 13:23 Thursday, December 26, 1996   Observation Length: 25106

Last Modified: 13:23 Thursday, December 26, 1996   Deleted Observations: 0

Protection: Compressed: NO

Data Set Type: Sorted: NO

-----Variables Ordered by Position-----

#	VARIABLE	TYPE	START	END	LENGTH	LABEL
1	FIPS	Char	1	5	5	5-DIGIT COUNTY FIPS CODE
2	STATE	Char	6	7	2	FIPS STATE CODE
3	COUNTY	Char	8	10	3	FIPS COUNTY CODE
4	NAMES	Char	11	30	20	COUNTY NAMES
5	SA	Char	31	31	1	1. STUDY AREA ONLY (for Florida, only Panhandle region); 0. ALL NON-PANHANDLE COUNTIES IN FLORIDA
6	COAST	Char	32	32	1	COASTAL AREA: 1. CA 2. NON-CA
7	D30001	Num	33	40	8	TOTAL PSNS
8	D30002	Num	41	48	8	TOTAL PSNS: URBAN
9	D30003	Num	49	56	8	TOTAL PSNS: URBAN-FARM
10	D30004	Num	57	64	8	TOTAL PSNS: RURAL
11	D30005	Num	65	72	8	TOTAL PSNS: RURAL-FARM
12	D30006	Num	73	80	8	TOTAL PSNS: RURAL-NONFARM
13	D30007	Num	81	88	8	TOTAL PSNS: URBAN (1920)
14	D30008	Num	89	96	8	TOTAL PSNS: RURAL (1920)
15	D30009	Num	97	104	8	TOTAL MALE PSNS
16	D30010	Num	105	112	8	TOTAL FEMALE PSNS
17	D30011	Num	113	120	8	TOTAL WHITE PSNS
18	D30012	Num	121	128	8	TOTAL NATIVE WHITE PSNS
19	D30013	Num	129	136	8	NATIVE WHITE MALE PSNS
20	D30014	Num	137	144	8	NATIVE WHITE FEMALE PSNS
21	D30015	Num	145	152	8	TOTAL FOREIGN-BORN WHITE PSNS
22	D30016	Num	153	160	8	FOREIGN BORN WHITE MALE PSNS
23	D30017	Num	161	168	8	FOREIGN BORN WHITE FEMALE PSNS

24	D30018	Num	169	176	8	TOTAL BLACK PSNS
25	D30019	Num	177	184	8	BLACK MALE PSNS
26	D30020	Num	185	192	8	BLACK FEMALE PSNS
27	D30021	Num	193	200	8	TOTAL OTHER RACES
28	D30022	Num	201	208	8	TOTAL PSNS 21 YRS+
29	D30023	Num	209	216	8	TOTAL MALE PSNS: 21 YRS AND OVER
30	D30024	Num	217	224	8	TOTAL FEMALE PSNS: 21 YRS+
31	D30025	Num	225	232	8	TOTAL WHITE PSNS 21 YRS+
32	D30026	Num	233	240	8	TOTAL WHITE MALE PSNS 21 YRS+
33	D30027	Num	241	248	8	TOTAL WHITE FEMALE PSNS 21 YRS+
34	D30028	Num	249	256	8	TOTAL NATIVE WHITE PSNS 21 YRS+
35	D30029	Num	257	264	8	TOTAL NATIVE WHITE MALE PSNS 21 YRS+
36	D30030	Num	265	272	8	TOTAL NATIVE WHITE FEMALE PSNS 21 YRS+
37	D30031	Num	273	280	8	TOTAL FOREIGN-BORN WHITE PSNS 21 YRS+
38	D30032	Num	281	288	8	FOREIGN BORN WHITE MALE PSNS 21 YRS+
39	D30033	Num	289	296	8	FOREIGN BORN WHITE FEMALE: 21 YRS+
40	D30034	Num	297	304	8	TOTAL BLACK PSNS 21 YRS+
41	D30035	Num	305	312	8	BLACK MALE PSNS 21 YRS+
42	D30036	Num	313	320	8	BLACK FEMALES: 21 YRS+
43	D30037	Num	321	328	8	TOTAL OTHER RACES: PSNS 21 YRS+
44	D30038	Num	329	336	8	OTHER RACES: MALE 21 YRS+
45	D30039	Num	337	344	8	OTHER RACES: FEMALE 21 YRS+
46	D30040	Num	345	352	8	TOTAL PSNS: 7-13 YRS
47	D30041	Num	353	360	8	TOTAL PSNS: 14-15 YRS
48	D30042	Num	361	368	8	TOTAL PSNS: 16-17
49	D30043	Num	369	376	8	TOTAL PSNS: 18-20 YRS
50	D30044	Num	377	384	8	TOTAL PSNS: 10 YRS & OVR
51	D30045	Num	385	392	8	ILLITERATE PSNS: 10 YRS+
52	D30046	Num	393	400	8	NATIVE WHITE PSNS: 10 YRS+
53	D30047	Num	401	408	8	ILLITERATE NATIVE WHITE PSNS: 10 YRS+
54	D30048	Num	409	416	8	FOREIGN BORN WHITE PSNS: 10 YRS+
55	D30049	Num	417	424	8	ILLITERATE FOREIGN BORN WHT PSNS: 10 YRS
56	D30050	Num	425	432	8	BLACK PSNS: 10 YRS+
57	D30051	Num	433	440	8	ILLITERATE BLACK PSNS: 10 YRS+
58	D30052	Num	441	448	8	TOTAL PSNS 15 YRS+: TOTAL
59	D30053	Num	449	456	8	TOTAL PSNS 15 YRS+: SINGLE
60	D30054	Num	457	464	8	TOTAL PSNS 15 YRS+: MARRIED
61	D30055	Num	465	472	8	TOTAL PSNS 15 YRS+: WIDOWED
62	D30056	Num	473	480	8	TOTAL PSNS 15 YRS+: DIVORCED
63	D30057	Num	481	488	8	TOTAL PSNS 15 YRS+: MAR STAT UNKNOWN
64	D30058	Num	489	496	8	MALE PSNS 15 YRS+: TOTAL

65	D30059	Num	497	504	8	MALE PSNS 15 YRS+: SINGLE
66	D30060	Num	505	512	8	MALE PSNS 15 YRS+: MARRIED
67	D30061	Num	513	520	8	MALE PSNS 15 YRS+: WIDOWED
68	D30062	Num	521	528	8	MALE PSNS 15 YRS+: DIVORCED
69	D30063	Num	529	536	8	MALE PSNS 15 YRS+: MAR STAT UNKNOWN
70	D30064	Num	537	544	8	FEMALE PSNS 15 YRS+: TOTAL
71	D30065	Num	545	552	8	FEMALE PSNS 15 YRS+: SINGLE
72	D30066	Num	553	560	8	FEMALE PSNS 15 YRS+: MARRIED
73	D30067	Num	561	568	8	FEMALE PSNS 15 YRS+: WIDOWED
74	D30068	Num	569	576	8	FEMALE PSNS 15 YRS+: DIVORCED
75	D30069	Num	577	584	8	FEMALE PSNS 15 YRS+: MAR STAT UNKNOWN
76	D40001	Num	585	592	8	TOTAL PSNS
77	D40002	Num	593	600	8	TOTAL PSNS: URBAN
78	D40003	Num	601	608	8	TOTAL PSNS: URBAN-FARM
79	D40004	Num	609	616	8	TOTAL PSNS: RURAL
80	D40005	Num	617	624	8	TOTAL PSNS: RURAL-FARM
81	D40006	Num	625	632	8	TOTAL PSNS: RURAL-NONFARM
82	D40007	Num	633	640	8	TOTAL MALE PSNS
83	D40008	Num	641	648	8	TOTAL FEMALE PSNS
84	D40009	Num	649	656	8	TOTAL NATIVE PSNS
85	D40010	Num	657	664	8	TOTAL FOREIGN-BORN PSNS
86	D40011	Num	665	672	8	NATIVE MALE PSNS
87	D40012	Num	673	680	8	NATIVE FEMALE PSNS
88	D40013	Num	681	688	8	FOREIGN BORN MALE PSNS
89	D40014	Num	689	696	8	FOREIGN BORN FEMALE PSNS
90	D40015	Num	697	704	8	TOTAL WHITE PSNS
91	D40016	Num	705	712	8	NATIVE WHITE PSNS
92	D40017	Num	713	720	8	FOREIGN BORN WHITE PSNS
93	D40018	Num	721	728	8	TOTAL BLACK PSNS
94	D40019	Num	729	736	8	OTHER RACES
95	D40020	Num	737	744	8	TOTAL PSNS 21 YRS+
96	D40021	Num	745	752	8	MALE PSNS: 21 YRS+
97	D40022	Num	753	760	8	FEMALE PSNS: 21 YRS+
98	D40023	Num	761	768	8	TOTAL NATIVE PSNS 21 YRS+
99	D40024	Num	769	776	8	NATIVE BORN MALES PSNS: 21 YRS+
100	D40025	Num	777	784	8	NATIVE BORN FEMALES PSNS: 21 YRS+
101	D40026	Num	785	792	8	TOTAL FOREIGN-BORN PSNS 21 YRS+
102	D40027	Num	793	800	8	FOREIGN-BORN MALE PSNS 21 YRS+
103	D40028	Num	801	808	8	FOREIGN-BORN FEMALE PSNS 21 YRS+
104	D40029	Num	809	816	8	TOTAL WHITE PSNS 21 YRS+

105	D40030	Num	817	824	8	NATIVE BORN WHITE PSNS: 21 YRS+
106	D40031	Num	825	832	8	NATIVE BORN WHITE MALE PSNS: 21 YRS+
107	D40032	Num	833	840	8	NATIVE BORN WHITE FEMALE PSNS: 21 YRS+
108	D40033	Num	841	848	8	FOREIGN-BORN WHITE PSNS 21 YRS+
109	D40034	Num	849	856	8	FOREIGN BORN WHITE MALE PSNS: 21 YRS+
110	D40035	Num	857	864	8	FOREIGN BORN WHITE FEMALE PSNS: 21 YRS+
111	D40036	Num	865	872	8	TOTAL BLACK PSNS 21 YRS+
112	D40037	Num	873	880	8	TOTAL BLACK MALE PSNS 21 YRS+
113	D40038	Num	881	888	8	TOTAL BLACK FEMALE PSNS 21 YRS+
114	D40039	Num	889	896	8	TOTAL OTHER RACES: PSNS 21 YRS+
115	D40040	Num	897	904	8	TOTAL OTHER RACES: MALE PSNS 21 YRS+
116	D40041	Num	905	912	8	TOTAL OTHER RACES: FEMALE PSNS 21 YRS+
117	D40042	Num	913	920	8	TOTAL PSNS 5-6 YRS
118	D40043	Num	921	928	8	TOTAL PSNS 7-13 YRS
119	D40044	Num	929	936	8	TOTAL PSNS 14-15 YRS
120	D40045	Num	937	944	8	TOTAL PSNS 16-17 YRS
121	D40046	Num	945	952	8	TOTAL PSNS 18-20 YRS
122	D40047	Num	953	960	8	TOTAL PSNS 21-24 YRS
123	D40048	Num	961	968	8	TOTA PSNS: 25 YRS+
124	D40049	Num	969	976	8	TOTAL PSNS 25 YRS+: NO SCHOOL
125	D40050	Num	977	984	8	TOTAL PSNS 25 YRS+: 1-4TH GRADE
126	D40051	Num	985	992	8	TOTAL PSNS 25 YRS+: 5 OR 6 GRADE
127	D40052	Num	993	1000	8	TOTAL PSNS 25 YRS+: 7 OR 8 GRADE
128	D40053	Num	1001	1008	8	TOTAL PSNS 25 YRS+: 9-11TH GRADE
129	D40054	Num	1009	1016	8	TOTAL PSNS 25 YRS+: 12 TH GRADE
130	D40055	Num	1017	1024	8	TOTAL PSNS 25 YRS+: COLLEGE 1-3 YRS
131	D40056	Num	1025	1032	8	TOTAL PSNS 25 YRS+: COLLEGE 4 YRS+
132	D40057	Num	1033	1040	8	TOTAL PSNS 25 YRS+: SCHOOL NOT RPRTD
133	D40058	Num	1041	1048	8	MALES PSNS: 25 YRS+
134	D40059	Num	1049	1056	8	MALE PSNS 25 YRS+: NO SCHOOL
135	D40060	Num	1057	1064	8	MALE PSNS 25 YRS+: 1-4TH GRADE
136	D40061	Num	1065	1072	8	MALE PSNS 25 YRS+: 5 OR 6 GRADE
137	D40062	Num	1073	1080	8	MALE PSNS 25 YRS+: 7 OR 8 GRADE
138	D40063	Num	1081	1088	8	MALE PSNS 25 YRS+: 9-11TH GRADE
139	D40064	Num	1089	1096	8	MALE PSNS 25 YRS+: 12 TH GRADE
140	D40065	Num	1097	1104	8	MALE PSNS 25 YRS+: COLLEGE 1-3 YRS
141	D40066	Num	1105	1112	8	MALE PSNS 25 YRS+: COLLEGE 4 YRS+
142	D40067	Num	1113	1120	8	MALE PSNS 25 YRS+: SCHOOL NOT RPRTD
143	D40068	Num	1121	1128	8	FEMALES PSNS: 25 YRS+
144	D40069	Num	1129	1136	8	FEMALE PSNS 25 YRS+: NO SCHOOL
145	D40070	Num	1137	1144	8	FEMALE PSNS 25 YRS+: 1-4TH GRADE

146	D40071	Num	1145	1152	8	FEMALE PSNS 25 YRS+: 5 OR 6 GRADE
147	D40072	Num	1153	1160	8	FEMALE PSNS 25 YRS+: 7 OR 8 GRADE
148	D40073	Num	1161	1168	8	FEMALE PSNS 25 YRS+: 9-11TH GRADE
149	D40074	Num	1169	1176	8	FEMALE PSNS 25 YRS+: 12 TH GRADE
150	D40075	Num	1177	1184	8	FEMALE PSNS 25 YRS+: COLLEGE 1-3 YRS
151	D40076	Num	1185	1192	8	FEMALE PSNS 25 YRS+: COLLEGE 4 YRS+
152	D40077	Num	1193	1200	8	FEMALE PSNS 25 YRS+: SCHOOL NOT RPRTD
153	D50001	Num	1201	1208	8	TOTAL PSNS
154	D50002	Num	1209	1216	8	TOTAL NUMBER OF FAMILIES
155	D50003	Num	1217	1224	8	TOTAL NUMBER OF UNRELATED INDIVIDUALS
156	D50004	Num	1225	1232	8	TOTAL NUMBER OF HOUSEHOLDS
157	D50005	Num	1233	1240	8	PSNS IN HOUSEHOLDS
158	D50006	Num	1241	1248	8	PSNS IN INSTITUTIONS
159	D50007	Num	1249	1256	8	TOTAL PSNS: URBAN
160	D50008	Num	1257	1264	8	TOTAL PSNS: URBAN-FARM
161	D50009	Num	1265	1272	8	TOTAL PSNS: RURAL
162	D50010	Num	1273	1280	8	TOTAL PSNS: RURAL -FARM
163	D50011	Num	1281	1288	8	TOTAL PSNS: RURAL-NONFARM
164	D50012	Num	1289	1296	8	TOTAL MALE PSNS
165	D50013	Num	1297	1304	8	TOTAL FEMALE PSNS
166	D50014	Num	1305	1312	8	TOTAL WHITE MALE PSNS
167	D50015	Num	1313	1320	8	TOTAL WHITE FEMALE PSNS
168	D50016	Num	1321	1328	8	TOTAL NATIVE WHITE PSNS
169	D50017	Num	1329	1336	8	NATIVE-WHITE MALE PSNS
170	D50018	Num	1337	1344	8	NATIVE-WHITE FEMALE PSNS
171	D50019	Num	1345	1352	8	TOTAL FOREIGN-BORN WHITE PSNS
172	D50020	Num	1353	1360	8	FOREIGN-BORN WHITE MALE PSNS
173	D50021	Num	1361	1368	8	FOREIGN-BORN WHITE FEMALE PSNS
174	D50022	Num	1369	1376	8	TOTAL BLACK PSNS
175	D50023	Num	1377	1384	8	BLACK MALE PSNS
176	D50024	Num	1385	1392	8	BLACK FEMALE PSNS
177	D50025	Num	1393	1400	8	TOTAL OTHER RACES
178	D50026	Num	1401	1408	8	OTHER RACES MALE PSNS
179	D50027	Num	1409	1416	8	OTHER RACES FEMALE PSNS
180	D50028	Num	1417	1424	8	TOTAL PSNS 21 YRS+
181	D50029	Num	1425	1432	8	NATIVE PSNS 21 YRS+
182	D50030	Num	1433	1440	8	FOREIGN-BORN PSNS 21 YRS+
183	D50031	Num	1441	1448	8	TOTAL NONWHITE PSNS 21 YRS+
184	D50032	Num	1449	1456	8	NONWHITE MALE PSNS: 21 YRS+
185	D50033	Num	1457	1464	8	NONWHITE FEMALE PSNS: 21 YRS+

186	D50034	Num	1465	1472	8	TOTAL PSNS UNDER 1 YEAR
187	D50035	Num	1473	1480	8	TOTAL PSNS UNDER 5 YRS
188	D50036	Num	1481	1488	8	TOTAL PSNS 5-9 YRS
189	D50037	Num	1489	1496	8	TOTAL PSNS 10-14 YRS
190	D50038	Num	1497	1504	8	TOTAL PSNS 15-19 YRS
191	D50039	Num	1505	1512	8	TOTAL PSNS 20-24 YRS
192	D50040	Num	1513	1520	8	TOTAL PSNS 25-29 YRS
193	D50041	Num	1521	1528	8	TOTAL PSNS 30-34 YRS
194	D50042	Num	1529	1536	8	TOTAL PSNS 35-39 YRS
195	D50043	Num	1537	1544	8	TOTAL PSNS 40-44 YRS
196	D50044	Num	1545	1552	8	TOTAL PSNS 45-49 YRS
197	D50045	Num	1553	1560	8	TOTAL PSNS 50-54 YRS
198	D50046	Num	1561	1568	8	TOTAL PSNS 55-59 YRS
199	D50047	Num	1569	1576	8	TOTAL PSNS 60-64 YRS
200	D50048	Num	1577	1584	8	TOTAL PSNS 65-69 YRS
201	D50049	Num	1585	1592	8	TOTAL PSNS 70-74 YRS
202	D50050	Num	1593	1600	8	TOTAL PSNS 75-84 YRS
203	D50051	Num	1601	1608	8	TOTAL PSNS 85 AND OVER
204	D50052	Num	1609	1616	8	TOTAL MALES UNDER 1 YEAR
205	D50053	Num	1617	1624	8	TOTAL MALES UNDER 5 YRS
206	D50054	Num	1625	1632	8	TOTAL MALES 5-9 YRS
207	D50055	Num	1633	1640	8	TOTAL MALES 10-14 YRS
208	D50056	Num	1641	1648	8	TOTAL MALES 15-19 YRS
209	D50057	Num	1649	1656	8	TOTAL MALES 20-24 YRS
210	D50058	Num	1657	1664	8	TOTAL MALES 25-29 YRS
211	D50059	Num	1665	1672	8	TOTAL MALES 30-34 YRS
212	D50060	Num	1673	1680	8	TOTAL MALES 35-39 YRS
213	D50061	Num	1681	1688	8	TOTAL MALES 40-44 YRS
214	D50062	Num	1689	1696	8	TOTAL MALES 45-49 YRS
215	D50063	Num	1697	1704	8	TOTAL MALES 50-54 YRS
216	D50064	Num	1705	1712	8	TOTAL MALES 55-59 YRS
217	D50065	Num	1713	1720	8	TOTAL MALES 60-64 YRS
218	D50066	Num	1721	1728	8	TOTAL MALES 65-69 YRS
219	D50067	Num	1729	1736	8	TOTAL MALES 70-74 YRS
220	D50068	Num	1737	1744	8	TOTAL MALES 75-84 YRS
221	D50069	Num	1745	1752	8	TOTAL MALES 85 AND OVER
222	D50070	Num	1753	1760	8	TOTAL FEMALES UNDER 1 YEAR
223	D50071	Num	1761	1768	8	TOTAL FEMALES UNDER 5 YRS
224	D50072	Num	1769	1776	8	TOTAL FEMALES 5-9 YRS
225	D50073	Num	1777	1784	8	TOTAL FEMALES 10-14 YRS
226	D50074	Num	1785	1792	8	TOTAL FEMALES 15-19 YRS

227	D50075	Num	1793	1800	8	TOTAL FEMALES 20-24 YRS
228	D50076	Num	1801	1808	8	TOTAL FEMALES 25-29 YRS
229	D50077	Num	1809	1816	8	TOTAL FEMALES 30-34 YRS
230	D50078	Num	1817	1824	8	TOTAL FEMALES 35-39 YRS
231	D50079	Num	1825	1832	8	TOTAL FEMALES 40-44 YRS
232	D50080	Num	1833	1840	8	TOTAL FEMALES 45-49 YRS
233	D50081	Num	1841	1848	8	TOTAL FEMALES 50-54 YRS
234	D50082	Num	1849	1856	8	TOTAL FEMALES 55-59 YRS
235	D50083	Num	1857	1864	8	TOTAL FEMALES 60-64 YRS
236	D50084	Num	1865	1872	8	TOTAL FEMALES 65-69 YRS
237	D50085	Num	1873	1880	8	TOTAL FEMALES 70-74 YRS
238	D50086	Num	1881	1888	8	TOTAL FEMALES 75-84 YRS
239	D50087	Num	1889	1896	8	TOTAL FEMALES 85 AND OVER
240	D50088	Num	1897	1904	8	TOTAL WHITE PSNS
241	D50089	Num	1905	1912	8	TOTAL WHITE PSNS: UNDER 1 YEAR
242	D50090	Num	1913	1920	8	TOTAL WHITE PSNS: UNDER 5 YEAR
243	D50091	Num	1921	1928	8	TOTAL WHITE PSNS: 5-9 YRS
244	D50092	Num	1929	1936	8	TOTAL WHITE PSNS: 10-14 YRS
245	D50093	Num	1937	1944	8	TOTAL WHITE PSNS: 15-19 YRS
246	D50094	Num	1945	1952	8	TOTAL WHITE PSNS: 20-24 YRS
247	D50095	Num	1953	1960	8	TOTAL WHITE PSNS: 25-29 YRS
248	D50096	Num	1961	1968	8	TOTAL WHITE PSNS: 30-34 YRS
249	D50097	Num	1969	1976	8	TOTAL WHITE PSNS: 35-39 YRS
250	D50098	Num	1977	1984	8	TOTAL WHITE PSNS: 40-44 YRS
251	D50099	Num	1985	1992	8	TOTAL WHITE PSNS: 45-49 YRS
252	D50100	Num	1993	2000	8	TOTAL WHITE PSNS: 50-54 YRS
253	D50101	Num	2001	2008	8	TOTAL WHITE PSNS: 55-59 YRS
254	D50102	Num	2009	2016	8	TOTAL WHITE PSNS: 60-64 YRS
255	D50103	Num	2017	2024	8	TOTAL WHITE PSNS: 65-69 YRS
256	D50104	Num	2025	2032	8	TOTAL WHITE PSNS: 70-74 YRS
257	D50105	Num	2033	2040	8	TOTAL WHITE PSNS: 75-84 YRS
258	D50106	Num	2041	2048	8	TOTAL WHITE PSNS: 85 AND OVER
259	D50107	Num	2049	2056	8	WHITE MALE PSNS: UNDER 1 YEAR
260	D50108	Num	2057	2064	8	WHITE MALE PSNS: UNDER 5 YEAR
261	D50109	Num	2065	2072	8	WHITE MALE PSNS: 5-9 YRS
262	D50110	Num	2073	2080	8	WHITE MALE PSNS: 10-14 YRS
263	D50111	Num	2081	2088	8	WHITE MALE PSNS: 15-19 YRS
264	D50112	Num	2089	2096	8	WHITE MALE PSNS: 20-24 YRS
265	D50113	Num	2097	2104	8	WHITE MALE PSNS: 25-29 YRS
266	D50114	Num	2105	2112	8	WHITE MALE PSNS: 30-34 YRS
267	D50115	Num	2113	2120	8	WHITE MALE PSNS: 35-39 YRS

268	D50116	Num	2121	2128	8	WHITE MALE PSNS: 40-44 YRS
269	D50117	Num	2129	2136	8	WHITE MALE PSNS: 45-49 YRS
270	D50118	Num	2137	2144	8	WHITE MALE PSNS: 50-54 YRS
271	D50119	Num	2145	2152	8	WHITE MALE PSNS: 55-59 YRS
272	D50120	Num	2153	2160	8	WHITE MALE PSNS: 60-64 YRS
273	D50121	Num	2161	2168	8	WHITE MALE PSNS: 65-69 YRS
274	D50122	Num	2169	2176	8	WHITE MALE PSNS: 70-74 YRS
275	D50123	Num	2177	2184	8	WHITE MALE PSNS: 75-84 YRS
276	D50124	Num	2185	2192	8	WHITE MALE PSNS: 85 AND OVER
277	D50125	Num	2193	2200	8	WHITE FEMALE PSNS: UNDER 1 YEAR
278	D50126	Num	2201	2208	8	WHITE FEMALE PSNS: UNDER 5 YEAR
279	D50127	Num	2209	2216	8	WHITE FEMALE PSNS: 5-9 YRS
280	D50128	Num	2217	2224	8	WHITE FEMALE PSNS: 10-14 YRS
281	D50129	Num	2225	2232	8	WHITE FEMALE PSNS: 15-19 YRS
282	D50130	Num	2233	2240	8	WHITE FEMALE PSNS: 20-24 YRS
283	D50131	Num	2241	2248	8	WHITE FEMALE PSNS: 25-29 YRS
284	D50132	Num	2249	2256	8	WHITE FEMALE PSNS: 30-34 YRS
285	D50133	Num	2257	2264	8	WHITE FEMALE PSNS: 35-39 YRS
286	D50134	Num	2265	2272	8	WHITE FEMALE PSNS: 40-44 YRS
287	D50135	Num	2273	2280	8	WHITE FEMALE PSNS: 45-49 YRS
288	D50136	Num	2281	2288	8	WHITE FEMALE PSNS: 50-54 YRS
289	D50137	Num	2289	2296	8	WHITE FEMALE PSNS: 55-59 YRS
290	D50138	Num	2297	2304	8	WHITE FEMALE PSNS: 60-64 YRS
291	D50139	Num	2305	2312	8	WHITE FEMALE PSNS: 65-69 YRS
292	D50140	Num	2313	2320	8	WHITE FEMALE PSNS: 70-74 YRS
293	D50141	Num	2321	2328	8	WHITE FEMALE PSNS: 75-84 YRS
294	D50142	Num	2329	2336	8	WHITE FEMALE PSNS: 85 AND OVER
295	D50143	Num	2337	2344	8	TOTAL NONWHITE PSNS
296	D50144	Num	2345	2352	8	TOTAL NONWHITE PSNS: UNDER 1 YEAR
297	D50145	Num	2353	2360	8	TOTAL NONWHITE PSNS: UNDER 5 YEAR
298	D50146	Num	2361	2368	8	TOTAL NONWHITE PSNS: 5-9 YRS
299	D50147	Num	2369	2376	8	TOTAL NONWHITE PSNS: 10-14 YRS
300	D50148	Num	2377	2384	8	TOTAL NONWHITE PSNS: 15-19 YRS
301	D50149	Num	2385	2392	8	TOTAL NONWHITE PSNS: 20-24 YRS
302	D50150	Num	2393	2400	8	TOTAL NONWHITE PSNS: 25-29 YRS
303	D50151	Num	2401	2408	8	TOTAL NONWHITE PSNS: 30-34 YRS
304	D50152	Num	2409	2416	8	TOTAL NONWHITE PSNS: 35-39 YRS
305	D50153	Num	2417	2424	8	TOTAL NONWHITE PSNS: 40-44 YRS
306	D50154	Num	2425	2432	8	TOTAL NONWHITE PSNS: 45-49 YRS
307	D50155	Num	2433	2440	8	TOTAL NONWHITE PSNS: 50-54 YRS
308	D50156	Num	2441	2448	8	TOTAL NONWHITE PSNS: 55-59 YRS

309	D50157	Num	2449	2456	8	TOTAL NONWHITE PSNS: 60-64 YRS
310	D50158	Num	2457	2464	8	TOTAL NONWHITE PSNS: 65-69 YRS
311	D50159	Num	2465	2472	8	TOTAL NONWHITE PSNS: 70-74 YRS
312	D50160	Num	2473	2480	8	TOTAL NONWHITE PSNS: 75-84 YRS
313	D50161	Num	2481	2488	8	TOTAL NONWHITE PSNS: 85 AND OVER
314	D50162	Num	2489	2496	8	TOTAL NONWHITE MALE PSNS
315	D50163	Num	2497	2504	8	NONWHITE MALE PSNS: UNDER 1 YEAR
316	D50164	Num	2505	2512	8	NONWHITE MALE PSNS: UNDER 5 YEAR
317	D50165	Num	2513	2520	8	NONWHITE MALE PSNS: 5-9 YRS
318	D50166	Num	2521	2528	8	NONWHITE MALE PSNS: 10-14 YRS
319	D50167	Num	2529	2536	8	NONWHITE MALE PSNS: 15-19 YRS
320	D50168	Num	2537	2544	8	NONWHITE MALE PSNS: 20-24 YRS
321	D50169	Num	2545	2552	8	NONWHITE MALE PSNS: 25-29 YRS
322	D50170	Num	2553	2560	8	NONWHITE MALE PSNS: 30-34 YRS
323	D50171	Num	2561	2568	8	NONWHITE MALE PSNS: 35-39 YRS
324	D50172	Num	2569	2576	8	NONWHITE MALE PSNS: 40-44 YRS
325	D50173	Num	2577	2584	8	NONWHITE MALE PSNS: 45-49 YRS
326	D50174	Num	2585	2592	8	NONWHITE MALE PSNS: 50-54 YRS
327	D50175	Num	2593	2600	8	NONWHITE MALE PSNS: 55-59 YRS
328	D50176	Num	2601	2608	8	NONWHITE MALE PSNS: 60-64 YRS
329	D50177	Num	2609	2616	8	NONWHITE MALE PSNS: 65-69 YRS
330	D50178	Num	2617	2624	8	NONWHITE MALE PSNS: 70-74 YRS
331	D50179	Num	2625	2632	8	NONWHITE MALE PSNS: 75-84 YRS
332	D50180	Num	2633	2640	8	NONWHITE MALE PSNS: 85 AND OVER
333	D50181	Num	2641	2648	8	TOTAL NONWHITE FEMALE PSNS
334	D50182	Num	2649	2656	8	NONWHITE FEMALE PSNS: UNDER 1 YEAR
335	D50183	Num	2657	2664	8	NONWHITE FEMALE PSNS: UNDER 5 YEAR
336	D50184	Num	2665	2672	8	NONWHITE FEMALE PSNS: 5-9 YRS
337	D50185	Num	2673	2680	8	NONWHITE FEMALE PSNS: 10-14 YRS
338	D50186	Num	2681	2688	8	NONWHITE FEMALE PSNS: 15-19 YRS
339	D50187	Num	2689	2696	8	NONWHITE FEMALE PSNS: 20-24 YRS
340	D50188	Num	2697	2704	8	NONWHITE FEMALE PSNS: 25-29 YRS
341	D50189	Num	2705	2712	8	NONWHITE FEMALE PSNS: 30-34 YRS
342	D50190	Num	2713	2720	8	NONWHITE FEMALE PSNS: 35-39 YRS
343	D50191	Num	2721	2728	8	NONWHITE FEMALE PSNS: 40-44 YRS
344	D50192	Num	2729	2736	8	NONWHITE FEMALE PSNS: 45-49 YRS
345	D50193	Num	2737	2744	8	NONWHITE FEMALE PSNS: 50-54 YRS
346	D50194	Num	2745	2752	8	NONWHITE FEMALE PSNS: 55-59 YRS
347	D50195	Num	2753	2760	8	NONWHITE FEMALE PSNS: 60-64 YRS
348	D50196	Num	2761	2768	8	NONWHITE FEMALE PSNS: 65-69 YRS
349	D50197	Num	2769	2776	8	NONWHITE FEMALE PSNS: 70-74 YRS

350	D50198	Num	2777	2784	8	NONWHITE FEMALE PSNS: 75-84 YRS
351	D50199	Num	2785	2792	8	NONWHITE FEMALE PSNS: 85 AND OVER
352	D50200	Num	2793	2800	8	TOTAL PSNS 5 AND 6 YRS
353	D50201	Num	2801	2808	8	TOTAL PSNS 7-13 YRS
354	D50202	Num	2809	2816	8	TOTAL PSNS 14 AND 15 YRS
355	D50203	Num	2817	2824	8	TOTAL PSNS 16 AND 17 YRS
356	D50204	Num	2825	2832	8	TOTAL PSNS 18 AND 19 YRS
357	D50205	Num	2833	2840	8	TOTAL PSNS 20-24 YRS
358	D50206	Num	2841	2848	8	TOTAL PSNS 25-29 YRS
359	D50207	Num	2849	2856	8	TOTAL PSNS 25 YRS+
360	D50208	Num	2857	2864	8	TOTAL PSNS 25 YRS+: NO SCHOOL CMPLETED
361	D50209	Num	2865	2872	8	TOTAL PSNS 25 YRS+: 1-4TH GRADE
362	D50210	Num	2873	2880	8	TOTAL PSNS 25 YRS+: 5-6TH GRADE
363	D50211	Num	2881	2888	8	TOTAL PSNS 25 YRS+: 7TH GRADE
364	D50212	Num	2889	2896	8	TOTAL PSNS 25 YRS+: 8TH GRADE
365	D50213	Num	2897	2904	8	TOTAL PSNS 25 YRS+: 9-11TH GRADE
366	D50214	Num	2905	2912	8	TOTAL PSNS 25 YRS+: 12TH GRADE
367	D50215	Num	2913	2920	8	TOTAL PSNS 25 YRS+: COLLEGE 1-3 YRS
368	D50216	Num	2921	2928	8	TOTAL PSNS 25 YRS+: COLLEGE 4 YRS+
369	D50217	Num	2929	2936	8	TOTAL PSNS 25 YRS+: NOT REPORTED
370	D50218	Num	2937	2944	8	TOTAL MALE PERSONS 25 YRS+
371	D50219	Num	2945	2952	8	MALE PSNS 25 YRS+: NO SCHOOL CMPLETED
372	D50220	Num	2953	2960	8	MALE PSNS 25 YRS+: 1-4TH GRADE
373	D50221	Num	2961	2968	8	MALE PSNS 25 YRS+: 5-6TH GRADE
374	D50222	Num	2969	2976	8	MALE PSNS 25 YRS+: 7TH GRADE
375	D50223	Num	2977	2984	8	MALE PSNS 25 YRS+: 8TH GRADE
376	D50224	Num	2985	2992	8	MALE PSNS 25 YRS+: 9-11TH GRADE
377	D50225	Num	2993	3000	8	MALE PSNS 25 YRS+: 12TH GRADE
378	D50226	Num	3001	3008	8	MALE PSNS 25 YRS+: COLLEGE 1-3 YRS
379	D50227	Num	3009	3016	8	MALE PSNS 25 YRS+: COLLEGE 4 YRS+
380	D50228	Num	3017	3024	8	MALE PSNS 25 YRS+: NOT REPORTED
381	D50229	Num	3025	3032	8	TOTAL FEMALE PERSONS 25 YRS+
382	D50230	Num	3033	3040	8	FEMALE PSNS 25 YRS+: NO SCHOOL CMPLETED
383	D50231	Num	3041	3048	8	FEMALE PSNS 25 YRS+: 1-4TH GRADE
384	D50232	Num	3049	3056	8	FEMALE PSNS 25 YRS+: 5-6TH GRADE
385	D50233	Num	3057	3064	8	FEMALE PSNS 25 YRS+: 7TH GRADE
386	D50234	Num	3065	3072	8	FEMALE PSNS 25 YRS+: 8TH GRADE
387	D50235	Num	3073	3080	8	FEMALE PSNS 25 YRS+: 9-11TH GRADE
388	D50236	Num	3081	3088	8	FEMALE PSNS 25 YRS+: 12TH GRADE
389	D50237	Num	3089	3096	8	FEMALE PSNS 25 YRS+: COLLEGE 1-3 YRS
390	D50238	Num	3097	3104	8	FEMALE PSNS 25 YRS+: COLLEGE 4 YRS+

391	D50239	Num	3105	3112	8	FEMALE PSNS 25 YRS+: NOT REPORTED
392	D50240	Num	3113	3120	8	TOTAL PSNS 14 YRS+: TOTAL
393	D50241	Num	3121	3128	8	TOTAL PSNS 14 YRS+: SINGLE
394	D50242	Num	3129	3136	8	TOTAL PSNS 14 YRS+: MARRIED
395	D50243	Num	3137	3144	8	TOTAL PSNS 14 YRS+: DIVORCED
396	D50244	Num	3145	3152	8	MALE PSNS 14 YRS+: TOTAL
397	D50245	Num	3153	3160	8	MALE PSNS 14 YRS+: SINGLE
398	D50246	Num	3161	3168	8	MALE PSNS 14 YRS+: MARRIED
399	D50247	Num	3169	3176	8	MALE PSNS 14 YRS+: DIVORCED
400	D50248	Num	3177	3184	8	FEMALE PSNS 14 YRS+: TOTAL
401	D50249	Num	3185	3192	8	FEMALE PSNS 14 YRS+: SINGLE
402	D50250	Num	3193	3200	8	FEMALE PSNS 14 YRS+: MARRIED
403	D50251	Num	3201	3208	8	FEMALE PSNS 14 YRS+: DIVORCED
404	D50252	Num	3209	3216	8	TOTAL NUMBER OF MARRIED COUPLES
405	D50253	Num	3217	3224	8	MARRIED COUPLES WITH OWN HOUSEHOLD
406	D50254	Num	3225	3232	8	MARRIED COUPLES WITHOUT OWN HOUSEHOLD
407	D50255	Num	3233	3240	8	TOTAL PSNS: 1 YRS+
408	D50256	Num	3241	3248	8	RES IN 1949 (PSNS 1 YRS+): SAME HOUSE
409	D50257	Num	3249	3256	8	RES IN 1949 (PSNS 1 YRS+): SAME CNTY
410	D50258	Num	3257	3264	8	RES IN 1949 (PSNS 1 YRS+): DIFF CNTY/ABR
411	D50259	Num	3265	3272	8	RESIDENCE NOT REPORTED
412	D60001	Num	3273	3280	8	TOTAL PSNS
413	D60002	Num	3281	3288	8	TOTAL NUMBER OF FAMILIES
414	D60003	Num	3289	3296	8	TOTAL PSNS: URBAN
415	D60004	Num	3297	3304	8	TOTAL PSNS: RURAL
416	D60005	Num	3305	3312	8	TOTAL PSNS: RURAL-FARM
417	D60006	Num	3313	3320	8	TOTAL PSNS: RURAL-NONFARM
418	D60007	Num	3321	3328	8	TOTAL MALE PSNS
419	D60008	Num	3329	3336	8	TOTAL FEMALE PSNS
420	D60009	Num	3337	3344	8	TOTAL WHITE PSNS
421	D60010	Num	3345	3352	8	TOTAL WHITE MALE PSNS
422	D60011	Num	3353	3360	8	TOTAL WHITE FEMALE PSNS
423	D60012	Num	3361	3368	8	TOTAL BLACK PSNS
424	D60013	Num	3369	3376	8	TOTAL BLACK MALE PSNS
425	D60014	Num	3377	3384	8	TOTAL BLACK FEMALE PSNS
426	D60015	Num	3385	3392	8	TOTAL NONWHITE PSNS
427	D60016	Num	3393	3400	8	TOTAL NONWHITE MALE PSNS
428	D60017	Num	3401	3408	8	TOTAL NONWHITE FEMALE PSNS
429	D60018	Num	3409	3416	8	TOTAL NONWHITE PSNS 21 YRS+
430	D60019	Num	3417	3424	8	NONWHITE MALE PSNS:21 YRS+

431	D60020	Num	3425	3432	8	NONWHITE FEMALE PSNS:21 YRS+
432	D60021	Num	3433	3440	8	TOTAL PSNS UNDER 1 YEAR
433	D60022	Num	3441	3448	8	TOTAL PSNS UNDER 5 YRS
434	D60023	Num	3449	3456	8	TOTAL PSNS 5-9 YRS
435	D60024	Num	3457	3464	8	TOTAL PSNS 10-14 YRS
436	D60025	Num	3465	3472	8	TOTAL PSNS 15-19 YRS
437	D60026	Num	3473	3480	8	TOTAL PSNS 20-24 YRS
438	D60027	Num	3481	3488	8	TOTAL PSNS 25-29 YRS
439	D60028	Num	3489	3496	8	TOTAL PSNS 30-34 YRS
440	D60029	Num	3497	3504	8	TOTAL PSNS 35-39 YRS
441	D60030	Num	3505	3512	8	TOTAL PSNS 40-44 YRS
442	D60031	Num	3513	3520	8	TOTAL PSNS 45-49 YRS
443	D60032	Num	3521	3528	8	TOTAL PSNS 50-54 YRS
444	D60033	Num	3529	3536	8	TOTAL PSNS 55-59 YRS
445	D60034	Num	3537	3544	8	TOTAL PSNS 60-64 YRS
446	D60035	Num	3545	3552	8	TOTAL PSNS 65-69 YRS
447	D60036	Num	3553	3560	8	TOTAL PSNS 70-74 YRS
448	D60037	Num	3561	3568	8	TOTAL PSNS 75-79 YRS
449	D60038	Num	3569	3576	8	TOTAL PSNS 80-84 YRS
450	D60039	Num	3577	3584	8	TOTAL PSNS 85 AND OVER
451	D60040	Num	3585	3592	8	TOTAL PSNS UNDER 18 YRS
452	D60041	Num	3593	3600	8	TOTAL MALES UNDER 1 YEAR
453	D60042	Num	3601	3608	8	TOTAL MALES UNDER 5 YRS
454	D60043	Num	3609	3616	8	TOTAL MALES 5-9 YRS
455	D60044	Num	3617	3624	8	TOTAL MALES 10-14 YRS
456	D60045	Num	3625	3632	8	TOTAL MALES 15-19 YRS
457	D60046	Num	3633	3640	8	TOTAL MALES 20-24 YRS
458	D60047	Num	3641	3648	8	TOTAL MALES 25-29 YRS
459	D60048	Num	3649	3656	8	TOTAL MALES 30-34 YRS
460	D60049	Num	3657	3664	8	TOTAL MALES 35-39 YRS
461	D60050	Num	3665	3672	8	TOTAL MALES 40-44 YRS
462	D60051	Num	3673	3680	8	TOTAL MALES 45-49 YRS
463	D60052	Num	3681	3688	8	TOTAL MALES 50-54 YRS
464	D60053	Num	3689	3696	8	TOTAL MALES 55-59 YRS
465	D60054	Num	3697	3704	8	TOTAL MALES 60-64 YRS
466	D60055	Num	3705	3712	8	TOTAL MALES 65-69 YRS
467	D60056	Num	3713	3720	8	TOTAL MALES 70-74 YRS
468	D60057	Num	3721	3728	8	TOTAL MALES 75-79 YRS
469	D60058	Num	3729	3736	8	TOTAL MALES 80-84 YRS
470	D60059	Num	3737	3744	8	TOTAL MALES 85 AND OVER
471	D60060	Num	3745	3752	8	TOTAL MALES UNDER 18 YRS

472	D60061	Num	3753	3760	8	TOTAL FEMALES UNDER 1 YEAR
473	D60062	Num	3761	3768	8	TOTAL FEMALES UNDER 5 YRS
474	D60063	Num	3769	3776	8	TOTAL FEMALES 5-9 YRS
475	D60064	Num	3777	3784	8	TOTAL FEMALES 10-14 YRS
476	D60065	Num	3785	3792	8	TOTAL FEMALES 15-19 YRS
477	D60066	Num	3793	3800	8	TOTAL FEMALES 20-24 YRS
478	D60067	Num	3801	3808	8	TOTAL FEMALES 25-29 YRS
479	D60068	Num	3809	3816	8	TOTAL FEMALES 30-34 YRS
480	D60069	Num	3817	3824	8	TOTAL FEMALES 35-39 YRS
481	D60070	Num	3825	3832	8	TOTAL FEMALES 40-44 YRS
482	D60071	Num	3833	3840	8	TOTAL FEMALES 45-49 YRS
483	D60072	Num	3841	3848	8	TOTAL FEMALES 50-54 YRS
484	D60073	Num	3849	3856	8	TOTAL FEMALES 55-59 YRS
485	D60074	Num	3857	3864	8	TOTAL FEMALES 60-64 YRS
486	D60075	Num	3865	3872	8	TOTAL FEMALES 65-69 YRS
487	D60076	Num	3873	3880	8	TOTAL FEMALES 70-74 YRS
488	D60077	Num	3881	3888	8	TOTAL FEMALES 75-79 YRS
489	D60078	Num	3889	3896	8	TOTAL FEMALES 80-84 YRS
490	D60079	Num	3897	3904	8	TOTAL FEMALES 85 AND OVER
491	D60080	Num	3905	3912	8	TOTAL FEMALES UNDER 18 YRS
492	D60081	Num	3913	3920	8	WHITE PSNS: UNDER 1 YEAR
493	D60082	Num	3921	3928	8	WHITE PSNS: UNDER 5 YEAR
494	D60083	Num	3929	3936	8	WHITE PSNS: 5-9 YRS
495	D60084	Num	3937	3944	8	WHITE PSNS: 10-14 YRS
496	D60085	Num	3945	3952	8	WHITE PSNS: 15-19 YRS
497	D60086	Num	3953	3960	8	WHITE PSNS: 20-24 YRS
498	D60087	Num	3961	3968	8	WHITE PSNS: 25-29 YRS
499	D60088	Num	3969	3976	8	WHITE PSNS: 30-34 YRS
500	D60089	Num	3977	3984	8	WHITE PSNS: 35-39 YRS
501	D60090	Num	3985	3992	8	WHITE PSNS: 40-44 YRS
502	D60091	Num	3993	4000	8	WHITE PSNS: 45-49 YRS
503	D60092	Num	4001	4008	8	WHITE PSNS: 50-54 YRS
504	D60093	Num	4009	4016	8	WHITE PSNS: 55-59 YRS
505	D60094	Num	4017	4024	8	WHITE PSNS: 60-64 YRS
506	D60095	Num	4025	4032	8	WHITE PSNS: 65-69 YRS
507	D60096	Num	4033	4040	8	WHITE PSNS: 70-74 YRS
508	D60097	Num	4041	4048	8	WHITE PSNS: 75-79 YRS
509	D60098	Num	4049	4056	8	WHITE PSNS: 80-84 YRS
510	D60099	Num	4057	4064	8	WHITE PSNS: 85 AND OVER
511	D60100	Num	4065	4072	8	WHITE PSNS: UNDER 18 YRS
512	D60101	Num	4073	4080	8	WHITE MALE PSNS: UNDER 1 YEAR

513	D60102	Num	4081	4088	8	WHITE MALE PSNS: UNDER 5 YEAR
514	D60103	Num	4089	4096	8	WHITE MALE PSNS: 5-9 YRS
515	D60104	Num	4097	4104	8	WHITE MALE PSNS: 10-14 YRS
516	D60105	Num	4105	4112	8	WHITE MALE PSNS: 15-19 YRS
517	D60106	Num	4113	4120	8	WHITE MALE PSNS: 20-24 YRS
518	D60107	Num	4121	4128	8	WHITE MALE PSNS: 25-29 YRS
519	D60108	Num	4129	4136	8	WHITE MALE PSNS: 30-34 YRS
520	D60109	Num	4137	4144	8	WHITE MALE PSNS: 35-39 YRS
521	D60110	Num	4145	4152	8	WHITE MALE PSNS: 40-44 YRS
522	D60111	Num	4153	4160	8	WHITE MALE PSNS: 45-49 YRS
523	D60112	Num	4161	4168	8	WHITE MALE PSNS: 50-54 YRS
524	D60113	Num	4169	4176	8	WHITE MALE PSNS: 55-59 YRS
525	D60114	Num	4177	4184	8	WHITE MALE PSNS: 60-64 YRS
526	D60115	Num	4185	4192	8	WHITE MALE PSNS: 65-69 YRS
527	D60116	Num	4193	4200	8	WHITE MALE PSNS: 70-74 YRS
528	D60117	Num	4201	4208	8	WHITE MALE PSNS: 75-79 YRS
529	D60118	Num	4209	4216	8	WHITE MALE PSNS: 80-84 YRS
530	D60119	Num	4217	4224	8	WHITE MALE PSNS: 85 AND OVER
531	D60120	Num	4225	4232	8	WHITE MALE PSNS: UNDER 18 YRS
532	D60121	Num	4233	4240	8	WHITE FEMALE PSNS: UNDER 1 YEAR
533	D60122	Num	4241	4248	8	WHITE FEMALE PSNS: UNDER 5 YEAR
534	D60123	Num	4249	4256	8	WHITE FEMALE PSNS: 5-9 YRS
535	D60124	Num	4257	4264	8	WHITE FEMALE PSNS: 10-14 YRS
536	D60125	Num	4265	4272	8	WHITE FEMALE PSNS: 15-19 YRS
537	D60126	Num	4273	4280	8	WHITE FEMALE PSNS: 20-24 YRS
538	D60127	Num	4281	4288	8	WHITE FEMALE PSNS: 25-29 YRS
539	D60128	Num	4289	4296	8	WHITE FEMALE PSNS: 30-34 YRS
540	D60129	Num	4297	4304	8	WHITE FEMALE PSNS: 35-39 YRS
541	D60130	Num	4305	4312	8	WHITE FEMALE PSNS: 40-44 YRS
542	D60131	Num	4313	4320	8	WHITE FEMALE PSNS: 45-49 YRS
543	D60132	Num	4321	4328	8	WHITE FEMALE PSNS: 50-54 YRS
544	D60133	Num	4329	4336	8	WHITE FEMALE PSNS: 55-59 YRS
545	D60134	Num	4337	4344	8	WHITE FEMALE PSNS: 60-64 YRS
546	D60135	Num	4345	4352	8	WHITE FEMALE PSNS: 65-69 YRS
547	D60136	Num	4353	4360	8	WHITE FEMALE PSNS: 70-74 YRS
548	D60137	Num	4361	4368	8	WHITE FEMALE PSNS: 75-79 YRS
549	D60138	Num	4369	4376	8	WHITE FEMALE PSNS: 80-84 YRS
550	D60139	Num	4377	4384	8	WHITE FEMALE PSNS: 85 AND OVER
551	D60140	Num	4385	4392	8	WHITE FEMALE PSNS: UNDER 18 YRS
552	D60141	Num	4393	4400	8	NONWHITE PSNS: UNDER 1 YEAR
553	D60142	Num	4401	4408	8	NONWHITE PSNS: UNDER 5 YEAR

554	D60143	Num	4409	4416	8	NONWHITE PSNS: 5-9 YRS
555	D60144	Num	4417	4424	8	NONWHITE PSNS: 10-14 YRS
556	D60145	Num	4425	4432	8	NONWHITE PSNS: 15-19 YRS
557	D60146	Num	4433	4440	8	NONWHITE PSNS: 20-24 YRS
558	D60147	Num	4441	4448	8	NONWHITE PSNS: 25-29 YRS
559	D60148	Num	4449	4456	8	NONWHITE PSNS: 30-34 YRS
560	D60149	Num	4457	4464	8	NONWHITE PSNS: 35-39 YRS
561	D60150	Num	4465	4472	8	NONWHITE PSNS: 40-44 YRS
562	D60151	Num	4473	4480	8	NONWHITE PSNS: 45-49 YRS
563	D60152	Num	4481	4488	8	NONWHITE PSNS: 50-54 YRS
564	D60153	Num	4489	4496	8	NONWHITE PSNS: 55-59 YRS
565	D60154	Num	4497	4504	8	NONWHITE PSNS: 60-64 YRS
566	D60155	Num	4505	4512	8	NONWHITE PSNS: 65-69 YRS
567	D60156	Num	4513	4520	8	NONWHITE PSNS: 70-74 YRS
568	D60157	Num	4521	4528	8	NONWHITE PSNS: 75-79 YRS
569	D60158	Num	4529	4536	8	NONWHITE PSNS: 80-84 YRS
570	D60159	Num	4537	4544	8	NONWHITE PSNS: 85 AND OVER
571	D60160	Num	4545	4552	8	NONWHITE PSNS: UNER 18 YRS
572	D60161	Num	4553	4560	8	NONWHITE MALE PSNS: UNDER 1 YEAR
573	D60162	Num	4561	4568	8	NONWHITE MALE PSNS: UNDER 5 YEAR
574	D60163	Num	4569	4576	8	NONWHITE MALE PSNS: 5-9 YRS
575	D60164	Num	4577	4584	8	NONWHITE MALE PSNS: 10-14 YRS
576	D60165	Num	4585	4592	8	NONWHITE MALE PSNS: 15-19 YRS
577	D60166	Num	4593	4600	8	NONWHITE MALE PSNS: 20-24 YRS
578	D60167	Num	4601	4608	8	NONWHITE MALE PSNS: 25-29 YRS
579	D60168	Num	4609	4616	8	NONWHITE MALE PSNS: 30-34 YRS
580	D60169	Num	4617	4624	8	NONWHITE MALE PSNS: 35-39 YRS
581	D60170	Num	4625	4632	8	NONWHITE MALE PSNS: 40-44 YRS
582	D60171	Num	4633	4640	8	NONWHITE MALE PSNS: 45-49 YRS
583	D60172	Num	4641	4648	8	NONWHITE MALE PSNS: 50-54 YRS
584	D60173	Num	4649	4656	8	NONWHITE MALE PSNS: 55-59 YRS
585	D60174	Num	4657	4664	8	NONWHITE MALE PSNS: 60-64 YRS
586	D60175	Num	4665	4672	8	NONWHITE MALE PSNS: 65-69 YRS
587	D60176	Num	4673	4680	8	NONWHITE MALE PSNS: 70-74 YRS
588	D60177	Num	4681	4688	8	NONWHITE MALE PSNS: 75-79 YRS
589	D60178	Num	4689	4696	8	NONWHITE MALE PSNS: 80-84 YRS
590	D60179	Num	4697	4704	8	NONWHITE MALE PSNS: 85 AND OVER
591	D60180	Num	4705	4712	8	NONWHITE MALE PSNS: UNER 18 YRS
592	D60181	Num	4713	4720	8	NONWHITE FEMALE PSNS: UNDER 1 YEAR
593	D60182	Num	4721	4728	8	NONWHITE FEMALE PSNS: UNDER 5 YEAR
594	D60183	Num	4729	4736	8	NONWHITE FEMALE PSNS: 5-9 YRS

595	D60184	Num	4737	4744	8	NONWHITE FEMALE PSNS: 10-14 YRS
596	D60185	Num	4745	4752	8	NONWHITE FEMALE PSNS: 15-19 YRS
597	D60186	Num	4753	4760	8	NONWHITE FEMALE PSNS: 20-24 YRS
598	D60187	Num	4761	4768	8	NONWHITE FEMALE PSNS: 25-29 YRS
599	D60188	Num	4769	4776	8	NONWHITE FEMALE PSNS: 30-34 YRS
600	D60189	Num	4777	4784	8	NONWHITE FEMALE PSNS: 35-39 YRS
601	D60190	Num	4785	4792	8	NONWHITE FEMALE PSNS: 40-44 YRS
602	D60191	Num	4793	4800	8	NONWHITE FEMALE PSNS: 45-49 YRS
603	D60192	Num	4801	4808	8	NONWHITE FEMALE PSNS: 50-54 YRS
604	D60193	Num	4809	4816	8	NONWHITE FEMALE PSNS: 55-59 YRS
605	D60194	Num	4817	4824	8	NONWHITE FEMALE PSNS: 60-64 YRS
606	D60195	Num	4825	4832	8	NONWHITE FEMALE PSNS: 65-69 YRS
607	D60196	Num	4833	4840	8	NONWHITE FEMALE PSNS: 70-74 YRS
608	D60197	Num	4841	4848	8	NONWHITE FEMALE PSNS: 75-79 YRS
609	D60198	Num	4849	4856	8	NONWHITE FEMALE PSNS: 80-84 YRS
610	D60199	Num	4857	4864	8	NONWHITE FEMALE PSNS: 85 AND OVER
611	D60200	Num	4865	4872	8	NONWHITE FEMALE PSNS: UNER 18 YRS
612	D60201	Num	4873	4880	8	TOTAL PSNS 14 YRS+: TOTAL
613	D60202	Num	4881	4888	8	TOTAL PSNS 14 YRS+: SINGLE
614	D60203	Num	4889	4896	8	TOTAL PSNS 14 YRS+: MARRIED
615	D60204	Num	4897	4904	8	TOTAL PSNS 14 YRS+: SEPARATED
616	D60205	Num	4905	4912	8	TOTAL PSNS 14 YRS+: WIDOWED
617	D60206	Num	4913	4920	8	TOTAL PSNS 14 YRS+: DIVORCED
618	D60207	Num	4921	4928	8	MALE PSNS 14 YRS+: TOTAL
619	D60208	Num	4929	4936	8	MALE PSNS 14 YRS+: SINGLE
620	D60209	Num	4937	4944	8	MALE PSNS 14 YRS+: MARRIED
621	D60210	Num	4945	4952	8	MALE PSNS 14 YRS+: SEPARATED
622	D60211	Num	4953	4960	8	MALE PSNS 14 YRS+: WIDOWED
623	D60212	Num	4961	4968	8	MALE PSNS 14 YRS+: DIVORCED
624	D60213	Num	4969	4976	8	FEMALE PSNS 14 YRS+: TOTAL
625	D60214	Num	4977	4984	8	FEMALE PSNS 14 YRS+: SINGLE
626	D60215	Num	4985	4992	8	FEMALE PSNS 14 YRS+: MARRIED
627	D60216	Num	4993	5000	8	REMALE PSNS 14 YRS+: SEPARATED
628	D60217	Num	5001	5008	8	FEMALE PSNS 14 YRS+: WIDOWED
629	D60218	Num	5009	5016	8	FEMALE PSNS 14 YRS+: DIVORCED
630	D60219	Num	5017	5024	8	RES IN 1955 (PSNS 5 YRS+): SAME HOUSE
631	D60220	Num	5025	5032	8	RES IN 1955 (PSNS 5 YRS+): SAME COUNTY
632	D60221	Num	5033	5040	8	RES IN 1955 (PSNS 5 YRS+): SAME STATE
633	D60222	Num	5041	5048	8	RES IN 1955 (PSNS 5 YRS+): DIFF STATE
634	D60223	Num	5049	5056	8	RES IN 1955 (PSNS 5 YRS+): ABROAD
635	D60224	Num	5057	5064	8	RES IN 1955 (PSNS 5 YRS+): NOT REPORTED

636	D70001	Num	5065	5072	8	TOTAL PSNS
637	D70002	Num	5073	5080	8	TOTAL NUMBER OF FAMILIES
638	D70003	Num	5081	5088	8	TOTAL NUMBER OF HOUSEHOLDS
639	D70004	Num	5089	5096	8	TOTAL PSNS: URBAN
640	D70005	Num	5097	5104	8	TOTAL PSNS: RURAL
641	D70006	Num	5105	5112	8	TOTAL PSNS: RURAL-FARM
642	D70007	Num	5113	5120	8	TOTAL PSNS: RURAL-NONFARM
643	D70008	Num	5121	5128	8	TOTAL MALE PSNS
644	D70009	Num	5129	5136	8	TOTAL FEMALE PSNS
645	D70010	Num	5137	5144	8	WHT PSNS
646	D70011	Num	5145	5152	8	WHT MALE PSNS
647	D70012	Num	5153	5160	8	WHT FEMALE PSNS
648	D70013	Num	5161	5168	8	BLK PSNS
649	D70014	Num	5169	5176	8	BLK MALE PSNS
650	D70015	Num	5177	5184	8	BLK FEMALE PSNS
651	D70016	Num	5185	5192	8	HISP PSNS
652	D70017	Num	5193	5200	8	HISP MALE PSNS
653	D70018	Num	5201	5208	8	HISP FEMALE PSNS
654	D70019	Num	5209	5216	8	TOTAL PSNS:0-4 YRS
655	D70020	Num	5217	5224	8	TOTAL PSNS:5-9 YRS
656	D70021	Num	5225	5232	8	TOTAL PSNS:10-14 YRS
657	D70022	Num	5233	5240	8	TOTAL PSNS:15-19 YRS
658	D70023	Num	5241	5248	8	TOTAL PSNS:20-24 YRS
659	D70024	Num	5249	5256	8	TOTAL PSNS:25-29 YRS
660	D70025	Num	5257	5264	8	TOTAL PSNS:30-34 YRS
661	D70026	Num	5265	5272	8	TOTAL PSNS:35-39 YRS
662	D70027	Num	5273	5280	8	TOTAL PSNS:40-44 YRS
663	D70028	Num	5281	5288	8	TOTAL PSNS:45-49 YRS
664	D70029	Num	5289	5296	8	TOTAL PSNS:50-54 YRS
665	D70030	Num	5297	5304	8	TOTAL PSNS:55-59 YRS
666	D70031	Num	5305	5312	8	TOTAL PSNS:60-64 YRS
667	D70032	Num	5313	5320	8	TOTAL PSNS:65-69 YRS
668	D70033	Num	5321	5328	8	TOTAL PSNS:70-74 YRS
669	D70034	Num	5329	5336	8	TOTAL PSNS:75 AND OVER
670	D70035	Num	5337	5344	8	TOTAL MALE PSNS:0-4 YRS
671	D70036	Num	5345	5352	8	TOTAL MALE PSNS:5-9 YRS
672	D70037	Num	5353	5360	8	TOTAL MALE PSNS:10-14 YRS
673	D70038	Num	5361	5368	8	TOTAL MALE PSNS:15-19 YRS
674	D70039	Num	5369	5376	8	TOTAL MALE PSNS:20-24 YRS
675	D70040	Num	5377	5384	8	TOTAL MALE PSNS:25-29 YRS

676	D70041	Num	5385	5392	8	TOTAL MALE PSNS:30-34 YRS
677	D70042	Num	5393	5400	8	TOTAL MALE PSNS:35-39 YRS
678	D70043	Num	5401	5408	8	TOTAL MALE PSNS:40-44 YRS
679	D70044	Num	5409	5416	8	TOTAL MALE PSNS:45-49 YRS
680	D70045	Num	5417	5424	8	TOTAL MALE PSNS:50-54 YRS
681	D70046	Num	5425	5432	8	TOTAL MALE PSNS:55-59 YRS
682	D70047	Num	5433	5440	8	TOTAL MALE PSNS:60-64 YRS
683	D70048	Num	5441	5448	8	TOTAL MALE PSNS:65-69 YRS
684	D70049	Num	5449	5456	8	TOTAL MALE PSNS:70-74 YRS
685	D70050	Num	5457	5464	8	TOTAL MALE PSNS:75 AND OVER
686	D70051	Num	5465	5472	8	TOTAL FEMALE PSNS:0-4 YRS
687	D70052	Num	5473	5480	8	TOTAL FEMALE PSNS:5-9 YRS
688	D70053	Num	5481	5488	8	TOTAL FEMALE PSNS:10-14 YRS
689	D70054	Num	5489	5496	8	TOTAL FEMALE PSNS:15-19 YRS
690	D70055	Num	5497	5504	8	TOTAL FEMALE PSNS:20-24 YRS
691	D70056	Num	5505	5512	8	TOTAL FEMALE PSNS:25-29 YRS
692	D70057	Num	5513	5520	8	TOTAL FEMALE PSNS:30-34 YRS
693	D70058	Num	5521	5528	8	TOTAL FEMALE PSNS:35-39 YRS
694	D70059	Num	5529	5536	8	TOTAL FEMALE PSNS:40-44 YRS
695	D70060	Num	5537	5544	8	TOTAL FEMALE PSNS:45-49 YRS
696	D70061	Num	5545	5552	8	TOTAL FEMALE PSNS:50-54 YRS
697	D70062	Num	5553	5560	8	TOTAL FEMALE PSNS:55-59 YRS
698	D70063	Num	5561	5568	8	TOTAL FEMALE PSNS:60-64 YRS
699	D70064	Num	5569	5576	8	TOTAL FEMALE PSNS:65-69 YRS
700	D70065	Num	5577	5584	8	TOTAL FEMALE PSNS:70-74 YRS
701	D70066	Num	5585	5592	8	TOTAL FEMALE PSNS:75 AND OVER
702	D70067	Num	5593	5600	8	TOTAL WHITE PSNS:0-4 YRS
703	D70068	Num	5601	5608	8	TOTAL WHITE PSNS:5-9 YRS
704	D70069	Num	5609	5616	8	TOTAL WHITE PSNS:10-14 YRS
705	D70070	Num	5617	5624	8	TOTAL WHITE PSNS:15-19 YRS
706	D70071	Num	5625	5632	8	TOTAL WHITE PSNS:20-24 YRS
707	D70072	Num	5633	5640	8	TOTAL WHITE PSNS:25-29 YRS
708	D70073	Num	5641	5648	8	TOTAL WHITE PSNS:30-34 YRS
709	D70074	Num	5649	5656	8	TOTAL WHITE PSNS:35-39 YRS
710	D70075	Num	5657	5664	8	TOTAL WHITE PSNS:40-44 YRS
711	D70076	Num	5665	5672	8	TOTAL WHITE PSNS:45-49 YRS
712	D70077	Num	5673	5680	8	TOTAL WHITE PSNS:50-54 YRS
713	D70078	Num	5681	5688	8	TOTAL WHITE PSNS:55-59 YRS
714	D70079	Num	5689	5696	8	TOTAL WHITE PSNS:60-64 YRS
715	D70080	Num	5697	5704	8	TOTAL WHITE PSNS:65-69 YRS
716	D70081	Num	5705	5712	8	TOTAL WHITE PSNS:70-74 YRS

717	D70082	Num	5713	5720	8	TOTAL WHITE PSNS:75 AND OVER
718	D70083	Num	5721	5728	8	WHT MALE PSNS:0-4 YRS
719	D70084	Num	5729	5736	8	WHT MALE PSNS:5-9 YRS
720	D70085	Num	5737	5744	8	WHT MALE PSNS:10-14 YRS
721	D70086	Num	5745	5752	8	WHT MALE PSNS:15-19 YRS
722	D70087	Num	5753	5760	8	WHT MALE PSNS:20-24 YRS
723	D70088	Num	5761	5768	8	WHT MALE PSNS:25-29 YRS
724	D70089	Num	5769	5776	8	WHT MALE PSNS:30-34 YRS
725	D70090	Num	5777	5784	8	WHT MALE PSNS:35-39 YRS
726	D70091	Num	5785	5792	8	WHT MALE PSNS:40-44 YRS
727	D70092	Num	5793	5800	8	WHT MALE PSNS:45-49 YRS
728	D70093	Num	5801	5808	8	WHT MALE PSNS:50-54 YRS
729	D70094	Num	5809	5816	8	WHT MALE PSNS:55-59 YRS
730	D70095	Num	5817	5824	8	WHT MALE PSNS:60-64 YRS
731	D70096	Num	5825	5832	8	WHT MALE PSNS:65-69 YRS
732	D70097	Num	5833	5840	8	WHT MALE PSNS:70-74 YRS
733	D70098	Num	5841	5848	8	WHT MALE PSNS:75 AND OVER
734	D70099	Num	5849	5856	8	WHT FEMALE PSNS:0-4 YRS
735	D70100	Num	5857	5864	8	WHT FEMALE PSNS:5-9 YRS
736	D70101	Num	5865	5872	8	WHT FEMALE PSNS:10-14 YRS
737	D70102	Num	5873	5880	8	WHT FEMALE PSNS:15-19 YRS
738	D70103	Num	5881	5888	8	WHT FEMALE PSNS:20-24 YRS
739	D70104	Num	5889	5896	8	WHT FEMALE PSNS:25-29 YRS
740	D70105	Num	5897	5904	8	WHT FEMALE PSNS:30-34 YRS
741	D70106	Num	5905	5912	8	WHT FEMALE PSNS:35-39 YRS
742	D70107	Num	5913	5920	8	WHT FEMALE PSNS:40-44 YRS
743	D70108	Num	5921	5928	8	WHT FEMALE PSNS:45-49 YRS
744	D70109	Num	5929	5936	8	WHT FEMALE PSNS:50-54 YRS
745	D70110	Num	5937	5944	8	WHT FEMALE PSNS:55-59 YRS
746	D70111	Num	5945	5952	8	WHT FEMALE PSNS:60-64 YRS
747	D70112	Num	5953	5960	8	WHT FEMALE PSNS:65-69 YRS
748	D70113	Num	5961	5968	8	WHT FEMALE PSNS:70-74 YRS
749	D70114	Num	5969	5976	8	WHT FEMALE PSNS:75 AND OVER
750	D70115	Num	5977	5984	8	TOTAL BLACK PSNS:0-4 YRS
751	D70116	Num	5985	5992	8	TOTAL BLACK PSNS:5-9 YRS
752	D70117	Num	5993	6000	8	TOTAL BLACK PSNS:10-14 YRS
753	D70118	Num	6001	6008	8	TOTAL BLACK PSNS:15-19 YRS
754	D70119	Num	6009	6016	8	TOTAL BLACK PSNS:20-24 YRS
755	D70120	Num	6017	6024	8	TOTAL BLACK PSNS:25-29 YRS
756	D70121	Num	6025	6032	8	TOTAL BLACK PSNS:30-34 YRS
757	D70122	Num	6033	6040	8	TOTAL BLACK PSNS:35-39 YRS

758	D70123	Num	6041	6048	8	TOTAL BLACK PSNS:40-44 YRS
759	D70124	Num	6049	6056	8	TOTAL BLACK PSNS:45-49 YRS
760	D70125	Num	6057	6064	8	TOTAL BLACK PSNS:50-54 YRS
761	D70126	Num	6065	6072	8	TOTAL BLACK PSNS:55-59 YRS
762	D70127	Num	6073	6080	8	TOTAL BLACK PSNS:60-64 YRS
763	D70128	Num	6081	6088	8	TOTAL BLACK PSNS:65-69 YRS
764	D70129	Num	6089	6096	8	TOTAL BLACK PSNS:70-74 YRS
765	D70130	Num	6097	6104	8	TOTAL BLACK PSNS:75 AND OVER
766	D70131	Num	6105	6112	8	BLK MALE PSNS:0-4 YRS
767	D70132	Num	6113	6120	8	BLK MALE PSNS:5-9 YRS
768	D70133	Num	6121	6128	8	BLK MALE PSNS:10-14 YRS
769	D70134	Num	6129	6136	8	BLK MALE PSNS:15-19 YRS
770	D70135	Num	6137	6144	8	BLK MALE PSNS:20-24 YRS
771	D70136	Num	6145	6152	8	BLK MALE PSNS:25-29 YRS
772	D70137	Num	6153	6160	8	BLK MALE PSNS:30-34 YRS
773	D70138	Num	6161	6168	8	BLK MALE PSNS:35-39 YRS
774	D70139	Num	6169	6176	8	BLK MALE PSNS:40-44 YRS
775	D70140	Num	6177	6184	8	BLK MALE PSNS:45-49 YRS
776	D70141	Num	6185	6192	8	BLK MALE PSNS:50-54 YRS
777	D70142	Num	6193	6200	8	BLK MALE PSNS:55-59 YRS
778	D70143	Num	6201	6208	8	BLK MALE PSNS:60-64 YRS
779	D70144	Num	6209	6216	8	BLK MALE PSNS:65-69 YRS
780	D70145	Num	6217	6224	8	BLK MALE PSNS:70-74 YRS
781	D70146	Num	6225	6232	8	BLK MALE PSNS:75 AND OVER
782	D70147	Num	6233	6240	8	BLK FEMALE PSNS:0-4 YRS
783	D70148	Num	6241	6248	8	BLK FEMALE PSNS:5-9 YRS
784	D70149	Num	6249	6256	8	BLK FEMALE PSNS:10-14 YRS
785	D70150	Num	6257	6264	8	BLK FEMALE PSNS:15-19 YRS
786	D70151	Num	6265	6272	8	BLK FEMALE PSNS:20-24 YRS
787	D70152	Num	6273	6280	8	BLK FEMALE PSNS:25-29 YRS
788	D70153	Num	6281	6288	8	BLK FEMALE PSNS:30-34 YRS
789	D70154	Num	6289	6296	8	BLK FEMALE PSNS:35-39 YRS
790	D70155	Num	6297	6304	8	BLK FEMALE PSNS:40-44 YRS
791	D70156	Num	6305	6312	8	BLK FEMALE PSNS:45-49 YRS
792	D70157	Num	6313	6320	8	BLK FEMALE PSNS:50-54 YRS
793	D70158	Num	6321	6328	8	BLK FEMALE PSNS:55-59 YRS
794	D70159	Num	6329	6336	8	BLK FEMALE PSNS:60-64 YRS
795	D70160	Num	6337	6344	8	BLK FEMALE PSNS:65-69 YRS
796	D70161	Num	6345	6352	8	BLK FEMALE PSNS:70-74 YRS
797	D70162	Num	6353	6360	8	BLK FEMALE PSNS:75 AND OVER
798	D70163	Num	6361	6368	8	TOTAL HISP PSNS:0-4 YRS

799	D70164	Num	6369	6376	8	TOTAL HISP PSNS:5-9 YRS
800	D70165	Num	6377	6384	8	TOTAL HISP PSNS:10-14 YRS
801	D70166	Num	6385	6392	8	TOTAL HISP PSNS:15-19 YRS
802	D70167	Num	6393	6400	8	TOTAL HISP PSNS:20-24 YRS
803	D70168	Num	6401	6408	8	TOTAL HISP PSNS:25-29 YRS
804	D70169	Num	6409	6416	8	TOTAL HISP PSNS:30-34 YRS
805	D70170	Num	6417	6424	8	TOTAL HISP PSNS:35-39 YRS
806	D70171	Num	6425	6432	8	TOTAL HISP PSNS:40-44 YRS
807	D70172	Num	6433	6440	8	TOTAL HISP PSNS:45-49 YRS
808	D70173	Num	6441	6448	8	TOTAL HISP PSNS:50-54 YRS
809	D70174	Num	6449	6456	8	TOTAL HISP PSNS:55-59 YRS
810	D70175	Num	6457	6464	8	TOTAL HISP PSNS:60-64 YRS
811	D70176	Num	6465	6472	8	TOTAL HISP PSNS:65-69 YRS
812	D70177	Num	6473	6480	8	TOTAL HISP PSNS:70-74 YRS
813	D70178	Num	6481	6488	8	TOTAL HISP PSNS:75 AND OVER
814	D70179	Num	6489	6496	8	HISP MALE PSNS:0-4 YRS
815	D70180	Num	6497	6504	8	HISP MALE PSNS:5-9 YRS
816	D70181	Num	6505	6512	8	HISP MALE PSNS:10-14 YRS
817	D70182	Num	6513	6520	8	HISP MALE PSNS:15-19 YRS
818	D70183	Num	6521	6528	8	HISP MALE PSNS:20-24 YRS
819	D70184	Num	6529	6536	8	HISP MALE PSNS:25-29 YRS
820	D70185	Num	6537	6544	8	HISP MALE PSNS:30-34 YRS
821	D70186	Num	6545	6552	8	HISP MALE PSNS:35-39 YRS
822	D70187	Num	6553	6560	8	HISP MALE PSNS:40-44 YRS
823	D70188	Num	6561	6568	8	HISP MALE PSNS:45-49 YRS
824	D70189	Num	6569	6576	8	HISP MALE PSNS:50-54 YRS
825	D70190	Num	6577	6584	8	HISP MALE PSNS:55-59 YRS
826	D70191	Num	6585	6592	8	HISP MALE PSNS:60-64 YRS
827	D70192	Num	6593	6600	8	HISP MALE PSNS:65-69 YRS
828	D70193	Num	6601	6608	8	HISP MALE PSNS:70-74 YRS
829	D70194	Num	6609	6616	8	HISP MALE PSNS:75 AND OVER
830	D70195	Num	6617	6624	8	HISP FEMALE PSNS:0-4 YRS
831	D70196	Num	6625	6632	8	HISP FEMALE PSNS:5-9 YRS
832	D70197	Num	6633	6640	8	HISP FEMALE PSNS:10-14 YRS
833	D70198	Num	6641	6648	8	HISP FEMALE PSNS:15-19 YRS
834	D70199	Num	6649	6656	8	HISP FEMALE PSNS:20-24 YRS
835	D70200	Num	6657	6664	8	HISP FEMALE PSNS:25-29 YRS
836	D70201	Num	6665	6672	8	HISP FEMALE PSNS:30-34 YRS
837	D70202	Num	6673	6680	8	HISP FEMALE PSNS:35-39 YRS
838	D70203	Num	6681	6688	8	HISP FEMALE PSNS:40-44 YRS
839	D70204	Num	6689	6696	8	HISP FEMALE PSNS:45-49 YRS

840	D70205	Num	6697	6704	8	HISP FEMALE PSNS:50-54 YRS
841	D70206	Num	6705	6712	8	HISP FEMALE PSNS:55-59 YRS
842	D70207	Num	6713	6720	8	HISP FEMALE PSNS:60-64 YRS
843	D70208	Num	6721	6728	8	HISP FEMALE PSNS:65-69 YRS
844	D70209	Num	6729	6736	8	HISP FEMALE PSNS:70-74 YRS
845	D70210	Num	6737	6744	8	HISP FEMALE PSNS:75 AND OVER
846	D70211	Num	6745	6752	8	HUS-WIFE FAM: W/OUT CHILD UNDER 18
847	D70212	Num	6753	6760	8	HUS-WIFE FAM: W/ OWN CHILD UNDER 6
848	D70213	Num	6761	6768	8	HUS-WIFE FAM: W/OUT CHILD UNDER 6
849	D70214	Num	6769	6776	8	MALE HD FAM: W/OUT CHILD UNDER 18
850	D70215	Num	6777	6784	8	MALE HD FAM: W/ OWN CHILD UNDER 6
851	D70216	Num	6785	6792	8	MALE HD FAM: W/OUT CHILD UNDER 6
852	D70217	Num	6793	6800	8	FEMALE HD FAM: W/OUT CHILD UNDER 18
853	D70218	Num	6801	6808	8	FEMALE HD FAM: W/OWN CHILD UNDER 6
854	D70219	Num	6809	6816	8	FEMALE HD FAM: W/OUT CHILD UNDER 6
855	D70220	Num	6817	6824	8	TOTAL PSNS 14 YRS+: NEVER MARRIED
856	D70221	Num	6825	6832	8	TOTAL PSNS 14 YRS+: MARR,SPOUSE PRESENT
857	D70222	Num	6833	6840	8	TOTAL PSNS 14 YRS+: MARR,SPOUSE ABSENT
858	D70223	Num	6841	6848	8	TOTAL PSNS 14 YRS+: SEPARATED
859	D70224	Num	6849	6856	8	TOTAL PSNS 14 YRS+: WIDOWED
860	D70225	Num	6857	6864	8	TOTAL PSNS 14 YRS+: DIVORCED
861	D70226	Num	6865	6872	8	MALE PSNS 14 YRS+: NEVER MARRIED
862	D70227	Num	6873	6880	8	MALE PSNS 14 YRS+: MARR,SPOUSE PRESENT
863	D70228	Num	6881	6888	8	MALE PSNS 14 YRS+: MARR,SPOUSE ABSENT
864	D70229	Num	6889	6896	8	MALE PSNS 14 YRS+: SEPARATED
865	D70230	Num	6897	6904	8	MALE PSNS 14 YRS+: WIDOWED
866	D70231	Num	6905	6912	8	MALE PSNS 14 YRS+: DIVORCED
867	D70232	Num	6913	6920	8	FEMALE PSNS 14 YRS+: NEVER MARRIED
868	D70233	Num	6921	6928	8	FEMALE PSNS 14 YRS+: MARR,SPOUSE PRESENT
869	D70234	Num	6929	6936	8	FEMALE PSNS 14 YRS+: MARR,SPOUSE ABSENT
870	D70235	Num	6937	6944	8	FEMALE PSNS 14 YRS+: SEPARATED
871	D70236	Num	6945	6952	8	FEMALE PSNS 14 YRS+: WIDOWED
872	D70237	Num	6953	6960	8	FEMALE PSNS 14 YRS+: DIVORCED
873	D70238	Num	6961	6968	8	EVER MARRIED 14-54 YRS: WIDOWED ONLY
874	D70239	Num	6969	6976	8	EVER MARRIED 14-54 YRS: DIVORCED ONLY
875	D70240	Num	6977	6984	8	EVER MARRIED 14-54 YRS: WIDOWED/DIVORCED
876	D70241	Num	6985	6992	8	EVER MARRIED 14-54 YRS: NIETHER WID/DIV
877	D70242	Num	6993	7000	8	NATIVE PSNS: UNDER 18 YRS
878	D70243	Num	7001	7008	8	NATIVE PSNS: 18 YRS
879	D70244	Num	7009	7016	8	NATIVE PSNS: 19 YRS
880	D70245	Num	7017	7024	8	NATIVE PSNS: 20 YRS

881	D70246	Num	7025	7032	8	NATIVE PSNS: 21 YRS AND OVER
882	D70247	Num	7033	7040	8	FOREIGN BORN, NATURALIZED: UNDER 18 YRS
883	D70248	Num	7041	7048	8	FOREIGN BORN, NATURALIZED: 18 YRS
884	D70249	Num	7049	7056	8	FOREIGN BORN, NATURALIZED: 19 YRS
885	D70250	Num	7057	7064	8	FOREIGN BORN, NATURALIZED: 20 YRS
886	D70251	Num	7065	7072	8	FOREIGN BORN, NATURALIZED: 21 YRS+
887	D70252	Num	7073	7080	8	FOREIGN BORN, ALIEN: UNDER 18 YRS
888	D70253	Num	7081	7088	8	FOREIGN BORN, ALIEN: 18 YRS
889	D70254	Num	7089	7096	8	FOREIGN BORN, ALIEN: 19 YRS
890	D70255	Num	7097	7104	8	FOREIGN BORN, ALIEN: 20 YRS
891	D70256	Num	7105	7112	8	FOREIGN BORN, ALIEN: 21 YRS AND OVER
892	D70257	Num	7113	7120	8	YEAR OF IMMIGRATION: 1960-70
893	D70258	Num	7121	7128	8	YEAR OF IMMIGRATION: 1945-59
894	D70259	Num	7129	7136	8	YEAR OF IMMIGRATION: 1925-44
895	D70260	Num	7137	7144	8	YEAR OF IMMIGRATION: BEFORE 1925
896	D70261	Num	7145	7152	8	YEAR OF IMMIGRATION: NOT REPORTED
897	D70262	Num	7153	7160	8	BIRTHPLACE: BORN IN STATE OF RESIDENCE
898	D70263	Num	7161	7168	8	BIRTHPLACE: BORN IN NORTHEAST
899	D70264	Num	7169	7176	8	BIRTHPLACE: BORN IN NORTH CENTRAL
900	D70265	Num	7177	7184	8	BIRTHPLACE: BORN IN SOUTH
901	D70266	Num	7185	7192	8	BIRTHPLACE: BORN IN WEST
902	D70267	Num	7193	7200	8	BIRTHPLACE: BORN ELSEWHERE
903	D70268	Num	7201	7208	8	BIRTHPLACE: STATE OF BIRTH NOT REPORTED
904	D70269	Num	7209	7216	8	RES IN 1965: SAME HOUSE
905	D70270	Num	7217	7224	8	RES IN 1965: SAME COUNTY
906	D70271	Num	7225	7232	8	RES IN 1965: SAME STATE
907	D70272	Num	7233	7240	8	RES IN 1965: NORTHEAST
908	D70273	Num	7241	7248	8	RES IN 1965: NORTH CENTRAL
909	D70274	Num	7249	7256	8	RES IN 1965: SOUTH
910	D70275	Num	7257	7264	8	RES IN 1965: WEST
911	D70276	Num	7265	7272	8	RES IN 1965: ABROAD, IN ARMED FORCES
912	D70277	Num	7273	7280	8	RES IN 1965: ABROAD, NOT IN ARMED FORCES
913	D70278	Num	7281	7288	8	RES IN 1965: MOVED,NOT REPORTED
914	D70279	Num	7289	7296	8	METRO RES 1970: SAME SMSA/SAME HUSE 1965
915	D70280	Num	7297	7304	8	METRO RES 1970: SAME SMSA/CENT CITY 1965
916	D70281	Num	7305	7312	8	METRO RES 1970: SAME SMSA/REMAINDER 1965
917	D70282	Num	7313	7320	8	METRO RES 1970:DIFF SMSA:NORTH/WEST 1965
918	D70283	Num	7321	7328	8	METRO RES 1970: DIFF SMSA: SOUTH 1965
919	D70284	Num	7329	7336	8	METRO RES 1970: ABROAD 1965
920	D70285	Num	7337	7344	8	METRO RES 1970: RES IN 1965 NOT REPORTED
921	D70286	Num	7345	7352	8	TOTAL PSNS 25 YRS+: NO SCHOOL

922	D70287	Num	7353	7360	8	TOTAL PSNS 25 YRS+: 1-4TH GRADE
923	D70288	Num	7361	7368	8	TOTAL PSNS 25 YRS+: 5-6TH GRADE
924	D70289	Num	7369	7376	8	TOTAL PSNS 25 YRS+: 7TH GRADE
925	D70290	Num	7377	7384	8	TOTAL PSNS 25 YRS+: 8TH GRADE
926	D70291	Num	7385	7392	8	TOTAL PSNS 25 YRS+: 9-11 GRADE
927	D70292	Num	7393	7400	8	TOTAL PSNS 25 YRS+: 12 GRADE
928	D70293	Num	7401	7408	8	TOTAL PSNS 25 YRS+: COLLEGE 1-3 YRS
929	D70294	Num	7409	7416	8	TOTAL PSNS 25 YRS+: COLLEGE 4 YRS
930	D70295	Num	7417	7424	8	TOTAL PSNS 25 YRS+: COLLEGE 5 YRS+
931	D70296	Num	7425	7432	8	MALE PSNS 25 YRS+: NO SCHOOL
932	D70297	Num	7433	7440	8	MALE PSNS 25 YRS+: 1-4TH GRADE
933	D70298	Num	7441	7448	8	MALE PSNS 25 YRS+: 5-6TH GRADE
934	D70299	Num	7449	7456	8	MALE PSNS 25 YRS+: 7TH GRADE
935	D70300	Num	7457	7464	8	MALE PSNS 25 YRS+: 8TH GRADE
936	D70301	Num	7465	7472	8	MALE PSNS 25 YRS+: 9-11 GRADE
937	D70302	Num	7473	7480	8	MALE PSNS 25 YRS+: 12 GRADE
938	D70303	Num	7481	7488	8	MALE PSNS 25 YRS+: COLLEGE 1-3 YRS
939	D70304	Num	7489	7496	8	MALE PSNS 25 YRS+: COLLEGE 4 YRS
940	D70305	Num	7497	7504	8	MALE PSNS 25 YRS+: COLLEGE 5 YRS+
941	D70306	Num	7505	7512	8	FEMALE PSNS 25 YRS+: NO SCHOOL
942	D70307	Num	7513	7520	8	FEMALE PSNS 25 YRS+: 1-4TH GRADE
943	D70308	Num	7521	7528	8	FEMALE PSNS 25 YRS+: 5-6TH GRADE
944	D70309	Num	7529	7536	8	FEMALE PSNS 25 YRS+: 7TH GRADE
945	D70310	Num	7537	7544	8	FEMALE PSNS 25 YRS+: 8TH GRADE
946	D70311	Num	7545	7552	8	FEMALE PSNS 25 YRS+: 9-11 GRADE
947	D70312	Num	7553	7560	8	FEMALE PSNS 25 YRS+: 12 GRADE
948	D70313	Num	7561	7568	8	FEMALE PSNS 25 YRS+: COLLEGE 1-3 YRS
949	D70314	Num	7569	7576	8	FEMALE PSNS 25 YRS+: COLLEGE 4 YRS
950	D70315	Num	7577	7584	8	FEMALE PSNS 25 YRS+: COLLEGE 5 YRS+
951	D80001	Num	7585	7592	8	TOTAL PSNS
952	D80002	Num	7593	7600	8	TOTAL NUMBER OF FAMILIES
953	D80003	Num	7601	7608	8	TOTAL NUMBER OF HOUSEHOLDS, REC 1, 1980
954	D80004	Num	7609	7616	8	TOTAL PSNS: INSIDE URBANIZED AREAS
955	D80005	Num	7617	7624	8	TOTAL PSNS: URBAN
956	D80006	Num	7625	7632	8	TOTAL PSNS: RURAL
957	D80007	Num	7633	7640	8	TOTAL PSNS: RURAL FARM (1980 DEF)
958	D80008	Num	7641	7648	8	TOTAL PSNS: RURAL NONFARM (1980 DEF)
959	D80009	Num	7649	7656	8	TOTAL PSNS: RURAL FARM (1970 DEF)
960	D80010	Num	7657	7664	8	TOTAL PSNS: RURAL NONFARM (1970 DEF)
961	D80011	Num	7665	7672	8	TOTAL PSNS: WHITE

962	D80012	Num	7673	7680	8	TOTAL PSNS: BLK
963	D80013	Num	7681	7688	8	PSNS OF HSPANIC ORIGIN: TOTAL
964	D80014	Num	7689	7696	8	PSNS OF HSPANIC ORIGIN: WHITE
965	D80015	Num	7697	7704	8	PSNS OF HSPANIC ORIGIN: BLACK
966	D80016	Num	7705	7712	8	TOTAL PSNS
967	D80017	Num	7713	7720	8	TOTAL MALE PSNS
968	D80018	Num	7721	7728	8	TOTAL FEMALE PSNS
969	D80019	Num	7729	7736	8	TOTAL WHT PSNS
970	D80020	Num	7737	7744	8	TOTAL WHT MALE PSNS
971	D80021	Num	7745	7752	8	TOTAL WHT FEMALE PSNS
972	D80022	Num	7753	7760	8	TOTAL BLK PSNS
973	D80023	Num	7761	7768	8	TOTAL BLK MALE PSNS
974	D80024	Num	7769	7776	8	TOTAL BLK FEMALE PSNS
975	D80025	Num	7777	7784	8	TOTAL HISP PSNS
976	D80026	Num	7785	7792	8	TOTAL HISP MALE PSNS
977	D80027	Num	7793	7800	8	TOTAL HISP FEMALE PSNS
978	D80028	Num	7801	7808	8	TOTAL PSNS: UNDER 1 YEAR
979	D80029	Num	7809	7816	8	TOTAL PSNS:0-4 YRS
980	D80030	Num	7817	7824	8	TOTAL PSNS:5-9 YRS
981	D80031	Num	7825	7832	8	TOTAL PSNS:10-14 YRS
982	D80032	Num	7833	7840	8	TOTAL PSNS:15-19 YRS
983	D80033	Num	7841	7848	8	TOTAL PSNS:20-24 YRS
984	D80034	Num	7849	7856	8	TOTAL PSNS:25-29 YRS
985	D80035	Num	7857	7864	8	TOTAL PSNS:30-34 YRS
986	D80036	Num	7865	7872	8	TOTAL PSNS:35-44 YRS
987	D80037	Num	7873	7880	8	TOTAL PSNS:45-54 YRS
988	D80038	Num	7881	7888	8	TOTAL PSNS:55-59 YRS
989	D80039	Num	7889	7896	8	TOTAL PSNS:60-64 YRS
990	D80040	Num	7897	7904	8	TOTAL PSNS:65-74 YRS
991	D80041	Num	7905	7912	8	TOTAL PSNS:75-84 YRS
992	D80042	Num	7913	7920	8	TOTAL PSNS:85 AND OVER
993	D80043	Num	7921	7928	8	TOTAL MALE PSNS: UNDER 1 YRS
994	D80044	Num	7929	7936	8	TOTAL MALE PSNS:0-4 YRS
995	D80045	Num	7937	7944	8	TOTAL MALE PSNS:5-9 YRS
996	D80046	Num	7945	7952	8	TOTAL MALE PSNS:10-14 YRS
997	D80047	Num	7953	7960	8	TOTAL MALE PSNS:15-19 YRS
998	D80048	Num	7961	7968	8	TOTAL MALE PSNS:20-24 YRS
999	D80049	Num	7969	7976	8	TOTAL MALE PSNS:25-29 YRS
1000	D80050	Num	7977	7984	8	TOTAL MALE PSNS:30-34 YRS
1001	D80051	Num	7985	7992	8	TOTAL MALE PSNS:35-44 YRS
1002	D80052	Num	7993	8000	8	TOTAL MALE PSNS:45-54 YRS

1003	D80053	Num	8001	8008	8	TOTAL MALE PSNS:55-59 YRS
1004	D80054	Num	8009	8016	8	TOTAL MALE PSNS:60-64 YRS
1005	D80055	Num	8017	8024	8	TOTAL MALE PSNS:65-74 YRS
1006	D80056	Num	8025	8032	8	TOTAL MALE PSNS:75-84 YRS
1007	D80057	Num	8033	8040	8	TOTAL MALE PSNS:85 AND OVER
1008	D80058	Num	8041	8048	8	TOTAL FEMALE PSNS: UNDER 1 YRS
1009	D80059	Num	8049	8056	8	TOTAL FEMALE PSNS:0-4 YRS
1010	D80060	Num	8057	8064	8	TOTAL FEMALE PSNS:5-9 YRS
1011	D80061	Num	8065	8072	8	TOTAL FEMALE PSNS:10-14 YRS
1012	D80062	Num	8073	8080	8	TOTAL FEMALE PSNS:15-19 YRS
1013	D80063	Num	8081	8088	8	TOTAL FEMALE PSNS:20-24 YRS
1014	D80064	Num	8089	8096	8	TOTAL FEMALE PSNS:25-29 YRS
1015	D80065	Num	8097	8104	8	TOTAL FEMALE PSNS:30-34 YRS
1016	D80066	Num	8105	8112	8	TOTAL FEMALE PSNS:35-44 YRS
1017	D80067	Num	8113	8120	8	TOTAL FEMALE PSNS:45-54 YRS
1018	D80068	Num	8121	8128	8	TOTAL FEMALE PSNS:55-59 YRS
1019	D80069	Num	8129	8136	8	TOTAL FEMALE PSNS:60-64 YRS
1020	D80070	Num	8137	8144	8	TOTAL FEMALE PSNS:65-74 YRS
1021	D80071	Num	8145	8152	8	TOTAL FEMALE PSNS:75-84 YRS
1022	D80072	Num	8153	8160	8	TOTAL FEMALE PSNS:85 AND OVER
1023	D80073	Num	8161	8168	8	WHITE PSNS: UNDER 5 YRS
1024	D80074	Num	8169	8176	8	WHITE PSNS: 5 TO 14 YRS
1025	D80075	Num	8177	8184	8	WHITE PSNS: 15-59 YRS
1026	D80076	Num	8185	8192	8	WHITE PSNS: 60-64 YRS
1027	D80077	Num	8193	8200	8	WHITE PSNS: 65 YRS AND OLDER
1028	D80078	Num	8201	8208	8	WHITE MALE PSNS: UNDER 5 YRS
1029	D80079	Num	8209	8216	8	WHITE MALE PSNS: 5-14 YRS
1030	D80080	Num	8217	8224	8	WHITE MALE PSNS: 15-59 YRS
1031	D80081	Num	8225	8232	8	WHITE MALE PSNS: 60-64 YRS
1032	D80082	Num	8233	8240	8	WHITE MALE PSNS: 65 AND OVER
1033	D80083	Num	8241	8248	8	WHITE FEMALE PSNS: UNDER 5 YRS
1034	D80084	Num	8249	8256	8	WHITE FEMALE PSNS: 5-14 YRS
1035	D80085	Num	8257	8264	8	WHITE FEMALE PSNS: 15-59 YRS
1036	D80086	Num	8265	8272	8	WHITE FEMALE PSNS: 60-64 YRS
1037	D80087	Num	8273	8280	8	WHITE FEMALE PSNS: 65 AND OVER
1038	D80088	Num	8281	8288	8	BLK PSNS: UNDER 5 YRS
1039	D80089	Num	8289	8296	8	BLK PSNS: 5 TO 14 YRS
1040	D80090	Num	8297	8304	8	BLK PSNS: 15-59 YRS
1041	D80091	Num	8305	8312	8	BLK PSNS: 60-64 YRS
1042	D80092	Num	8313	8320	8	BLK PSNS: 65 YRS AND OLDER
1043	D80093	Num	8321	8328	8	BLK MALE PSNS: UNDER 5 YRS

1044	D80094	Num	8329	8336	8	BLK MALE PSNS: 5-14 YRS
1045	D80095	Num	8337	8344	8	BLK MALE PSNS: 15-59 YRS
1046	D80096	Num	8345	8352	8	BLK MALE PSNS: 60-64 YRS
1047	D80097	Num	8353	8360	8	BLK MALE PSNS: 65 AND OVER
1048	D80098	Num	8361	8368	8	BLK FEMALE PSNS: UNDER 5 YRS
1049	D80099	Num	8369	8376	8	BLK FEMALE PSNS: 5-14 YRS
1050	D80100	Num	8377	8384	8	BLK FEMALE PSNS: 15-59 YRS
1051	D80101	Num	8385	8392	8	BLK FEMALE PSNS: 60-64 YRS
1052	D80102	Num	8393	8400	8	BLK FEMALE PSNS: 65 AND OVER
1053	D80103	Num	8401	8408	8	TOTAL HISP ORIGIN PSNS:UNDER 5 YRS
1054	D80104	Num	8409	8416	8	TOTAL HISP ORIGIN PSNS: 5 TO 14 YRS
1055	D80105	Num	8417	8424	8	TOTAL HISP ORIGIN PSNS: 15 TO 59 YRS
1056	D80106	Num	8425	8432	8	TOTAL HISP ORIGIN PSNS: 60 TO 64 YRS
1057	D80107	Num	8433	8440	8	TOTAL HISP ORIGIN PSNS: 65 YRS AND OVER.
1058	D80108	Num	8441	8448	8	TOTAL MALE HISP ORIGIN PSNS:UNDER 5 YRS
1059	D80109	Num	8449	8456	8	TOTAL MALE HISP ORIGIN PSNS: 5-14 YRS
1060	D80110	Num	8457	8464	8	TOTAL MALE HISP ORIGIN PSNS: 15-59 YRS
1061	D80111	Num	8465	8472	8	TOTAL MALE HISP ORIGIN PSNS: 60-64 YRS
1062	D80112	Num	8473	8480	8	TOTAL MALE HISP ORIGIN PSNS: 65 YRS+
1063	D80113	Num	8481	8488	8	TOTAL FEMALE HISP ORIGIN PSNS:UNDER 5
1064	D80114	Num	8489	8496	8	TOTAL FEMALE HISP ORIGIN PSNS: 5-14 YRS
1065	D80115	Num	8497	8504	8	TOTAL FEMALE HISP ORIGIN PSNS: 15-59 YRS
1066	D80116	Num	8505	8512	8	TOTAL FEMALE HISP ORIGIN PSNS: 60-64 YRS
1067	D80117	Num	8513	8520	8	TOTAL FEMALE HISP ORIGIN PSNS: 65 YRS+
1068	D80118	Num	8521	8528	8	TTL HUS-WIFE FAM: W/ OWN CHILD UNDER 18
1069	D80119	Num	8529	8536	8	TTL HUS-WIFE FAM: W/OUT CHILD UNDER 18
1070	D80120	Num	8537	8544	8	TTL MALE HD FAM: W/ OWN CHILD UNDER 18
1071	D80121	Num	8545	8552	8	TTL MALE HD FAM: W/OUT CHILD UNDER 18
1072	D80122	Num	8553	8560	8	TTL FEMALE HD FAM: W/ OWN CHILD UNDER 18
1073	D80123	Num	8561	8568	8	TTL FEMALE HD FAM: W/OUT CHILD UNDER 18
1074	D80124	Num	8569	8576	8	TTL NONFAMILY HOUSEHOLDS
1075	D80125	Num	8577	8584	8	WHT HUS-WIFE FAM: W/ OWN CHILD UNDER 18
1076	D80126	Num	8585	8592	8	WHT HUS-WIFE FAM: W/OUT CHILD UNDER 18
1077	D80127	Num	8593	8600	8	WHT MALE HD FAM: W/ OWN CHILD UNDER 18
1078	D80128	Num	8601	8608	8	WHT MALE HD FAM: W/OUT CHILD UNDER 18
1079	D80129	Num	8609	8616	8	WHT FEMALE HD FAM: W/ OWN CHILD UNDER 18
1080	D80130	Num	8617	8624	8	WHT FEMALE HD FAM: W/OUT CHILD UNDER 18
1081	D80131	Num	8625	8632	8	WHT NONFAMILY HOUSEHOLDS
1082	D80132	Num	8633	8640	8	BLK HUS-WIFE FAM: W/ OWN CHILD UNDER 18
1083	D80133	Num	8641	8648	8	BLK HUS-WIFE FAM: W/OUT CHILD UNDER 18
1084	D80134	Num	8649	8656	8	BLK MALE HD FAM: W/ OWN CHILD UNDER 18

1085	D80135	Num	8657	8664	8	BLK MALE HD FAM: W/OUT CHILD UNDER 18
1086	D80136	Num	8665	8672	8	BLK FEMALE HD FAM: W/ OWN CHILD UNDER 18
1087	D80137	Num	8673	8680	8	BLK FEMALE HD FAM: W/OUT CHILD UNDER 18
1088	D80138	Num	8681	8688	8	BLK NONFAMILY HOUSEHOLDS
1089	D80139	Num	8689	8696	8	HISP HUS-WIFE FAM: W/ OWN CHILD UNDER 18
1090	D80140	Num	8697	8704	8	HISP HUS-WIFE FAM: W/OUT CHILD UNDER 18
1091	D80141	Num	8705	8712	8	HISP MALE HD FAM: W/ OWN CHILD UNDER 18
1092	D80142	Num	8713	8720	8	HISP MALE HD FAM: W/OUT CHILD UNDER 18
1093	D80143	Num	8721	8728	8	HISP FEMALE HD FAM: W/ OWN CHILD UNDER 1
1094	D80144	Num	8729	8736	8	HISP FEMALE HD FAM: W/OUT CHILD UNDER 18
1095	D80145	Num	8737	8744	8	HISP NONFAMILY HOUSEHOLDS
1096	D80146	Num	8745	8752	8	TOTAL PSNS 15 YRS+: SINGLE
1097	D80147	Num	8753	8760	8	TOTAL PSNS 15 YRS+: MARRIED
1098	D80148	Num	8761	8768	8	TOTAL PSNS 15 YRS+: SEPARATED
1099	D80149	Num	8769	8776	8	TOTAL PSNS 15 YRS+: WIDOWED
1100	D80150	Num	8777	8784	8	TOTAL PSNS 15 YRS+: DIVORCED
1101	D80151	Num	8785	8792	8	MALE PSNS 15 YRS+: SINGLE
1102	D80152	Num	8793	8800	8	MALE PSNS 15 YRS+: MARRIED
1103	D80153	Num	8801	8808	8	MALE PSNS 15 YRS+: SEPARATED
1104	D80154	Num	8809	8816	8	MALE PSNS 15 YRS+: WIDOWED
1105	D80155	Num	8817	8824	8	MALE PSNS 15 YRS+: DIVORCED
1106	D80156	Num	8825	8832	8	FEMALE PSNS 15 YRS+: SINGLE
1107	D80157	Num	8833	8840	8	FEMALE PSNS 15 YRS+: MARRIED
1108	D80158	Num	8841	8848	8	FEMALE PSNS 15 YRS+: SEPARATED
1109	D80159	Num	8849	8856	8	FEMALE PSNS 15 YRS+: WIDOWED
1110	D80160	Num	8857	8864	8	FEMALE PSNS 15 YRS+: DIVORCED
1111	D80161	Num	8865	8872	8	BIRTHPLACE: BORN IN STATE OF RESIDENCE
1112	D80162	Num	8873	8880	8	BIRTHPLACE: BORN IN DIFFERENT STATE
1113	D80163	Num	8881	8888	8	BIRTHPLACE: BORN ABROAD
1114	D80164	Num	8889	8896	8	BIRTHPLACE: FOREIGN BORN PSNS
1115	D80165	Num	8897	8904	8	RES IN 1975: SAME HOUSE
1116	D80166	Num	8905	8912	8	RES IN 1975: SAME COUNTY
1117	D80167	Num	8913	8920	8	RES IN 1975: SAME STATE
1118	D80168	Num	8921	8928	8	RES IN 1975: NORTHEAST
1119	D80169	Num	8929	8936	8	RES IN 1975: NORTH CENTRAL
1120	D80170	Num	8937	8944	8	RES IN 1975: SOUTH
1121	D80171	Num	8945	8952	8	RES IN 1975: WEST
1122	D80172	Num	8953	8960	8	RES IN 1975: ABROAD
1123	D80173	Num	8961	8968	8	METRO RES 1980: SAME SMSA/CENT CITY 1975
1124	D80174	Num	8969	8976	8	METRO RES 1980: SAME SMSA/REMAINDER 1975
1125	D80175	Num	8977	8984	8	METRO RES 1980: DIFF SMSA 1975

1126	D80176 Num	8985	8992	8	METRO RES 1980: NOT IN SMSA 1975
1127	D80177 Num	8993	9000	8	NONMETRO RES 1980: IN SMSA 1975
1128	D80178 Num	9001	9008	8	NONMETRO RES 1980: NOT IN SMSA 1975
1129	D80179 Num	9009	9016	8	PSNS 25 YRS+: 0-8TH GRADE
1130	D80180 Num	9017	9024	8	PSNS 25 YRS+: 9-11TH GRADE
1131	D80181 Num	9025	9032	8	PSNS 25 YRS+: 12TH GRADE
1132	D80182 Num	9033	9040	8	PSNS 25 YRS+: COLLEGE (1-3 YRS)
1133	D80183 Num	9041	9048	8	PSNS 25 YRS+: COLLEGE (4+ YRS)
1134	D80184 Num	9049	9056	8	WHT PSNS 25 YRS+: 0-8TH GRADE
1135	D80185 Num	9057	9064	8	WHT PSNS 25 YRS+: 9-11TH GRADE
1136	D80186 Num	9065	9072	8	WHT PSNS 25 YRS+: 12TH GRADE
1137	D80187 Num	9073	9080	8	WHT PSNS 25 YRS+: COLLEGE (1-3 YRS)
1138	D80188 Num	9081	9088	8	WHT PSNS 25 YRS+: COLLEGE (4+ YRS)
1139	D80189 Num	9089	9096	8	BLK PSNS 25 YRS+: 0-8TH GRADE
1140	D80190 Num	9097	9104	8	BLK PSNS 25 YRS+: 9-11TH GRADE
1141	D80191 Num	9105	9112	8	BLK PSNS 25 YRS+: 12TH GRADE
1142	D80192 Num	9113	9120	8	BLK PSNS 25 YRS+: COLLEGE (1-3 YRS)
1143	D80193 Num	9121	9128	8	BLK PSNS 25 YRS+: COLLEGE (4+ YRS)
1144	D80194 Num	9129	9136	8	HISP PSNS 25 YRS+: 0-8TH GRADE
1145	D80195 Num	9137	9144	8	HISP PSNS 25 YRS+: 9-11TH GRADE
1146	D80196 Num	9145	9152	8	HISP PSNS 25 YRS+: 12TH GRADE
1147	D80197 Num	9153	9160	8	HISP PSNS 25 YRS+: COLLEGE (1-3 YRS)
1148	D80198 Num	9161	9168	8	HISP PSNS 25 YRS+: COLLEGE (4+ YRS)
1149	D80FLG1 Char	9169	9169	1	TOTAL POPULATION SUPPRESSION FLAG
1150	D80FLG2 Char	9170	9170	1	WHITE POPULATION SUPPRESSION FLAG
1151	D80FLG3 Char	9171	9171	1	BLACK POPULATION SUPPRESSION FLAG
1152	D80FLG4 Char	9172	9172	1	HISPANIC POPULATION SUPPRESSION FLAG
1153	D90001 Num	9173	9180	8	TOTAL PERSONS
1154	D90002 Num	9181	9188	8	TOTAL NUMBER OF FAMILIES
1155	D90003 Num	9189	9196	8	TOTAL NUMBER OF HOUSEHOLDS
1156	D90004 Num	9197	9204	8	TOTAL PSNS: INSIDE URBANIZED AREA
1157	D90005 Num	9205	9212	8	TOTAL PSNS: OUTSIDE URBANIZED AREA
1158	D90006 Num	9213	9220	8	TOTAL PSNS: URBAN
1159	D90007 Num	9221	9228	8	TOTAL PSNS: RURAL
1160	D90008 Num	9229	9236	8	TOTAL PSNS: RURAL FARM
1161	D90009 Num	9237	9244	8	TOTAL PSNS: RURAL NONFARM
1162	D90010 Num	9245	9252	8	TOTAL MALE PSNS
1163	D90011 Num	9253	9260	8	TOTAL FEMALE PSNS
1164	D90012 Num	9261	9268	8	TOTAL PSNS: WHITE
1165	D90013 Num	9269	9276	8	TOTAL WHITE MALE PSNS

1166	D90014	Num	9277	9284	8	TOTAL WHITE FEMALE PSNS
1167	D90015	Num	9285	9292	8	TOTAL PSNS: BLACK
1168	D90016	Num	9293	9300	8	TOTAL BLACK MALE PSNS
1169	D90017	Num	9301	9308	8	TOTAL BLACK FEMALE PSNS
1170	D90018	Num	9309	9316	8	PSNS OF HISPANIC ORIGIN: TOTAL
1171	D90019	Num	9317	9324	8	PSNS OF HISPANIC ORIGIN: TOTAL MALE
1172	D90020	Num	9325	9332	8	PSNS OF HISPANIC ORIGIN: TOTAL FEMALE
1173	D90021	Num	9333	9340	8	PSNS OF HISPANIC ORIGIN: WHITE
1174	D90022	Num	9341	9348	8	PSNS OF HISPANIC ORIGIN: BLACK
1175	D90023	Num	9349	9356	8	TOTAL PSNS: UNDER 1 YEAR
1176	D90024	Num	9357	9364	8	TOTAL PSNS: 0-4 YRS
1177	D90025	Num	9365	9372	8	TOTAL PSNS: 5-9 YRS
1178	D90026	Num	9373	9380	8	TOTAL PSNS: 10-14 YRS
1179	D90027	Num	9381	9388	8	TOTAL PSNS: 15-19 YRS
1180	D90028	Num	9389	9396	8	TOTAL PSNS: 20-24 YRS
1181	D90029	Num	9397	9404	8	TOTAL PSNS: 25-29 YRS
1182	D90030	Num	9405	9412	8	TOTAL PSNS: 30-34 YRS
1183	D90031	Num	9413	9420	8	TOTAL PSNS: 35-39 YRS
1184	D90032	Num	9421	9428	8	TOTAL PSNS: 40-44 YRS
1185	D90033	Num	9429	9436	8	TOTAL PSNS: 45-49 YRS
1186	D90034	Num	9437	9444	8	TOTAL PSNS: 50-54 YRS
1187	D90035	Num	9445	9452	8	TOTAL PSNS: 55-59 YRS
1188	D90036	Num	9453	9460	8	TOTAL PSNS: 60-64 YRS
1189	D90037	Num	9461	9468	8	TOTAL PSNS: 65-69 YRS
1190	D90038	Num	9469	9476	8	TOTAL PSNS: 70-74 YRS
1191	D90039	Num	9477	9484	8	TOTAL PSNS: 75-79 YRS
1192	D90040	Num	9485	9492	8	TOTAL PSNS: 80-84 YRS
1193	D90041	Num	9493	9500	8	TOTAL PSNS: 85 AND OVER
1194	D90042	Num	9501	9508	8	TOTAL MALE PSNS: UNDER 1 YEAR
1195	D90043	Num	9509	9516	8	TOTAL MALE PSNS: 0-4 YRS
1196	D90044	Num	9517	9524	8	TOTAL MALE PSNS: 5-9 YRS
1197	D90045	Num	9525	9532	8	TOTAL MALE PSNS: 10-14 YRS
1198	D90046	Num	9533	9540	8	TOTAL MALE PSNS: 15-19 YRS
1199	D90047	Num	9541	9548	8	TOTAL MALE PSNS: 20-24 YRS
1200	D90048	Num	9549	9556	8	TOTAL MALE PSNS: 25-29 YRS
1201	D90049	Num	9557	9564	8	TOTAL MALE PSNS: 30-34 YRS
1202	D90050	Num	9565	9572	8	TOTAL MALE PSNS: 35-39 YRS
1203	D90051	Num	9573	9580	8	TOTAL MALE PSNS: 40-44 YRS
1204	D90052	Num	9581	9588	8	TOTAL MALE PSNS: 45-49 YRS
1205	D90053	Num	9589	9596	8	TOTAL MALE PSNS: 50-54 YRS
1206	D90054	Num	9597	9604	8	TOTAL MALE PSNS: 55-59 YRS

1207	D90055	Num	9605	9612	8	TOTAL MALE PSNS: 60-64 YRS
1208	D90056	Num	9613	9620	8	TOTAL MALE PSNS: 65-69 YRS
1209	D90057	Num	9621	9628	8	TOTAL MALE PSNS: 70-74 YRS
1210	D90058	Num	9629	9636	8	TOTAL MALE PSNS: 75-79 YRS
1211	D90059	Num	9637	9644	8	TOTAL MALE PSNS: 80-84 YRS
1212	D90060	Num	9645	9652	8	TOTAL MALE PSNS: 85 AND OVER
1213	D90061	Num	9653	9660	8	TOTAL FEMALE PSNS: UNDER 1 YEAR
1214	D90062	Num	9661	9668	8	TOTAL FEMALE PSNS: 0-4 YRS
1215	D90063	Num	9669	9676	8	TOTAL FEMALE PSNS: 5-9 YRS
1216	D90064	Num	9677	9684	8	TOTAL FEMALE PSNS: 10-14 YRS
1217	D90065	Num	9685	9692	8	TOTAL FEMALE PSNS: 15-19 YRS
1218	D90066	Num	9693	9700	8	TOTAL FEMALE PSNS: 20-24 YRS
1219	D90067	Num	9701	9708	8	TOTAL FEMALE PSNS: 25-29 YRS
1220	D90068	Num	9709	9716	8	TOTAL FEMALE PSNS: 30-34 YRS
1221	D90069	Num	9717	9724	8	TOTAL FEMALE PSNS: 35-39 YRS
1222	D90070	Num	9725	9732	8	TOTAL FEMALE PSNS: 40-44 YRS
1223	D90071	Num	9733	9740	8	TOTAL FEMALE PSNS: 45-49 YRS
1224	D90072	Num	9741	9748	8	TOTAL FEMALE PSNS: 50-54 YRS
1225	D90073	Num	9749	9756	8	TOTAL FEMALE PSNS: 55-59 YRS
1226	D90074	Num	9757	9764	8	TOTAL FEMALE PSNS: 60-64 YRS
1227	D90075	Num	9765	9772	8	TOTAL FEMALE PSNS: 65-69 YRS
1228	D90076	Num	9773	9780	8	TOTAL FEMALE PSNS: 70-74 YRS
1229	D90077	Num	9781	9788	8	TOTAL FEMALE PSNS: 75-79 YRS
1230	D90078	Num	9789	9796	8	TOTAL FEMALE PSNS: 80-84 YRS
1231	D90079	Num	9797	9804	8	TOTAL FEMALE PSNS: 85 AND OVER
1232	D90080	Num	9805	9812	8	TOTAL WHITE PSNS: 0-4 YRS
1233	D90081	Num	9813	9820	8	TOTAL WHITE PSNS: 5-9 YRS
1234	D90082	Num	9821	9828	8	TOTAL WHITE PSNS: 10-14 YRS
1235	D90083	Num	9829	9836	8	TOTAL WHITE PSNS: 15-19 YRS
1236	D90084	Num	9837	9844	8	TOTAL WHITE PSNS: 20-24 YRS
1237	D90085	Num	9845	9852	8	TOTAL WHITE PSNS: 25-29 YRS
1238	D90086	Num	9853	9860	8	TOTAL WHITE PSNS: 30-34 YRS
1239	D90087	Num	9861	9868	8	TOTAL WHITE PSNS: 35-39 YRS
1240	D90088	Num	9869	9876	8	TOTAL WHITE PSNS: 40-44 YRS
1241	D90089	Num	9877	9884	8	TOTAL WHITE PSNS: 45-49 YRS
1242	D90090	Num	9885	9892	8	TOTAL WHITE PSNS: 50-54 YRS
1243	D90091	Num	9893	9900	8	TOTAL WHITE PSNS: 55-59 YRS
1244	D90092	Num	9901	9908	8	TOTAL WHITE PSNS: 60-64 YRS
1245	D90093	Num	9909	9916	8	TOTAL WHITE PSNS: 65-69 YRS
1246	D90094	Num	9917	9924	8	TOTAL WHITE PSNS: 70-74 YRS
1247	D90095	Num	9925	9932	8	TOTAL WHITE PSNS: 75-79 YRS

1248	D90096	Num	9933	9940	8	TOTAL WHITE PSNS: 80-84 YRS
1249	D90097	Num	9941	9948	8	TOTAL WHITE PSNS: 85 AND OVER
1250	D90098	Num	9949	9956	8	WHT MALE PSNS: 0-4 YEYRS
1251	D90099	Num	9957	9964	8	WHT MALE PSNS: 5-9 YRS
1252	D90100	Num	9965	9972	8	WHT MALE PSNS: 10-14 YRS
1253	D90101	Num	9973	9980	8	WHT MALE PSNS: 15-19 YRS
1254	D90102	Num	9981	9988	8	WHT MALE PSNS: 20-24 YRS
1255	D90103	Num	9989	9996	8	WHT MALE PSNS: 25-29 YRS
1256	D90104	Num	9997	10004	8	WHT MALE PSNS: 30-34 YRS
1257	D90105	Num	10005	10012	8	WHT MALE PSNS: 35-39 YRS
1258	D90106	Num	10013	10020	8	WHT MALE PSNS: 40-44 YRS
1259	D90107	Num	10021	10028	8	WHT MALE PSNS: 45-49 YRS
1260	D90108	Num	10029	10036	8	WHT MALE PSNS: 50-54 YRS
1261	D90109	Num	10037	10044	8	WHT MALE PSNS: 55-59 YRS
1262	D90110	Num	10045	10052	8	WHT MALE PSNS: 60-64 YRS
1263	D90111	Num	10053	10060	8	WHT MALE PSNS: 65-69 YRS
1264	D90112	Num	10061	10068	8	WHT MALE PSNS: 70-74 YRS
1265	D90113	Num	10069	10076	8	WHT MALE PSNS: 75-79 YRS
1266	D90114	Num	10077	10084	8	WHT MALE PSNS: 80-84 YRS
1267	D90115	Num	10085	10092	8	WHT MALE PSNS: 85 AND OVER
1268	D90116	Num	10093	10100	8	WHT FEMALE PSNS: 0-4 YRS
1269	D90117	Num	10101	10108	8	WHT FEMALE PSNS: 5-9 YRS
1270	D90118	Num	10109	10116	8	WHT FEMALE PSNS: 10-14 YRS
1271	D90119	Num	10117	10124	8	WHT FEMALE PSNS: 15-19 YRS
1272	D90120	Num	10125	10132	8	WHT FEMALE PSNS: 20-24 YRS
1273	D90121	Num	10133	10140	8	WHT FEMALE PSNS: 25-29 YRS
1274	D90122	Num	10141	10148	8	WHT FEMALE PSNS: 30-34 YRS
1275	D90123	Num	10149	10156	8	WHT FEMALE PSNS: 35-39 YRS
1276	D90124	Num	10157	10164	8	WHT FEMALE PSNS: 40-44 YRS
1277	D90125	Num	10165	10172	8	WHT FEMALE PSNS: 45-49 YRS
1278	D90126	Num	10173	10180	8	WHT FEMALE PSNS: 50-54 YRS
1279	D90127	Num	10181	10188	8	WHT FEMALE PSNS: 55-59 YRS
1280	D90128	Num	10189	10196	8	WHT FEMALE PSNS: 60-64 YRS
1281	D90129	Num	10197	10204	8	WHT FEMALE PSNS: 65-69 YRS
1282	D90130	Num	10205	10212	8	WHT FEMALE PSNS: 70-74 YRS
1283	D90131	Num	10213	10220	8	WHT FEMALE PSNS: 75-79 YRS
1284	D90132	Num	10221	10228	8	WHT FEMALE PSNS: 80-84 YRS
1285	D90133	Num	10229	10236	8	WHT FEMALE PSNS: 85 AND OVER
1286	D90134	Num	10237	10244	8	TOTAL BLACK PSNS: 0-4 YRS
1287	D90135	Num	10245	10252	8	TOTAL BLACK PSNS: 5-9 YRS
1288	D90136	Num	10253	10260	8	TOTAL BLACK PSNS: 10-14 YRS

1289	D90137	Num	10261	10268	8	TOTAL BLACK PSNS: 15-19 YRS
1290	D90138	Num	10269	10276	8	TOTAL BLACK PSNS: 20-24 YRS
1291	D90139	Num	10277	10284	8	TOTAL BLACK PSNS: 25-29 YRS
1292	D90140	Num	10285	10292	8	TOTAL BLACK PSNS: 30-34 YRS
1293	D90141	Num	10293	10300	8	TOTAL BLACK PSNS: 35-39 YRS
1294	D90142	Num	10301	10308	8	TOTAL BLACK PSNS: 40-44 YRS
1295	D90143	Num	10309	10316	8	TOTAL BLACK PSNS: 45-49 YRS
1296	D90144	Num	10317	10324	8	TOTAL BLACK PSNS: 50-54 YRS
1297	D90145	Num	10325	10332	8	TOTAL BLACK PSNS: 55-59 YRS
1298	D90146	Num	10333	10340	8	TOTAL BLACK PSNS: 60-64 YRS
1299	D90147	Num	10341	10348	8	TOTAL BLACK PSNS: 65-69 YRS
1300	D90148	Num	10349	10356	8	TOTAL BLACK PSNS: 70-74 YRS
1301	D90149	Num	10357	10364	8	TOTAL BLACK PSNS: 75-79 YRS
1302	D90150	Num	10365	10372	8	TOTAL BLACK PSNS: 80-84 YRS
1303	D90151	Num	10373	10380	8	TOTAL BLACK PSNS: 85 AND OVER
1304	D90152	Num	10381	10388	8	BLK MALE PSNS: 0-4 YRS
1305	D90153	Num	10389	10396	8	BLK MALE PSNS: 5-9 YRS
1306	D90154	Num	10397	10404	8	BLK MALE PSNS: 10-14 YRS
1307	D90155	Num	10405	10412	8	BLK MALE PSNS: 15-19 YRS
1308	D90156	Num	10413	10420	8	BLK MALE PSNS: 20-24 YRS
1309	D90157	Num	10421	10428	8	BLK MALE PSNS: 25-29 YRS
1310	D90158	Num	10429	10436	8	BLK MALE PSNS: 30-34 YRS
1311	D90159	Num	10437	10444	8	BLK MALE PSNS: 35-39 YRS
1312	D90160	Num	10445	10452	8	BLK MALE PSNS: 40-44 YRS
1313	D90161	Num	10453	10460	8	BLK MALE PSNS: 45-49 YRS
1314	D90162	Num	10461	10468	8	BLK MALE PSNS: 50-54 YRS
1315	D90163	Num	10469	10476	8	BLK MALE PSNS: 55-59 YRS
1316	D90164	Num	10477	10484	8	BLK MALE PSNS: 60-64 YRS
1317	D90165	Num	10485	10492	8	BLK MALE PSNS: 65-69 YRS
1318	D90166	Num	10493	10500	8	BLK MALE PSNS: 70-74 YRS
1319	D90167	Num	10501	10508	8	BLK MALE PSNS: 75-79 YRS
1320	D90168	Num	10509	10516	8	BLK MALE PSNS: 80-84 YRS
1321	D90169	Num	10517	10524	8	BLK MALE PSNS: 85 AND OVER
1322	D90170	Num	10525	10532	8	BLK FEMALE PSNS: 0-4 YRS
1323	D90171	Num	10533	10540	8	BLK FEMALE PSNS: 5-9 YRS
1324	D90172	Num	10541	10548	8	BLK FEMALE PSNS: 10-14 YRS
1325	D90173	Num	10549	10556	8	BLK FEMALE PSNS: 15-19 YRS
1326	D90174	Num	10557	10564	8	BLK FEMALE PSNS: 20-24 YRS
1327	D90175	Num	10565	10572	8	BLK FEMALE PSNS: 25-29 YRS
1328	D90176	Num	10573	10580	8	BLK FEMALE PSNS: 30-34 YRS
1329	D90177	Num	10581	10588	8	BLK FEMALE PSNS: 35-39 YRS

1330	D90178	Num	10589	10596	8	BLK FEMALE PSNS: 40-44 YRS
1331	D90179	Num	10597	10604	8	BLK FEMALE PSNS: 45-49 YRS
1332	D90180	Num	10605	10612	8	BLK FEMALE PSNS: 50-54 YRS
1333	D90181	Num	10613	10620	8	BLK FEMALE PSNS: 55-59 YRS
1334	D90182	Num	10621	10628	8	BLK FEMALE PSNS: 60-64 YRS
1335	D90183	Num	10629	10636	8	BLK FEMALE PSNS: 64-69 YRS
1336	D90184	Num	10637	10644	8	BLK FEMALE PSNS: 70-74 YRS
1337	D90185	Num	10645	10652	8	BLK FEMALE PSNS: 75-79 YRS
1338	D90186	Num	10653	10660	8	BLK FEMALE PSNS: 80-84 YRS
1339	D90187	Num	10661	10668	8	BLK FEMALE PSNS: 85 AND OVER
1340	D90188	Num	10669	10676	8	HISP ORIGIN TOTAL PSNS: 0-4 YRS
1341	D90189	Num	10677	10684	8	HISP ORIGIN TOTAL PSNS: 5-9 YRS
1342	D90190	Num	10685	10692	8	HISP ORIGIN TOTAL PSNS: 10-14 YRS
1343	D90191	Num	10693	10700	8	HISP ORIGIN TOTAL PSNS: 15-19 YRS
1344	D90192	Num	10701	10708	8	HISP ORIGIN TOTAL PSNS: 20-24 YRS
1345	D90193	Num	10709	10716	8	HISP ORIGIN TOTAL PSNS: 25-29 YRS
1346	D90194	Num	10717	10724	8	HISP ORIGIN TOTAL PSNS: 30-34 YRS
1347	D90195	Num	10725	10732	8	HISP ORIGIN TOTAL PSNS: 35-39 YRS
1348	D90196	Num	10733	10740	8	HISP ORIGIN TOTAL PSNS: 40-44 YRS
1349	D90197	Num	10741	10748	8	HISP ORIGIN TOTAL PSNS: 45-49 YRS
1350	D90198	Num	10749	10756	8	HISP ORIGIN TOTAL PSNS: 50-54 YRS
1351	D90199	Num	10757	10764	8	HISP ORIGIN TOTAL PSNS: 55-59 YRS
1352	D90200	Num	10765	10772	8	HISP ORIGIN TOTAL PSNS: 60-64 YRS
1353	D90201	Num	10773	10780	8	HISP ORIGIN TOTAL PSNS: 65-69 YRS
1354	D90202	Num	10781	10788	8	HISP ORIGIN TOTAL PSNS: 70-74 YRS
1355	D90203	Num	10789	10796	8	HISP ORIGIN TOTAL PSNS: 75-79 YRS
1356	D90204	Num	10797	10804	8	HISP ORIGIN TOTAL PSNS: 80-84 YRS
1357	D90205	Num	10805	10812	8	HISP ORIGIN TOTAL PSNS: 85 AND OVER
1358	D90206	Num	10813	10820	8	HISP ORIGIN MALE PSNS: 0-4 YRS
1359	D90207	Num	10821	10828	8	HISP ORIGIN MALE PSNS: 5-9 YRS
1360	D90208	Num	10829	10836	8	HISP ORIGIN MALE PSNS: 10-14 YRS
1361	D90209	Num	10837	10844	8	HISP ORIGIN MALE PSNS: 15-19 YRS
1362	D90210	Num	10845	10852	8	HISP ORIGIN MALE PSNS: 20-24 YRS
1363	D90211	Num	10853	10860	8	HISP ORIGIN MALE PSNS: 25-29 YRS
1364	D90212	Num	10861	10868	8	HISP ORIGIN MALE PSNS: 30-34 YRS
1365	D90213	Num	10869	10876	8	HISP ORIGIN MALE PSNS: 35-39 YRS
1366	D90214	Num	10877	10884	8	HISP ORIGIN MALE PSNS: 40-44 YRS
1367	D90215	Num	10885	10892	8	HISP ORIGIN MALE PSNS: 45-49 YRS
1368	D90216	Num	10893	10900	8	HISP ORIGIN MALE PSNS: 50-54 YRS
1369	D90217	Num	10901	10908	8	HISP ORIGIN MALE PSNS: 55-59 YRS
1370	D90218	Num	10909	10916	8	HISP ORIGIN MALE PSNS: 60-64 YRS

1371	D90219	Num	10917	10924	8	HISP ORIGIN MALE PSNS: 65-69 YRS
1372	D90220	Num	10925	10932	8	HISP ORIGIN MALE PSNS: 70-74 YRS
1373	D90221	Num	10933	10940	8	HISP ORIGIN MALE PSNS: 75-79 YRS
1374	D90222	Num	10941	10948	8	HISP ORIGIN MALE PSNS: 80-84 YRS
1375	D90223	Num	10949	10956	8	HISP ORIGIN MALE PSNS: 85 AND OVER
1376	D90224	Num	10957	10964	8	HISP ORIGIN FEMALE PSNS: 0-4 YRS
1377	D90225	Num	10965	10972	8	HISP ORIGIN FEMALE PSNS: 5-9 YRS
1378	D90226	Num	10973	10980	8	HISP ORIGIN FEMALE PSNS: 10-14 YRS
1379	D90227	Num	10981	10988	8	HISP ORIGIN FEMALE PSNS: 15-19 YRS
1380	D90228	Num	10989	10996	8	HISP ORIGIN FEMALE PSNS: 20-24 YRS
1381	D90229	Num	10997	11004	8	HISP ORIGIN FEMALE PSNS: 25-29 YRS
1382	D90230	Num	11005	11012	8	HISP ORIGIN FEMALE PSNS: 30-34 YRS
1383	D90231	Num	11013	11020	8	HISP ORIGIN FEMALE PSNS: 35-39 YRS
1384	D90232	Num	11021	11028	8	HISP ORIGIN FEMALE PSNS: 40-44 YRS
1385	D90233	Num	11029	11036	8	HISP ORIGIN FEMALE PSNS: 45-49 YRS
1386	D90234	Num	11037	11044	8	HISP ORIGIN FEMALE PSNS: 50-54 YRS
1387	D90235	Num	11045	11052	8	HISP ORIGIN FEMALE PSNS: 55-59 YRS
1388	D90236	Num	11053	11060	8	HISP ORIGIN FEMALE PSNS: 60-64 YRS
1389	D90237	Num	11061	11068	8	HISP ORIGIN FEMALE PSNS: 65-69 YRS
1390	D90238	Num	11069	11076	8	HISP ORIGIN FEMALE PSNS: 70-74 YRS
1391	D90239	Num	11077	11084	8	HISP ORIGIN FEMALE PSNS: 75-79 YRS
1392	D90240	Num	11085	11092	8	HISP ORIGIN FEMALE PSNS: 80-84 YRS
1393	D90241	Num	11093	11100	8	HISP ORIGIN FEMALE PSNS: 85 AND OVER
1394	D90242	Num	11101	11108	8	TTL HUS-WIF FAM: W/ OWN CHILD UNDER 18
1395	D90243	Num	11109	11116	8	TTL HUS-WIF FAM: W/OUT CHILD UNDER 18
1396	D90244	Num	11117	11124	8	TTL MALE HD FAM: W/ OWN CHILD UNDER 18
1397	D90245	Num	11125	11132	8	TTL MALE HD FAM: W/OUT CHILD UNDER 18
1398	D90246	Num	11133	11140	8	TTL FEMALE HD FAM: W/ OWN CHILD UNDER 18
1399	D90247	Num	11141	11148	8	TTL FEMALE HD FAM: W/OUT CHILD UNDER 18
1400	D90248	Num	11149	11156	8	TTL NONFAMILY HOUSEHOLDS
1401	D90249	Num	11157	11164	8	WHT HUS-WIF FAM: W/ OWN CHILD UNDER 18
1402	D90250	Num	11165	11172	8	WHT HUS-WIF FAM: W/OUT CHILD UNDER 18
1403	D90251	Num	11173	11180	8	WHT MALE HD FAM: W/ OWN CHILD UNDER 18
1404	D90252	Num	11181	11188	8	WHT MALE HD FAM: W/OUT CHILD UNDER 18
1405	D90253	Num	11189	11196	8	WHT FEMALE HD FAM: W/ OWN CHILD UNDER 18
1406	D90254	Num	11197	11204	8	WHT FEMALE HD FAM: W/OUT CHILD UNDER 18
1407	D90255	Num	11205	11212	8	WHT NONFAMILY HOUSEHOLDS
1408	D90256	Num	11213	11220	8	BLK HUS-WIF FAM: W/ OWN CHILD UNDER 18
1409	D90257	Num	11221	11228	8	BLK HUS-WIF FAM: W/OUT CHILD UNDER 18
1410	D90258	Num	11229	11236	8	BLK MALE HD FAM: W/ OWN CHILD UNDER 18
1411	D90259	Num	11237	11244	8	BLK MALE HD FAM: W/OUT CHILD UNDER 18

1412	D90260	Num	11245	11252	8	BLK FEMALE HD FAM: W/ OWN CHILD UNDER 18
1413	D90261	Num	11253	11260	8	BLK FEMALE HD FAM: W/OUT CHILD UNDER 18
1414	D90262	Num	11261	11268	8	BLK NONFAMILY HOUSEHOLDS
1415	D90263	Num	11269	11276	8	HISP HUS-WIF FAM: W/ OWN CHILD UNDER 18
1416	D90264	Num	11277	11284	8	HISP HUS-WIF FAM: W/OUT CHILD UNDER 18
1417	D90265	Num	11285	11292	8	HISP MALE HD FAM: W/ OWN CHILD UNDER 18
1418	D90266	Num	11293	11300	8	HISP MALE HD FAM: W/OUT CHILD UNDER 18
1419	D90267	Num	11301	11308	8	HISP FEMALE HD FAM: W/ OWN CHILD UNDER 1
1420	D90268	Num	11309	11316	8	HISP FEMALE HD FAM: W/OUT CHILD UNDER 18
1421	D90269	Num	11317	11324	8	HISP NONFAMILY HOUSEHOLDS
1422	D90270	Num	11325	11332	8	TOTAL PSNS 15 YRS+: NEVER MARRIED
1423	D90271	Num	11333	11340	8	TOTAL PSNS 15 YRS+: MARR, SPO PRESENT
1424	D90272	Num	11341	11348	8	TOTAL PSNS 15 YRS+: SPO ABSEN,SEPARATED
1425	D90273	Num	11349	11356	8	TOTAL PSNS 15 YRS+: SPO ABSEN,OTHER RSN
1426	D90274	Num	11357	11364	8	TOTAL PSNS 15 YRS+: WIDOWED
1427	D90275	Num	11365	11372	8	TOTAL PSNS 15 YRS+: DIVORCED
1428	D90276	Num	11373	11380	8	MALE PSNS 15 YRS+: NEVER MARRIED
1429	D90277	Num	11381	11388	8	MALE PSNS 15 YRS+: MARR, SPOUSE PRESENT
1430	D90278	Num	11389	11396	8	MALE PSNS 15 YRS+: SPO ABSEN,SEPARATED
1431	D90279	Num	11397	11404	8	MALE PSNS 15 YRS+: SPO ABSEN,OTHER RSN
1432	D90280	Num	11405	11412	8	MALE PSNS 15 YRS+: WIDOWED
1433	D90281	Num	11413	11420	8	MALE PSNS 15 YRS+: DIVORCED
1434	D90282	Num	11421	11428	8	FEMALE PSNS 15 YRS+: NEVER MARRIED
1435	D90283	Num	11429	11436	8	FEMALE PSNS 15 YRS+: MARR, SPO PRESENT
1436	D90284	Num	11437	11444	8	FEMALE PSNS 15 YRS+: SPO ABSEN,SEPARATED
1437	D90285	Num	11445	11452	8	FEMALE PSNS 15 YRS+: SPO ABSEN,OTHER RSN
1438	D90286	Num	11453	11460	8	FEMALE PSNS 15 YRS+: WIDOWED
1439	D90287	Num	11461	11468	8	FEMALE PSNS 15 YRS+: DIVORCED
1440	D90288	Num	11469	11476	8	FOREIGN-BORN PSNS ENTRY YR: 1987 TO 1990
1441	D90289	Num	11477	11484	8	FOREIGN-BORN PSNS ENTRY YR: 1985 OR 1986
1442	D90290	Num	11485	11492	8	FOREIGN-BORN PSNS ENTRY YR: 1982 TO 1984
1443	D90291	Num	11493	11500	8	FOREIGN-BORN PSNS ENTRY YR: 1980 OR 1981
1444	D90292	Num	11501	11508	8	FOREIGN-BORN PSNS ENTRY YR: 1975 TO 1979
1445	D90293	Num	11509	11516	8	FOREIGN-BORN PSNS ENTRY YR: 1970 TO 1974
1446	D90294	Num	11517	11524	8	FOREIGN-BORN PSNS ENTRY YR: 1965 TO 1969
1447	D90295	Num	11525	11532	8	FOREIGN-BORN PSNS ENTRY YR: 1960 TO 1964
1448	D90296	Num	11533	11540	8	FOREIGN-BORN PSNS ENTRY YR: 1950 TO 1959
1449	D90297	Num	11541	11548	8	FOREIGN-BORN PSNS ENTRY YR: BEFORE 1950
1450	D90298	Num	11549	11556	8	BIRTHPLACE: BORN IN STATE OF RESIDENCE
1451	D90299	Num	11557	11564	8	BIRTHPLACE: BORN IN NORTHEAST
1452	D90300	Num	11565	11572	8	BIRTHPLACE: BORN IN MIDWEST

1453	D90301	Num	11573	11580	8	BIRTHPLACE: BORN IN SOUTH
1454	D90302	Num	11581	11588	8	BIRTHPLACE: BORN IN WEST
1455	D90303	Num	11589	11596	8	BIRTHPLACE: PUERTO RICO
1456	D90304	Num	11597	11604	8	BIRTHPLACE: OUTLYING AREA
1457	D90305	Num	11605	11612	8	BIRTHPLACE: BORN ABROAD OF AME PARENTS
1458	D90306	Num	11613	11620	8	BIRTHPLACE: FOREIGN BORN
1459	D90307	Num	11621	11628	8	RES IN 1985: SAME HOUSE
1460	D90308	Num	11629	11636	8	RES IN 1985: SAME COUNTY
1461	D90309	Num	11637	11644	8	RES IN 1985: SAME STATE
1462	D90310	Num	11645	11652	8	RES IN 1985: NORTHEAST
1463	D90311	Num	11653	11660	8	RES IN 1985: MIDWEST
1464	D90312	Num	11661	11668	8	RES IN 1985: SOUTH
1465	D90313	Num	11669	11676	8	RES IN 1985: WEST
1466	D90314	Num	11677	11684	8	RES IN 1985: PUERTO RICO
1467	D90315	Num	11685	11692	8	RES IN 1985: OUTLYING AREA
1468	D90316	Num	11693	11700	8	RES IN 1985: FOREIGN COUNTRY
1469	D90317	Num	11701	11708	8	METRO RES 1990: SAME MET/SAME HOUSE 1985
1470	D90318	Num	11709	11716	8	METRO RES 1990: SAME MET/CENT CITY 1985
1471	D90319	Num	11717	11724	8	METRO RES 1990: SAME MET/REMAINDER 1985
1472	D90320	Num	11725	11732	8	METRO RES 1990: DIFF MET/CENT CITY 1985
1473	D90321	Num	11733	11740	8	METRO RES 1990: DIFF METR/REMAINDER 1985
1474	D90322	Num	11741	11748	8	METRO RES 1990: NONMETRO AREAS 1985
1475	D90323	Num	11749	11756	8	METRO RES 1990: ABROAD 1985
1476	D90324	Num	11757	11764	8	NONMET RES 1990: SAME HOUSE 1985
1477	D90325	Num	11765	11772	8	NONMET RES 1990: DIFF HUSE/CEN CITY 1985
1478	D90326	Num	11773	11780	8	NONMET RES 1990: DIFF HOUSE/SUBURBS 1985
1479	D90327	Num	11781	11788	8	NONMET RES 1990: DIFF HOUSE/NONMET AREAS
1480	D90328	Num	11789	11796	8	NONMET RES 1990: ABROAD 1985
1481	D90329	Num	11797	11804	8	PSNS 25 YRS+: 0-8TH GRADE
1482	D90330	Num	11805	11812	8	PSNS 25 YRS+: 9-12TH GRADE, NO DIPLOMA
1483	D90331	Num	11813	11820	8	PSNS 25 YRS+: HIGH SCHOOL GRADUATE
1484	D90332	Num	11821	11828	8	PSNS 25 YRS+: SOME COLLEGE,NO DEGREE
1485	D90333	Num	11829	11836	8	PSNS 25 YRS+: ASSOCIATE DEGREE
1486	D90334	Num	11837	11844	8	PSNS 25 YRS+: BACHELOR'S DEGREE
1487	D90335	Num	11845	11852	8	PSNS 25 YRS+: GRADUATE/PROF DEGREE
1488	D90336	Num	11853	11860	8	WHT PSNS 25 YRS+: 0-8TH GRADE
1489	D90337	Num	11861	11868	8	WHT PSNS 25 YRS+: 9-12TH GRADE,NO DIPL
1490	D90338	Num	11869	11876	8	WHT PSNS 25 YRS+: HIGH SCHOOL GRADUATE
1491	D90339	Num	11877	11884	8	WHT PSNS 25 YRS+: SOME COLL,NO DEGREE
1492	D90340	Num	11885	11892	8	WHT PSNS 25 YRS+: ASSOCIATE DEGREE
1493	D90341	Num	11893	11900	8	WHT PSNS 25 YRS+: BACHELOR'S DEGREE

1494	D90342	Num	11901	11908	8	WHT PSNS 25 YRS+: GRADUATE/PROF DEGREE
1495	D90343	Num	11909	11916	8	BLK PSNS 25 YRS+: 0-8TH GRADE
1496	D90344	Num	11917	11924	8	BLK PSNS 25 YRS+: 9-12TH GRADE, NO DIPL
1497	D90345	Num	11925	11932	8	BLK PSNS 25 YRS+: HIGH SCHOOL GRADUATE
1498	D90346	Num	11933	11940	8	BLK PSNS 25 YRS+: SOME COLL,NO DEGREE
1499	D90347	Num	11941	11948	8	BLK PSNS 25 YRS+: ASSOCIATE DEGREE
1500	D90348	Num	11949	11956	8	BLK PSNS 25 YRS+: BACHELOR'S DEGREE
1501	D90349	Num	11957	11964	8	BLK PSNS 25 YRS+: GRADUATE/PROF DEGREE
1502	D90350	Num	11965	11972	8	HISP PSNS 25 YRS+: 0-8TH GRADE
1503	D90351	Num	11973	11980	8	HISP PSNS 25 YRS+: 9-12TH GRADE, NO DIPL
1504	D90352	Num	11981	11988	8	HISP PSNS 25 YRS+: HIGH SCHOOL GRADUATE
1505	D90353	Num	11989	11996	8	HISP PSNS 25 YRS+: SOME COLL,NO DEGREE
1506	D90354	Num	11997	12004	8	HISP PSNS 25 YRS+: ASSOCIATE DEGREE
1507	D90355	Num	12005	12012	8	HISP PSNS 25 YRS+: BACHELOR'S DEGREE
1508	D90356	Num	12013	12020	8	HISP PSNS 25 YRS+: GRADUATE/PROF DEGREE
1509	VS00148	Num	12021	12028	8	LIVE BIRTHS 1948
1510	VS00150	Num	12029	12036	8	LIVE BIRTHS 1950
1511	VS00154	Num	12037	12044	8	LIVE BIRTHS 1954
1512	VS00160	Num	12045	12052	8	LIVE BIRTHS 1960
1513	VS00244	Num	12053	12060	8	BIRTHS 1944
1514	VS00260	Num	12061	12068	8	BIRTHS 1960
1515	VS00264	Num	12069	12076	8	BIRTHS 1964
1516	VS00270	Num	12077	12084	8	BIRTHS 1970
1517	VS00275	Num	12085	12092	8	BIRTHS 1975
1518	VS00278	Num	12093	12100	8	BIRTHS 1978
1519	VS00279	Num	12101	12108	8	BIRTHS 1979
1520	VS00280	Num	12109	12116	8	BIRTHS 1980
1521	VS00282	Num	12117	12124	8	BIRTHS 1982
1522	VS00284	Num	12125	12132	8	BIRTHS 1984
1523	VS00285	Num	12133	12140	8	BIRTHS 1985
1524	VS00286	Num	12141	12148	8	BIRTHS 1986
1525	VS00287	Num	12149	12156	8	BIRTHS 1987
1526	VS00288	Num	12157	12164	8	BIRTHS 1988
1527	VS00360	Num	12165	12172	8	BIRTHS PER 1000 POPULATION 1960
1528	VS00370	Num	12173	12180	8	BIRTHS PER 1000 POPULATION 1970
1529	VS00375	Num	12181	12188	8	BIRTHS PER 1000 POPULATION 1975
1530	VS00378	Num	12189	12196	8	BIRTHS PER 1000 POPULATION 1978
1531	VS00379	Num	12197	12204	8	BIRTHS PER 1000 POPULATION 1979
1532	VS00380	Num	12205	12212	8	BIRTHS PER 1000 POPULATION 1980
1533	VS00382	Num	12213	12220	8	BIRTHS PER 1000 POPULATION 1982
1534	VS00384	Num	12221	12228	8	BIRTHS PER 1000 POPULATION 1984

1535	VS00385 Num	12229	12236	8	BIRTHS PER 1000 POPULATION 1985
1536	VS00386 Num	12237	12244	8	BIRTHS PER 1000 POPULATION 1986
1537	VS00387 Num	12245	12252	8	BIRTHS PER 1000 POPULATION 1987
1538	VS00388 Num	12253	12260	8	BIRTHS PER 1000 POPULATION 1988
1539	VS00470 Num	12261	12268	8	WHITE BIRTHS 1970
1540	VS00478 Num	12269	12276	8	WHITE BIRTHS 1978
1541	VS00570 Num	12277	12284	8	BLACK BIRTHS 1970
1542	VS00578 Num	12285	12292	8	BLACK BIRTHS 1978
1543	VS00582 Num	12293	12300	8	BLACK BIRTHS 1982
1544	VS00644 Num	12301	12308	8	DEATHS 1944
1545	VS00648 Num	12309	12316	8	DEATHS 1948
1546	VS00650 Num	12317	12324	8	DEATHS 1950
1547	VS00654 Num	12325	12332	8	DEATHS 1954
1548	VS00659 Num	12333	12340	8	DEATHS 1959
1549	VS00664 Num	12341	12348	8	DEATHS 1964
1550	VS00670 Num	12349	12356	8	DEATHS 1970
1551	VS00675 Num	12357	12364	8	DEATHS 1975
1552	VS00678 Num	12365	12372	8	DEATHS 1978
1553	VS00679 Num	12373	12380	8	DEATHS 1979
1554	VS00680 Num	12381	12388	8	DEATHS 1980
1555	VS00682 Num	12389	12396	8	DEATHS 1982
1556	VS00684 Num	12397	12404	8	DEATHS 1984
1557	VS00685 Num	12405	12412	8	DEATHS 1985
1558	VS00686 Num	12413	12420	8	DEATHS 1986
1559	VS00687 Num	12421	12428	8	DEATHS 1987
1560	VS00688 Num	12429	12436	8	DEATHS 1988
1561	VS00770 Num	12437	12444	8	DEATHS PER 1000 POPULATION 1970
1562	VS00775 Num	12445	12452	8	DEATHS PER 1000 POPULATION 1975
1563	VS00778 Num	12453	12460	8	DEATHS PER 1000 POPULATION 1978
1564	VS00779 Num	12461	12468	8	DEATHS PER 1000 POPULATION 1979
1565	VS00780 Num	12469	12476	8	DEATHS PER 1000 POPULATION 1980
1566	VS00782 Num	12477	12484	8	DEATHS PER 1000 POPULATION 1982
1567	VS00784 Num	12485	12492	8	DEATHS PER 1000 POPULATION 1984
1568	VS00785 Num	12493	12500	8	DEATHS PER 1000 POPULATION 1985
1569	VS00786 Num	12501	12508	8	DEATHS PER 1000 POPULATION 1986
1570	VS00787 Num	12509	12516	8	DEATHS PER 1000 POPULATION 1987
1571	VS00788 Num	12517	12524	8	DEATHS PER 1000 POPULATION 1988
1572	VS00848 Num	12525	12532	8	INFANT DEATHS UNDER ONE YEAR 1948
1573	VS00850 Num	12533	12540	8	INFANT DEATHS UNDER ONE YEAR 1950
1574	VS00878 Num	12541	12548	8	INFANT DEATHS UNDER ONE YEAR 1978
1575	VS00882 Num	12549	12556	8	INFANT DEATHS UNDER ONE YEAR 1982

1576	VS00884 Num	12557	12564	8	INFANT DEATHS UNDER ONE YEAR 1984
1577	VS00885 Num	12565	12572	8	INFANT DEATHS UNDER ONE YEAR 1985
1578	VS00886 Num	12573	12580	8	INFANT DEATHS UNDER ONE YEAR 1986
1579	VS00887 Num	12581	12588	8	INFANT DEATHS UNDER ONE YEAR 1987
1580	VS00948 Num	12589	12596	8	INFANT DEATHS PER 1000 LIVE BIRTHS 1948
1581	VS00950 Num	12597	12604	8	INFANT DEATHS PER 1000 LIVE BIRTHS 1950
1582	VS00978 Num	12605	12612	8	INFANT DEATHS PER 1000 LIVE BIRTHS 1978
1583	VS00982 Num	12613	12620	8	INFANT DEATHS PER 1000 LIVE BIRTHS 1982
1584	VS00984 Num	12621	12628	8	INFANT DEATHS PER 1000 LIVE BIRTHS 1984
1585	VS00985 Num	12629	12636	8	INFANT DEATHS PER 1000 LIVE BIRTHS 1985
1586	VS00986 Num	12637	12644	8	INFANT DEATHS PER 1000 LIVE BIRTHS 1986
1587	VS00987 Num	12645	12652	8	INFANT DEATHS PER 1000 LIVE BIRTHS 1987
1588	VS00988 Num	12653	12660	8	INFANT DEATHS PER 1000 LIVE BIRTHS 1988
1589	VS01048 Num	12661	12668	8	MARRIAGES 1948
1590	VS01050 Num	12669	12676	8	MARRIAGES 1950
1591	VS01054 Num	12677	12684	8	MARRIAGES 1954
1592	VS01060 Num	12685	12692	8	MARRIAGES 1960
1593	VS01064 Num	12693	12700	8	MARRIAGES 1964
1594	VS01070 Num	12701	12708	8	MARRIAGES 1970
1595	VS01075 Num	12709	12716	8	MARRIAGES 1975
1596	VS01078 Num	12717	12724	8	MARRIAGES 1978
1597	VS01079 Num	12725	12732	8	MARRIAGES 1979
1598	VS01080 Num	12733	12740	8	MARRIAGES 1980
1599	VS01082 Num	12741	12748	8	MARRIAGES 1982
1600	VS01084 Num	12749	12756	8	MARRIAGES 1984
1601	VS01170 Num	12757	12764	8	MARRIAGES PER 1000 POPULATION 1970
1602	VS01175 Num	12765	12772	8	MARRIAGES PER 1000 POPULATION 1975
1603	VS01178 Num	12773	12780	8	MARRIAGES PER 1000 POPULATION 1978
1604	VS01179 Num	12781	12788	8	MARRIAGES PER 1000 POPULATION 1979
1605	VS01180 Num	12789	12796	8	MARRIAGES PER 1000 POPULATION 1980
1606	VS01182 Num	12797	12804	8	MARRIAGES PER 1000 POPULATION 1982
1607	VS01184 Num	12805	12812	8	MARRIAGES PER 1000 POPULATION 1984
1608	VS01270 Num	12813	12820	8	DIVORCES 1970
1609	VS01278 Num	12821	12828	8	DIVORCES 1978
1610	VS01279 Num	12829	12836	8	DIVORCES 1979
1611	VS01280 Num	12837	12844	8	DIVORCES 1980
1612	VS01282 Num	12845	12852	8	DIVORCES 1982
1613	VS01284 Num	12853	12860	8	DIVORCES 1984
1614	VS01370 Num	12861	12868	8	DIVORCES PER 1000 POPULATION 1970
1615	VS01375 Num	12869	12876	8	DIVORCES PER 1000 POPULATION 1975
1616	VS01378 Num	12877	12884	8	DIVORCES PER 1000 POPULATION 1978

1617	VS01379 Num	12885	12892	8	DIVORCES PER 1000 POPULATION 1979
1618	VS01380 Num	12893	12900	8	DIVORCES PER 1000 POPULATION 1980
1619	VS01382 Num	12901	12908	8	DIVORCES PER 1000 POPULATION 1982
1620	VS01384 Num	12909	12916	8	DIVORCES PER 1000 POPULATION 984
1621	EM30001 Num	12917	12924	8	PSNS 10 YRS+: GAINFUL WORKERS
1622	EM30002 Num	12925	12932	8	PSNS 10 YRS+: UNEMPLOYED
1623	EM30003 Num	12933	12940	8	MALE PSNS 10 YRS+: UNEMPLOYED
1624	EM30004 Num	12941	12948	8	FEMALE PSNS 10 YRS+: UNEMPLOYED
1625	EM30005 Num	12949	12956	8	PSNS 10 YRS+: LAID OFF
1626	EM30006 Num	12957	12964	8	MALE PSNS 10 YRS+: LAID OFF
1627	EM30007 Num	12965	12972	8	FEMALE PSNS 10 YRS+: LAID OFF
1628	EM40001 Num	12973	12980	8	TOTAL PSNS 14 YRS+
1629	EM40002 Num	12981	12988	8	TOTAL PSNS 14 YRS+ IN LF
1630	EM40003 Num	12989	12996	8	TOTAL EMPLOYED PSNS 14 YRS+
1631	EM40004 Num	12997	13004	8	TOTAL PSNS 14 YRS+: UNEMPLOYED
1632	EM40005 Num	13005	13012	8	MALE PSNS 14 YRS+
1633	EM40006 Num	13013	13020	8	MALE PSNS 14 YRS+ IN LF
1634	EM40007 Num	13021	13028	8	EMPLOYED MALE PSNS 14 YRS+ IN LF
1635	EM40008 Num	13029	13036	8	MALE PSNS 14 YRS+: UNEMPLOYED
1636	EM40009 Num	13037	13044	8	FEMALE PSNS 14 YRS+
1637	EM40010 Num	13045	13052	8	FEMALE PSNS 14 YRS+ IN LF
1638	EM40011 Num	13053	13060	8	EMPLOYED FEMALE PSNS 14 YRS+ IN LF
1639	EM40012 Num	13061	13068	8	FEMALE PSNS 14 YRS+: UNEMPLOYED
1640	EM40013 Num	13069	13076	8	CLASS (EMP PSNS 14+): WAGE/SALARY
1641	EM40014 Num	13077	13084	8	CLASS (EMP PSNS 14+): EMPLYRS/SLEF EMP
1642	EM40015 Num	13085	13092	8	CLASS (EMP PSNS 14+): UMPAID FAM WKR
1643	EM40016 Num	13093	13100	8	CLASS (EMP PSNS 14+): NOT REPORTED
1644	EM40017 Num	13101	13108	8	CLASS (EMP PSNS 14+): EMERGENCY
1645	EM40018 Num	13109	13116	8	CLASS (EMP M PSNS 14+): WAGE/SALARY
1646	EM40019 Num	13117	13124	8	CLASS (EMP M PSNS 14+): EMPLYRS/SLEF EMP
1647	EM40020 Num	13125	13132	8	CLASS (EMP M PSNS 14+): UMPAID FAM WKR
1648	EM40021 Num	13133	13140	8	CLASS (EMP M PSNS 14+): NOT REPORTED
1649	EM40022 Num	13141	13148	8	MALE PSNS 14+: EMERGENCY WORK
1650	EM40023 Num	13149	13156	8	CLASS (EMP F PSNS 14+): WAGE/SALARY
1651	EM40024 Num	13157	13164	8	CLASS (EMP F PSNS 14+): EMPLYRS/SLEF EMP
1652	EM40025 Num	13165	13172	8	CLASS (EMP F PSNS 14+): UMPAID FAM WKR
1653	EM40026 Num	13173	13180	8	CLASS (EMP F PSNS 14+): NOT REPORTED
1654	EM40027 Num	13181	13188	8	FEMALE PSNS 14+: EMERGENCY WORK
1655	EM40028 Num	13189	13196	8	OCCUP (EMP PSNS 14+): PROFESSIONAL
1656	EM40029 Num	13197	13204	8	OCCUP (EMP PSNS 14+): SEMIPROFESSIONAL

1657	EM40030	Num	13205	13212	8	OCCUP (EMP PSNS 14+): FARMERS
1658	EM40031	Num	13213	13220	8	OCCUP (EMP PSNS 14+): ADMIN/MANAGER
1659	EM40032	Num	13221	13228	8	OCCUP (EMP PSNS 14+): CLERICAL/SALES
1660	EM40033	Num	13229	13236	8	OCCUP (EMP PSNS 14+): PROD/CRAFT
1661	EM40034	Num	13237	13244	8	OCCUP (EMP PSNS 14+): OPERATIVES
1662	EM40035	Num	13245	13252	8	OCCUP (EMP PSNS 14+): PRVT HH SERVICES
1663	EM40036	Num	13253	13260	8	OCCUP (EMP PSNS 14+): OTHER SERVICES
1664	EM40037	Num	13261	13268	8	OCCUP (EMP PSNS 14+): FARM WAGE LABOR
1665	EM40038	Num	13269	13276	8	OCCUP (EMP PSNS 14+): UNPAID FARM LABOR
1666	EM40039	Num	13277	13284	8	OCCUP (EMP PSNS 14+): NONFARM LABORERS
1667	EM40040	Num	13285	13292	8	OCCUP (EMP PSNS 14+): NOT REPORTED
1668	EM40041	Num	13293	13300	8	OCCUP (EMP M PSNS 14+): PROFESSIONAL
1669	EM40042	Num	13301	13308	8	OCCUP (EMP M PSNS 14+): SEMIPROFESSIONAL
1670	EM40043	Num	13309	13316	8	OCCUP (EMP M PSNS 14+): FARMERS
1671	EM40044	Num	13317	13324	8	OCCUP (EMP M PSNS 14+): ADMIN/MANAGER
1672	EM40045	Num	13325	13332	8	OCCUP (EMP M PSNS 14+): CLERICAL/SALES
1673	EM40046	Num	13333	13340	8	OCCUP (EMP M PSNS 14+): PROD/CRAFT
1674	EM40047	Num	13341	13348	8	OCCUP (EMP M PSNS 14+): OPERATIVES
1675	EM40048	Num	13349	13356	8	OCCUP (EMP M PSNS 14+): PRVT HH SERVICES
1676	EM40049	Num	13357	13364	8	OCCUP (EMP M PSNS 14+): OTHER SERVICES
1677	EM40050	Num	13365	13372	8	OCCUP (EMP M PSNS 14+): FARM WAGE LABOR
1678	EM40051	Num	13373	13380	8	OCCUP (EMP M PSNS 14+): UNPAI FARM LABOR
1679	EM40052	Num	13381	13388	8	OCCUP (EMP M PSNS 14+): NONFARM LABORERS
1680	EM40053	Num	13389	13396	8	OCCUP (EMP M PSNS 14+): NOT REPORTED
1681	EM40054	Num	13397	13404	8	OCCUP (EMP F PSNS 14+): PROFESSIONAL
1682	EM40055	Num	13405	13412	8	OCCUP (EMP F PSNS 14+): SEMIPROFESSIONAL
1683	EM40056	Num	13413	13420	8	OCCUP (EMP F PSNS 14+): FARMERS
1684	EM40057	Num	13421	13428	8	OCCUP (EMP F PSNS 14+): ADMIN/MANAGER
1685	EM40058	Num	13429	13436	8	OCCUP (EMP F PSNS 14+): CLERICAL/SALES
1686	EM40059	Num	13437	13444	8	OCCUP (EMP F PSNS 14+): PROD/CRAFT
1687	EM40060	Num	13445	13452	8	OCCUP (EMP F PSNS 14+): OPERATIVES
1688	EM40061	Num	13453	13460	8	OCCUP (EMP F PSNS 14+): PRVT HH SERVICES
1689	EM40062	Num	13461	13468	8	OCCUP (EMP F PSNS 14+): OTHER SERVICES
1690	EM40063	Num	13469	13476	8	OCCUP (EMP F PSNS 14+): FARM WAGE LABOR
1691	EM40064	Num	13477	13484	8	OCCUP (EMP F PSNS 14+): UNPAID FARM LABOR
1692	EM40065	Num	13485	13492	8	OCCUP (EMP F PSNS 14+): NONFARM LABORERS
1693	EM40066	Num	13493	13500	8	OCCUP (EMP F PSNS 14+): NOT REPORTED
1694	EM40067	Num	13501	13508	8	IND (EMP PSNS 14+): AGRICULTURE
1695	EM40068	Num	13509	13516	8	IND (EMP PSNS 14+): MINING
1696	EM40069	Num	13517	13524	8	IND (EMP PSNS 14+): CONSTRUCTION
1697	EM40070	Num	13525	13532	8	IND (EMP PSNS 14+): MANUFACTURING

1698	EM40071 Num	13533	13540	8	IND (EMP PSNS 14+): TRANS/COM/PUB UTIL
1699	EM40072 Num	13541	13548	8	IND (EMP PSNS 14+): WHOLESALE/RETAIL TRADE
1700	EM40073 Num	13549	13556	8	IND (EMP PSNS 14+): BUSINESS/PERSOAL SERVICE
1701	EM50001 Num	13557	13564	8	TOTAL PSNS 14 YRS+
1702	EM50002 Num	13565	13572	8	TOTAL PSNS 14 YRS+ IN LF
1703	EM50003 Num	13573	13580	8	TOTAL EMPLOYED PSNS 14 YRS+
1704	EM50004 Num	13581	13588	8	TOTAL PSNS 14 YRS+ IN CIVIL LF
1705	EM50005 Num	13589	13596	8	TOTAL PSNS 14+: UNEMPLOYED
1706	EM50006 Num	13597	13604	8	MALE PSNS 14 YRS+
1707	EM50007 Num	13605	13612	8	MALE PSNS 14 YRS+ IN LF
1708	EM50008 Num	13613	13620	8	MALE PSNS 14 YRS+ IN CIVIL. LF
1709	EM50009 Num	13621	13628	8	EMPLOYED MALE PSNS 14 YRS+
1710	EM50010 Num	13629	13636	8	MALE PSNS 14+: UNEMPLOYED
1711	EM50011 Num	13637	13644	8	FEMALE PSNS 14 YRS+
1712	EM50012 Num	13645	13652	8	FEMALE PSNS 14 YRS+ IN LF
1713	EM50013 Num	13653	13660	8	FEMALE PSNS 14 YRS+ IN CIVIL. LF
1714	EM50014 Num	13661	13668	8	EMPLOYED FEMALE PSNS 14 YRS+
1715	EM50015 Num	13669	13676	8	FEMALE PSNS 14+: UNEMPLOYED
1716	EM50016 Num	13677	13684	8	CLASS (EMP PSNS 14+): TOTAL
1717	EM50017 Num	13685	13692	8	CLASS (EMP PSNS 14+): WAGE/SALARY WORK
1718	EM50018 Num	13693	13700	8	CLASS (EMP PSNS 14+): GOVT WORKER
1719	EM50019 Num	13701	13708	8	CLASS (EMP PSNS 14+): SELF-EMPLOYED
1720	EM50020 Num	13709	13716	8	CLASS (EMP PSNS 14+): UNPAID FAM WRKER
1721	EM50021 Num	13717	13724	8	CLASS (EMP M PSNS 14+): WAGE/SALARY WORK
1722	EM50022 Num	13725	13732	8	CLASS (EMP M PSNS 14+): GOVT WORKER
1723	EM50023 Num	13733	13740	8	CLASS (EMP M PSNS 14+): SELF-EMPLOYED
1724	EM50024 Num	13741	13748	8	CLASS (EMP M PSNS 14+): UNPAID FAM WRKER
1725	EM50025 Num	13749	13756	8	CLASS (EMP F PSNS 14+): WAGE/SALARY WORK
1726	EM50026 Num	13757	13764	8	CLASS (EMP F PSNS 14+): GOVT WORKER
1727	EM50027 Num	13765	13772	8	CLASS (EMP F PSNS 14+): SELF-EMPLOYED
1728	EM50028 Num	13773	13780	8	CLASS (EMP F PSNS 14+): UNPAID FAM WRKER
1729	EM50029 Num	13781	13788	8	OCCUP (EMP PSNS 14+): PROFESSIONAL
1730	EM50030 Num	13789	13796	8	OCCUP (EMP PSNS 14+): FARMERS
1731	EM50031 Num	13797	13804	8	OCCUP (EMP PSNS 14+): ADMI/MANAGERS
1732	EM50032 Num	13805	13812	8	OCCUP (EMP PSNS 14+): CLERICAL
1733	EM50033 Num	13813	13820	8	OCCUP (EMP PSNS 14+): SALES
1734	EM50034 Num	13821	13828	8	OCCUP (EMP PSNS 14+): PROD/CRAFT
1735	EM50035 Num	13829	13836	8	OCCUP (EMP PSNS 14+): OPERATIVES
1736	EM50036 Num	13837	13844	8	OCCUP (EMP PSNS 14+): PRVT HH SERVICES
1737	EM50037 Num	13845	13852	8	OCCUP (EMP PSNS 14+): OTHER SERVICES

1738	EM50038	Num	13853	13860	8	OCCUP (EMP PSNS 14+): FARM LABOR-UNPAID
1739	EM50039	Num	13861	13868	8	OCCUP (EMP PSNS 14+): FARM WAGE LABOR
1740	EM50040	Num	13869	13876	8	OCCUP (EMP PSNS 14+): NONFARM LABOR
1741	EM50041	Num	13877	13884	8	OCCUP (EMP PSNS 14+): NOT REPORTED
1742	EM50042	Num	13885	13892	8	OCCUP (EMP M PSNS 14+): PROFESSIONAL
1743	EM50043	Num	13893	13900	8	OCCUP (EMP M PSNS 14+): FARMERS
1744	EM50044	Num	13901	13908	8	OCCUP (EMP M PSNS 14+): ADMI/MANAGERS
1745	EM50045	Num	13909	13916	8	OCCUP (EMP M PSNS 14+): CLERICAL
1746	EM50046	Num	13917	13924	8	OCCUP (EMP M PSNS 14+): SALES
1747	EM50047	Num	13925	13932	8	OCCUP (EMP M PSNS 14+): PROD/CRAFT
1748	EM50048	Num	13933	13940	8	OCCUP (EMP M PSNS 14+): OPERATIVES
1749	EM50049	Num	13941	13948	8	OCCUP (EMP M PSNS 14+): PRVT HH SERVICES
1750	EM50050	Num	13949	13956	8	OCCUP (EMP M PSNS 14+): OTHER SERVICES
1751	EM50051	Num	13957	13964	8	OCCUP (EMP M PSNS 14+): FARM LABOR-UNPAI
1752	EM50052	Num	13965	13972	8	OCCUP (EMP M PSNS 14+): FARM WAGE LABOR
1753	EM50053	Num	13973	13980	8	OCCUP (EMP M PSNS 14+): NONFARM LABOR
1754	EM50054	Num	13981	13988	8	OCCUP (EMP M PSNS 14+): NOT REPORTED
1755	EM50055	Num	13989	13996	8	OCCUP (EMP F PSNS 14+): PROFESSIONAL
1756	EM50056	Num	13997	14004	8	OCCUP (EMP F PSNS 14+): FARMERS
1757	EM50057	Num	14005	14012	8	OCCUP (EMP F PSNS 14+): ADMI/MANAGERS
1758	EM50058	Num	14013	14020	8	OCCUP (EMP F PSNS 14+): CLERICAL
1759	EM50059	Num	14021	14028	8	OCCUP (EMP F PSNS 14+): SALES
1760	EM50060	Num	14029	14036	8	OCCUP (EMP F PSNS 14+): PROD/CRAFT
1761	EM50061	Num	14037	14044	8	OCCUP (EMP F PSNS 14+): OPERATIVES
1762	EM50062	Num	14045	14052	8	OCCUP (EMP F PSNS 14+): PRVT HH SERVICES
1763	EM50063	Num	14053	14060	8	OCCUP (EMP F PSNS 14+): OTHER SERVICES
1764	EM50064	Num	14061	14068	8	OCCUP (EMP F PSNS 14+): FARM LABOR-UNPAID
1765	EM50065	Num	14069	14076	8	OCCUP (EMP F PSNS 14+): FARM WAGE LABOR
1766	EM50066	Num	14077	14084	8	OCCUP (EMP F PSNS 14+): NONFARM LABOR
1767	EM50067	Num	14085	14092	8	OCCUP (EMP F PSNS 14+): NOT REPORTED
1768	EM50068	Num	14093	14100	8	IND (EMP PSNS 14+): AGRICULTURE
1769	EM50069	Num	14101	14108	8	IND (EMP PSNS 14+): MINING
1770	EM50070	Num	14109	14116	8	IND (EMP PSNS 14+): CONSTRUCTION
1771	EM50071	Num	14117	14124	8	IND (EMP PSNS 14+): MANUFACTIROMG
1772	EM50072	Num	14125	14132	8	IND (EMP PSNS 14+): TRANS/COM/PUB UTIL
1773	EM50073	Num	14133	14140	8	IND (EMP PSNS 14+): WHOLE/RETAIL TRADE
1774	EM50074	Num	14141	14148	8	IND (EMP PSNS 14+): BUSINESS/PER SERVICES
1775	EM50075	Num	14149	14156	8	IND (EMP PSNS 14+): PROF/RELATED SERVICES
1776	EM50076	Num	14157	14164	8	IND (EMP PSNS 14+): FINANCE/INSURANCE/REAL EST
1777	EM60001	Num	14165	14172	8	TOTAL PSNS 14 YRS+

1778	EM60002 Num	14173	14180	8	TOTAL PSNS 14 YRS+ IN CIVIL. LF
1779	EM60003 Num	14181	14188	8	EMPLOYED PSNS 14 YRS+ IN CIVIL. LF
1780	EM60004 Num	14189	14196	8	UNEMPLOYED PSNS 14 YRS+ IN CIVIL. LF
1781	EM60005 Num	14197	14204	8	TOTAL MALE PSNS 14 YRS+
1782	EM60006 Num	14205	14212	8	MALE PSNS 14 YRS+ IN CIVIL. LF
1783	EM60007 Num	14213	14220	8	EMPLOYED MALE PSNS 14+
1784	EM60008 Num	14221	14228	8	MALE UNEMP PSNS 14 YRS+ IN CIVIL. LF
1785	EM60009 Num	14229	14236	8	TOTAL FEMALE PSNS 14 YRS+
1786	EM60010 Num	14237	14244	8	FEMALE PSNS 14 YRS+ IN CIVIL. LF
1787	EM60011 Num	14245	14252	8	EMPLOYED FEMALE PSNS 14+
1788	EM60012 Num	14253	14260	8	FEMALE UNEMP PSNS 14 YRS+ IN CIVIL.LF
1789	EM60013 Num	14261	14268	8	CLASS (EMP 14+ AGRI): TOTAL
1790	EM60014 Num	14269	14276	8	CLASS (EMP 14+ AGRI): WAGE/SALARY WORK
1791	EM60015 Num	14277	14284	8	CLASS (EMP 14+ AGRI): GOVT WORKER
1792	EM60016 Num	14285	14292	8	CLASS (EMP 14+ AGRI): SELF-EMPLOYED
1793	EM60017 Num	14293	14300	8	CLASS (EMP 14+ AGRI): UNPAID FAM WORK
1794	EM60018 Num	14301	14308	8	CLASS (EMP 14+ NONAGRI): TOTAL
1795	EM60019 Num	14309	14316	8	CLASS (EMP 14+ NONAGRI): WAGE/SALARY
1796	EM60020 Num	14317	14324	8	CLASS (EMP 14+ NONAGRI): GOVT WORKER
1797	EM60021 Num	14325	14332	8	CLASS (EMP 14+ NONAGRI): SELF-EMPLOYED
1798	EM60022 Num	14333	14340	8	CLASS (EMP 14+ NONAGRI): UNPAID FAM WK
1799	EM60023 Num	14341	14348	8	CLASS (EMP M 14+ AGRI): TOTAL
1800	EM60024 Num	14349	14356	8	CLASS (EMP M 14+ AGRI): WAGE/SALARY WORK
1801	EM60025 Num	14357	14364	8	CLASS (EMP M 14+ AGRI): GOVT WORKER
1802	EM60026 Num	14365	14372	8	CLASS (EMP M 14+ AGRI): SELF-EMPLOYED
1803	EM60027 Num	14373	14380	8	CLASS (EMP M 14+ AGRI): UNPAID FAM WORK
1804	EM60028 Num	14381	14388	8	CLASS (EMP F 14+ AGRI): TOTAL
1805	EM60029 Num	14389	14396	8	CLASS (EMP F 14+ AGRI): WAGE/SALARY WORK
1806	EM60030 Num	14397	14404	8	CLASS (EMP F 14+ AGRI): GOVT WORKER
1807	EM60031 Num	14405	14412	8	CLASS (EMP F 14+ AGRI): SELF-EMPLOYED
1808	EM60032 Num	14413	14420	8	CLASS (EMP F 14+ AGRI): UNPAID FAM WORK
1809	EM60033 Num	14421	14428	8	CLASS (EMP M 14+ NONAGRI): TOTAL
1810	EM60034 Num	14429	14436	8	CLASS (EMP M 14+ NONAGRI): WAGE/SALARY
1811	EM60035 Num	14437	14444	8	CLASS (EMP M 14+ NONAGRI): GOVT WORKER
1812	EM60036 Num	14445	14452	8	CLASS (EMP M 14+ NONAGRI): SELF-EMPLOYED
1813	EM60037 Num	14453	14460	8	CLASS (EMP M 14+ NONAGRI): UNPAID FAM WK
1814	EM60038 Num	14461	14468	8	CLASS (EMP F 14+ NONAGRI): TOTAL
1815	EM60039 Num	14469	14476	8	CLASS (EMP F 14+ NONAGRI): WAGE/SALARY
1816	EM60040 Num	14477	14484	8	CLASS (EMP F 14+ NONAGRI): GOVT WORKER
1817	EM60041 Num	14485	14492	8	CLASS (EMP F 14+ NONAGRI): SELF-EMPLOYED
1818	EM60042 Num	14493	14500	8	CLASS (EMP F 14+ NONAGRI): UNPAID FAM WK

1819	EM60043	Num	14501	14508	8	OCCUP (EMP PSNS 14+): PROFESSIONAL
1820	EM60044	Num	14509	14516	8	OCCUP (EMP PSNS 14+): FARMERS
1821	EM60045	Num	14517	14524	8	OCCUP (EMP PSNS 14+): MANAGER
1822	EM60046	Num	14525	14532	8	OCCUP (EMP PSNS 14+): CLERICAL
1823	EM60047	Num	14533	14540	8	OCCUP (EMP PSNS 14+): SALES
1824	EM60048	Num	14541	14548	8	OCCUP (EMP PSNS 14+): PROD/CRAFT
1825	EM60049	Num	14549	14556	8	OCCUP (EMP PSNS 14+): OPERATIVE
1826	EM60050	Num	14557	14564	8	OCCUP (EMP PSNS 14+): PRVT HH SERVICES
1827	EM60051	Num	14565	14572	8	OCCUP (EMP PSNS 14+): OTHER SERVICES-PROTECT
1828	EM60052	Num	14573	14580	8	OCCUP (EMP PSNS 14+): OTHER SERVICES-RESTAU
1829	EM60053	Num	14581	14588	8	OCCUP (EMP PSNS 14+): OTHER SERVICES-OTHER
1830	EM60054	Num	14589	14596	8	OCCUP (EMP PSNS 14+): FARM LABORER
1831	EM60055	Num	14597	14604	8	OCCUP (EMP PSNS 14+): NONFARM LABORER
1832	EM60056	Num	14605	14612	8	OCCUP (EMP PSNS 14+): NOT REPORTED
1833	EM60057	Num	14613	14620	8	OCCUP (EMP M PSNS 14+): PROFESSIONAL
1834	EM60058	Num	14621	14628	8	OCCUP (EMP M PSNS 14+): FARMERS
1835	EM60059	Num	14629	14636	8	OCCUP (EMP M PSNS 14+): MANAGER
1836	EM60060	Num	14637	14644	8	OCCUP (EMP M PSNS 14+): CLERICAL
1837	EM60061	Num	14645	14652	8	OCCUP (EMP M PSNS 14+): SALES
1838	EM60062	Num	14653	14660	8	OCCUP (EMP M PSNS 14+): PROD/CRAFT
1839	EM60063	Num	14661	14668	8	OCCUP (EMP M PSNS 14+): OPERATIVE
1840	EM60064	Num	14669	14676	8	OCCUP (EMP M PSNS 14+): PRVT HH SERVICES
1841	EM60065	Num	14677	14684	8	OCCUP (EMP M PSNS 14+): OTHER SERVICES-PROTECT
1842	EM60066	Num	14685	14692	8	OCCUP (EMP M PSNS 14+): OTHER SERVICES-RESTAU
1843	EM60067	Num	14693	14700	8	OCCUP (EMP M PSNS 14+): OTHER SERVICES-OTHER
1844	EM60068	Num	14701	14708	8	OCCUP (EMP M PSNS 14+): FARM LABORER
1845	EM60069	Num	14709	14716	8	OCCUP (EMP M PSNS 14+): NONFARM LABORER
1846	EM60070	Num	14717	14724	8	OCCUP (EMP M PSNS 14+): NOT REPORTED
1847	EM60071	Num	14725	14732	8	OCCUP (EMP F PSNS 14+): PROFESSIONAL
1848	EM60072	Num	14733	14740	8	OCCUP (EMP F PSNS 14+): FARMERS
1849	EM60073	Num	14741	14748	8	OCCUP (EMP F PSNS 14+): MANAGER
1850	EM60074	Num	14749	14756	8	OCCUP (EMP F PSNS 14+): CLERICAL
1851	EM60075	Num	14757	14764	8	OCCUP (EMP F PSNS 14+): SALES
1852	EM60076	Num	14765	14772	8	OCCUP (EMP F PSNS 14+): PROD/CRAFT
1853	EM60077	Num	14773	14780	8	OCCUP (EMP F PSNS 14+): OPERATIVE
1854	EM60078	Num	14781	14788	8	OCCUP (EMP F PSNS 14+): PRVT HH SERVICES
1855	EM60079	Num	14789	14796	8	OCCUP (EMP F PSNS 14+): OTHER SERVICES-RESTAU
1856	EM60080	Num	14797	14804	8	OCCUP (EMP F PSNS 14+): OTHER SERVICES-OTHER
1857	EM60081	Num	14805	14812	8	OCCUP (EMP F PSNS 14+): FARM LABORER
1858	EM60082	Num	14813	14820	8	OCCUP (EMP F PSNS 14+): NONFARM LABORER
1859	EM60083	Num	14821	14828	8	OCCUP (EMP F PSNS 14+): NOT REPORTED

1860	EM60084	Num	14829	14836	8	IND (EMP PSNS 14+): AGRICULTURE
1861	EM60085	Num	14837	14844	8	IND (EMP PSNS 14+): FORESTRY/FISHING
1862	EM60086	Num	14845	14852	8	IND (EMP PSNS 14+): MINING
1863	EM60087	Num	14853	14860	8	IND (EMP PSNS 14+): CONSTRUCTION
1864	EM60088	Num	14861	14868	8	IND (EMP PSNS 14+): MANUF (DURABLE)
1865	EM60089	Num	14869	14876	8	IND (EMP PSNS 14+): MANUF (NONDURABLE)
1866	EM60090	Num	14877	14884	8	IND (EMP PSNS 14+): TRANSPORTATION
1867	EM60091	Num	14885	14892	8	IND (EMP PSNS 14+): COMMUNI/PUB UTILS
1868	EM60092	Num	14893	14900	8	IND (EMP PSNS 14+): WHOLESALE TRADE
1869	EM60093	Num	14901	14908	8	IND (EMP PSNS 14+): RETAIL TRADE
1870	EM60094	Num	14909	14916	8	IND (EMP PSNS 14+): FINANCE/INSURANCE/REAL EST
1871	EM60095	Num	14917	14924	8	IND (EMP PSNS 14+): BUSINESS/REPAIR SERVICES
1872	EM60096	Num	14925	14932	8	IND (EMP PSNS 14+): PERSONAL SERVICES
1873	EM60097	Num	14933	14940	8	IND (EMP PSNS 14+): ENTERTN/RECREATON SERVICES
1874	EM60098	Num	14941	14948	8	IND (EMP PSNS 14+): PROFESSIONAL SERVICES (HEALTH)
1875	EM60099	Num	14949	14956	8	IND (EMP PSNS 14+): PROFESSIONAL SERVICES (EDUC)
1876	EM60100	Num	14957	14964	8	IND (EMP PSNS 14+): PROFESSIONAL SERVICES (OTHERS)
1877	EM60101	Num	14965	14972	8	IND (EMP PSNS 14+): PUB ADMINISTRATION
1878	EM60102	Num	14973	14980	8	IND (EMP PSNS 14+): NOT REPORTED
1879	EM60103	Num	14981	14988	8	IND (EMP M PSNS 14+): AGRI/FOREST/FISH
1880	EM60104	Num	14989	14996	8	IND (EMP M PSNS 14+): CONST/MINING
1881	EM60105	Num	14997	15004	8	IND (EMP M PSNS 14+): MANUF (DURABLE)
1882	EM60106	Num	15005	15012	8	IND (EMP M PSNS 14+): MANUF (NONDURABLE)
1883	EM60107	Num	15013	15020	8	IND (EMP M PSNS 14+): TRANS/COMM/PUB UTIL
1884	EM60108	Num	15021	15028	8	IND (EMP M PSNS 14+): WHOLESALE TRADE
1885	EM60109	Num	15029	15036	8	IND (EMP M PSNS 14+): RETAIL TRADE
1886	EM60110	Num	15037	15044	8	IND (EMP M PSNS 14+): FINANCE/INSURANCE/REAL EST
1887	EM60111	Num	15045	15052	8	IND (EMP M PSNS 14+): BUSINES/REPAIR SERVICES
1888	EM60112	Num	15053	15060	8	IND (EMP M PSNS 14+): PERSONAL SERVICES
1889	EM60113	Num	15061	15068	8	IND (EMP M PSNS 14+): ENTERTAIN/RECREATION SERVICE
1890	EM60114	Num	15069	15076	8	IND (EMP M PSNS 14+): PROFESSIONAL SERVICE (HEALTH)
1891	EM60115	Num	15077	15084	8	IND (EMP M PSNS 14+): PROFESSIONAL SERVICE (EDUC)
1892	EM60116	Num	15085	15092	8	IND (EMP M PSNS 14+): PROFESSIONAL SERVICE (OTHERS)
1893	EM60117	Num	15093	15100	8	IND (EMP M PSNS 14+): PUB ADMINISTRATION
1894	EM60118	Num	15101	15108	8	IND (EMP M PSNS 14+): NOT REPORTED
1895	EM60119	Num	15109	15116	8	IND (EMP F PSNS 14+): AGRI/FOREST/FISH
1896	EM60120	Num	15117	15124	8	IND (EMP F PSNS 14+): CONST/MINING
1897	EM60121	Num	15125	15132	8	IND (EMP F PSNS 14+): MANUF (DURABLE)
1898	EM60122	Num	15133	15140	8	IND (EMP F PSNS 14+): MANUF (NONDURABLE)
1899	EM60123	Num	15141	15148	8	IND (EMP F PSNS 14+): TRANS/COMM/PUB UTIL
1900	EM60124	Num	15149	15156	8	IND (EMP F PSNS 14+): WHOLESALE TRADE

1901	EM60125 Num	15157	15164	8	IND (EMP F PSNS 14+): RETAIL TRADE
1902	EM60126 Num	15165	15172	8	IND (EMP F PSNS 14+): FINANCE/INSURANCE/REAL EST
1903	EM60127 Num	15173	15180	8	IND (EMP F PSNS 14+): BUSINES/REPAIR SERVICE
1904	EM60128 Num	15181	15188	8	IND (EMP F PSNS 14+): PERSONAL SERVICES
1905	EM60129 Num	15189	15196	8	IND (EMP F PSNS 14+): ENTERTN/RECREATION SERVI
1906	EM60130 Num	15197	15204	8	IND (EMP F PSNS 14+): PROFESSIONAL SERVICE (HEALTH)
1907	EM60131 Num	15205	15212	8	IND (EMP F PSNS 14+): PROFESSIONAL SERVICE (EDUC)
1908	EM60132 Num	15213	15220	8	IND (EMP F PSNS 14+): PROFESSIONAL SERVICE (OTHERS)
1909	EM60133 Num	15221	15228	8	IND (EMP F PSNS 14+): PUB ADMINISTRATION
1910	EM60134 Num	15229	15236	8	IND (EMP F PSNS 14+): NOT REPORTED
1911	EM70001 Num	15237	15244	8	TOTAL PSNS 16 YRS+
1912	EM70002 Num	15245	15252	8	TOTAL PSNS IN LF 16 YRS+
1913	EM70003 Num	15253	15260	8	TOTAL PSNS IN CVL LF 16 YRS+
1914	EM70004 Num	15261	15268	8	MALE PSNS 16 YRS+
1915	EM70005 Num	15269	15276	8	MALE PSNS IN LF 16 YRS+
1916	EM70006 Num	15277	15284	8	MALE PSNS IN CVL LF 16 YRS+
1917	EM70007 Num	15285	15292	8	FEMALE PSNS 16 YRS+
1918	EM70008 Num	15293	15300	8	FEMALE PSNS IN LF 16 YRS+
1919	EM70009 Num	15301	15308	8	FEMALE PSNS IN CVL LF 16 YRS+
1920	EM70010 Num	15309	15316	8	TOTAL PSNS 16 YRS+: IN ARMED FORCES
1921	EM70011 Num	15317	15324	8	TOTAL PSNS 16 YRS+ IN CVL LF: EMPLOYED
1922	EM70012 Num	15325	15332	8	TOTAL PSNS 16 YRS+ IN CVL LF: UNEMPLOYED
1923	EM70013 Num	15333	15340	8	TOTAL PSNS 16-64 YRS NOT IN LF: INMATE
1924	EM70014 Num	15341	15348	8	TOTAL PSNS 16-64 YRS NOT IN LF: IN SCHL
1925	EM70015 Num	15349	15356	8	TOTAL PSNS 16-64 YRS NOT IN LF: OTHER
1926	EM70016 Num	15357	15364	8	TOTAL PSNS 65 YRS+ NOT IN LF: INMATE
1927	EM70017 Num	15365	15372	8	TOTAL PSNS 65 YRS+ NOT IN LF: IN SCHOOL
1928	EM70018 Num	15373	15380	8	TOTAL PSNS 65 YRS+ NOT IN LF: OTHER
1929	EM70019 Num	15381	15388	8	MALE PSNS 16 YRS+: IN ARMED FORCES
1930	EM70020 Num	15389	15396	8	MALE PSNS 16 YRS+ IN CVL LF: EMPLOYED
1931	EM70021 Num	15397	15404	8	MALE PSNS 16 YRS+ IN CVL LF: UNEMPLOYED
1932	EM70022 Num	15405	15412	8	MALE PSNS 16-64 YRS NOT IN LF: INMATE
1933	EM70023 Num	15413	15420	8	MALE PSNS 16-64 YRS NOT IN LF: IN SCHOOL
1934	EM70024 Num	15421	15428	8	MALE PSNS 16-64 YRS NOT IN LF: OTHER
1935	EM70025 Num	15429	15436	8	MALE PSNS 65 YRS+ NOT IN LF: INMATE
1936	EM70026 Num	15437	15444	8	MALE PSNS 65 YRS+ NOT IN LF: IN SCHOOL
1937	EM70027 Num	15445	15452	8	MALE PSNS 65 YRS+ NOT IN LF: OTHER
1938	EM70028 Num	15453	15460	8	FEMALE PSNS 16 YRS+: IN ARMED FORCES
1939	EM70029 Num	15461	15468	8	FEMALE PSNS 16 YRS+ IN CVL LF: EMPLOYED
1940	EM70030 Num	15469	15476	8	FEMALE PSNS 16 YRS+ IN CVL LF: UNEMPLOYED

1941	EM70031 Num	15477	15484	8	FEMALE PSNS 16-64 YRS NOT IN LF: INMATE
1942	EM70032 Num	15485	15492	8	FEMALE PSNS 16-64 YRS NOT IN LF: IN SCHL
1943	EM70033 Num	15493	15500	8	FEMALE PSNS 16-64 YRS NOT IN LF: OTHER
1944	EM70034 Num	15501	15508	8	FEMALE PSNS 65 YRS+ NOT IN LF: INMATE
1945	EM70035 Num	15509	15516	8	FEMALE PSNS 65 YRS+ NOT IN LF: IN SCHOOL
1946	EM70036 Num	15517	15524	8	FEMALE PSNS 65 YRS+ NOT IN LF: OTHER
1947	EM70037 Num	15525	15532	8	TOTAL PSNS 14-15 YRS: IN ARMED FORCES
1948	EM70038 Num	15533	15540	8	TOTAL PSNS 14-15 YRS IN CVL LF: EMPLOYED
1949	EM70039 Num	15541	15548	8	TOTAL PSNS 14-15 YRS IN CVL LF: UNEMPLYD
1950	EM70040 Num	15549	15556	8	TOTAL PSNS 14-15 YRS IN NOT LF
1951	EM70041 Num	15557	15564	8	MALE PSNS 14-15 YRS: IN ARMED FORCES
1952	EM70042 Num	15565	15572	8	MALE PSNS 14-15 YRS IN CVL LF: EMPLOYED
1953	EM70043 Num	15573	15580	8	MALE PSNS 14-15 YRS IN CVL LF:UNEMPLOYED
1954	EM70044 Num	15581	15588	8	MALE PSNS 14-15 YRS IN NOT LF
1955	EM70045 Num	15589	15596	8	FEMALE PSNS 14-15 YRS: IN ARMED FORCES
1956	EM70046 Num	15597	15604	8	FEMALE PSNS 14-15 YRS IN CVL LF:EMPLOYED
1957	EM70047 Num	15605	15612	8	FEMALE PSNS 14-15 YRS IN CVL LF:UNEMPLYD
1958	EM70048 Num	15613	15620	8	FEMALE PSNS 14-15 YRS IN NOT LF
1959	EM70049 Num	15621	15628	8	EMP PSNS 14-15 YR: WHITE COLLAR (+SALES)
1960	EM70050 Num	15629	15636	8	EMPLOYD PSNS 14-15 YRS: BLUE COLLAR
1961	EM70051 Num	15637	15644	8	EMPLOYED PSNS 14-15 YRS: FARM WKR
1962	EM70052 Num	15645	15652	8	EMP PSNS 14-15 YRS: SERVICE/PRVT HH WKR
1963	EM70053 Num	15653	15660	8	EMPLOYED MALES 14-15 YRS: SALES
1964	EM70054 Num	15661	15668	8	EMP MALES 14-15 YRS: OTHR WHITE COLLAR
1965	EM70055 Num	15669	15676	8	EMPLOYED MALES 14-15 YRS: BLUE COLLAR
1966	EM70056 Num	15677	15684	8	EMPLOYED MALES 14-15 YRS: FARM WKR
1967	EM70057 Num	15685	15692	8	EMP MALES 14-15 YRS: SERVICE/PRVT HH WKR
1968	EM70058 Num	15693	15700	8	EMPLOYED FEMALES 14-15 YR: WHITE COLLAR
1969	EM70059 Num	15701	15708	8	EMPLOYED FEMALES 14-15 YRS: BLUE COLLAR
1970	EM70060 Num	15709	15716	8	EMPLOYED FEMALES 14-15 YRS: FARM WKR
1971	EM70061 Num	15717	15724	8	EMPLOYED FEMALES 14-15 YRS: SERVICE WKR
1972	EM70062 Num	15725	15732	8	EMPLOYED FEMALES 14-15 YRS: PRVT HH WKR
1973	EM70063 Num	15733	15740	8	EMPLOYED PSNS 14-15 YRS: AGRICULTURE
1974	EM70064 Num	15741	15748	8	EMPLOYED PSNS 14-15 YRS: NONAGRICULTURE
1975	EM70065 Num	15749	15756	8	EMPLOYED MALES 14-15 YRS: AGRICULTURE
1976	EM70066 Num	15757	15764	8	EMPLOYED MALES 14-15 YRS IN LF: NONAGRI
1977	EM70067 Num	15765	15772	8	WHT PSNS 14-15 YRS: IN ARMED FORCES
1978	EM70068 Num	15773	15780	8	WHT PSNS 14-15 YRS IN CVL LF: EMPLOYED
1979	EM70069 Num	15781	15788	8	WHT PSNS 14-15 YRS IN CVL LF: UNEMPLOYED
1980	EM70070 Num	15789	15796	8	WHT PSNS 14-15 YRS IN NOT LF
1981	EM70071 Num	15797	15804	8	WHT MALES 14-15 YRS: IN ARMED FORCES

1982	EM70072	Num	15805	15812	8	WHT MALES 14-15 YRS IN CVL LF: EMPLOYED
1983	EM70073	Num	15813	15820	8	WHT MALES 14-15 YRS IN CVL LF:UNEMPLOYED
1984	EM70074	Num	15821	15828	8	WHT MALES 14-15 YRS IN NOT LF
1985	EM70075	Num	15829	15836	8	WHT FEMALES 14-15 YRS: IN ARMED FORCES
1986	EM70076	Num	15837	15844	8	WHT FEM 14-15 YRS IN CVL LF: EMPLOYED
1987	EM70077	Num	15845	15852	8	WHT FEM 14-15 YRS IN CVL LF: UNEMPLOYED
1988	EM70078	Num	15853	15860	8	WHT FEMALES 14-15 YRS IN NOT LF
1989	EM70079	Num	15861	15868	8	BLK PSNS 14-15 YRS: IN ARMED FORCES
1990	EM70080	Num	15869	15876	8	BLK PSNS 14-15 YRS IN CVL LF: EMPLOYED
1991	EM70081	Num	15877	15884	8	BLK PSNS 14-15 YRS IN CVL LF: UNEMPLOYED
1992	EM70082	Num	15885	15892	8	BLK PSNS 14-15 YRS IN NOT LF
1993	EM70083	Num	15893	15900	8	BLK MALES 14-15 YRS: IN ARMED FORCES
1994	EM70084	Num	15901	15908	8	BLK MALES 14-15 YRS IN CVL LF: EMPLOYED
1995	EM70085	Num	15909	15916	8	BLK MALES 14-15 YRS IN CVL LF: UNEMPLOYE
1996	EM70086	Num	15917	15924	8	BLK MALES 14-15 YRS IN NOT LF
1997	EM70087	Num	15925	15932	8	BLK FEM 14-15 YRS: IN ARMED FORCES
1998	EM70088	Num	15933	15940	8	BLK FEM 14-15 YRS IN CVL LF: EMPLOYED
1999	EM70089	Num	15941	15948	8	BLK FEM 14-15 YRS IN CVL LF: UNEMPLOYED
2000	EM70090	Num	15949	15956	8	BLK FEM 14-15 YRS IN NOT LF
2001	EM70091	Num	15957	15964	8	HISP PSNS 14-15 YRS: IN ARMED FORCES
2002	EM70092	Num	15965	15972	8	HISP PSNS 14-15 YRS IN CVL LF: EMPLOYED
2003	EM70093	Num	15973	15980	8	HISP PSNS 14-15 YRS IN CVL LF: UNEMPLOYED
2004	EM70094	Num	15981	15988	8	HISP PSNS 14-15 YRS IN NOT LF
2005	EM70095	Num	15989	15996	8	HISP MALES 14-15 YRS: IN ARMED FORCES
2006	EM70096	Num	15997	16004	8	HISP MALES 14-15 YRS IN CVL LF: EMPLOYED
2007	EM70097	Num	16005	16012	8	HISP MALES 14-15 YRS IN CVL LF: UNEMPLOYD
2008	EM70098	Num	16013	16020	8	HISP MALES 14-15 YRS IN NOT LF
2009	EM70099	Num	16021	16028	8	HISP FEM 14-15 YRS: IN ARMED FORCES
2010	EM70100	Num	16029	16036	8	HISP FEM 14-15 YRS IN CVL LF: EMPLOYED
2011	EM70101	Num	16037	16044	8	HISP FEM 14-15 YRS IN CVL LF: UNEMPLOYED
2012	EM70102	Num	16045	16052	8	HISP FEM 14-15 YRS IN NOT LF
2013	EM70103	Num	16053	16060	8	CLASS (EMP PSNS 14+): WAGE/SALARY WKR
2014	EM70104	Num	16061	16068	8	CLASS (EMP PSNS 14+): NONFARM SELF-EMP
2015	EM70105	Num	16069	16076	8	CLASS (EMP PSNS 14+): FARM SELF-EMPLOY
2016	EM70106	Num	16077	16084	8	CLASS (EMP PSNS 14+): SOC SEC/RAIL RET
2017	EM70107	Num	16085	16092	8	CLASS (EMP PSNS 14+): PUB ASSIST/WEL
2018	EM70108	Num	16093	16100	8	CLASS (EMP PSNS 14+): OTHER INCOME
2019	EM70109	Num	16101	16108	8	CLASS (EMP M PSNS 14+): WAGE/SALARY WKR
2020	EM70110	Num	16109	16116	8	CLASS (EMP M PSNS 14+): NONFARM SELF-EMP
2021	EM70111	Num	16117	16124	8	CLASS (EMP M PSNS 14+): FARM SELF-EMPLOY
2022	EM70112	Num	16125	16132	8	CLASS (EMP M PSNS 14+): SOC SEC/RAIL RET

2023	EM70113 Num	16133	16140	8	CLASS (EMP M PSNS 14+): PUB ASSIST/WELFA
2024	EM70114 Num	16141	16148	8	CLASS (EMP M PSNS 14+): OTHER INCOME
2025	EM70115 Num	16149	16156	8	CLASS (EMP F PSNS 14+): WAGE/SALARY WKR
2026	EM70116 Num	16157	16164	8	CLASS (EMP F PSNS 14+): NONFARM SELF-EMP
2027	EM70117 Num	16165	16172	8	CLASS (EMP F PSNS 14+): FARM SELF-EMPLOY
2028	EM70118 Num	16173	16180	8	CLASS (EMP F PSNS 14+): SOC SEC/RAIL RET
2029	EM70119 Num	16181	16188	8	CLASS (EMP F PSNS 14+): PUB ASSIST/WEL
2030	EM70120 Num	16189	16196	8	CLASS (EMP F PSNS 14+): OTHER INCOME
2031	EM70121 Num	16197	16204	8	CLASS (EMP PSNS 16+): WAGE/SALARY WKR
2032	EM70122 Num	16205	16212	8	CLASS (EMP PSNS 16+): FED GOVT WORKER
2033	EM70123 Num	16213	16220	8	CLASS (EMP PSNS 16+): STATE GOVT WORKER
2034	EM70124 Num	16221	16228	8	CLASS (EMP PSNS 16+): LOCAL GOVT WORKER
2035	EM70125 Num	16229	16236	8	CLASS (EMP PSNS 16+): SELF-EMPLYD WORKER
2036	EM70126 Num	16237	16244	8	CLASS (EMP PSNS 16+): UNPAID FAM WORKER
2037	EM70127 Num	16245	16252	8	CLASS (EMP M PSNS 16+): WAGE/SALARY WKR
2038	EM70128 Num	16253	16260	8	CLASS (EMP M PSNS 16+): FED GOVT WORKER
2039	EM70129 Num	16261	16268	8	CLASS (EMP M PSNS 16+): STATE GOVT WORKER
2040	EM70130 Num	16269	16276	8	CLASS (EMP M PSNS 16+): LOCAL GOVT WORKER
2041	EM70131 Num	16277	16284	8	CLASS (EMP M PSNS 16+): SELF-EMP WORKER
2042	EM70132 Num	16285	16292	8	CLASS (EMP M PSNS 16+): UNPAID FAM WORKER
2043	EM70133 Num	16293	16300	8	CLASS (EMP F PSNS 16+): WAGE/SALARY WKR
2044	EM70134 Num	16301	16308	8	CLASS (EMP F PSNS 16+): FED GOVT WORKER
2045	EM70135 Num	16309	16316	8	CLASS (EMP F PSNS 16+): STATE GOVT WORKER
2046	EM70136 Num	16317	16324	8	CLASS (EMP F PSNS 16+): LOCAL GOVT WORKER
2047	EM70137 Num	16325	16332	8	CLASS (EMP F PSNS 16+): SELF-EMP WORKER
2048	EM70138 Num	16333	16340	8	CLASS (EMP F PSNS 16+): UNPAID FAM WORKER
2049	EM70139 Num	16341	16348	8	OCCUP (EMP PSNS 16+): PROF/TECHNICAL
2050	EM70140 Num	16349	16356	8	OCCUP (EMP PSNS 16+): MANAGER/ADMINI
2051	EM70141 Num	16357	16364	8	OCCUP (EMP PSNS 16+): SALES
2052	EM70142 Num	16365	16372	8	OCCUP (EMP PSNS 16+): CLERICAL
2053	EM70143 Num	16373	16380	8	OCCUP (EMP PSNS 16+): PROD/CRAFT/REPAIR
2054	EM70144 Num	16381	16388	8	OCCUP (EMP PSNS 16+): MACHINE OPERATOR/ASSEMBLER
2055	EM70145 Num	16389	16396	8	OCCUP (EMP PSNS 16+): TRANSPORT/MATERIAL MOVING
2056	EM70146 Num	16397	16404	8	OCCUP (EMP PSNS 16+): OTHER LABORERS
2057	EM70147 Num	16405	16412	8	OCCUP (EMP PSNS 16+): FARMING
2058	EM70148 Num	16413	16420	8	OCCUP (EMP PSNS 16+): OTHER SERVICES
2059	EM70149 Num	16421	16428	8	OCCUP (EMP PSNS 16+): PROTECTIVE SERVICES
2060	EM70150 Num	16429	16436	8	OCCUP (EMP PSNS 16+): PRIVATE HH SERVICES
2061	EM70151 Num	16437	16444	8	IND (EMP PSNS 16+): AGRICULTURE
2062	EM70152 Num	16445	16452	8	IND (EMP PSNS 16+): MINING
2063	EM70153 Num	16453	16460	8	IND (EMP PSNS 16+): CONSTRUCTION

2064	EM70154 Num	16461	16468	8	IND (EMP PSNS 16+): MANUF (DURABLE)
2065	EM70155 Num	16469	16476	8	IND (EMP PSNS 16+): MANUF (NONDURABLE)
2066	EM70156 Num	16477	16484	8	IND (EMP PSNS 16+): TRANSPORTATION
2067	EM70157 Num	16485	16492	8	IND (EMP PSNS 16+): COMMUNI/ PUBLIC UTIL
2068	EM70158 Num	16493	16500	8	IND (EMP PSNS 16+): WHOLESALE TRADE
2069	EM70159 Num	16501	16508	8	IND (EMP PSNS 16+): RETAIL TRADE
2070	EM70160 Num	16509	16516	8	IND (EMP PSNS 16+): FINANCE/INSURANCE/REAL ESTATE
2071	EM70161 Num	16517	16524	8	IND (EMP PSNS 16+): BUSINESS/REPAIR SERVICES
2072	EM70162 Num	16525	16532	8	IND (EMP PSNS 16+): PERSONAL SERVICES
2073	EM70163 Num	16533	16540	8	IND (EMP PSNS 16+): ENTERTAIN/RECREATION SERVICES
2074	EM70164 Num	16541	16548	8	IND (EMP PSNS 16+): PROFESSIONAL SERVICES (HEALTH)
2075	EM70165 Num	16549	16556	8	IND (EMP PSNS 16+): PROFESSIONAL SERVICES (EDUC)
2076	EM70166 Num	16557	16564	8	IND (EMP PSNS 16+): PROFESSIONAL SERVICES (OTHERS)
2077	EM70167 Num	16565	16572	8	IND (EMP PSNS 16+): PUB ADMINISTRATION
2078	EM80001 Num	16573	16580	8	TOTAL PSNS 16 YRS+
2079	EM80002 Num	16581	16588	8	TOTAL PSNS IN LF 16 YRS+
2080	EM80003 Num	16589	16596	8	TOTAL PSNS IN CVL LF 16 YRS+
2081	EM80004 Num	16597	16604	8	MALE PSNS 16 YRS+
2082	EM80005 Num	16605	16612	8	MALE PSNS IN LF 16 YRS+
2083	EM80006 Num	16613	16620	8	MALE PSNS IN CVL LF 16 YRS+
2084	EM80007 Num	16621	16628	8	FEMALE PSNS 16 YRS+
2085	EM80008 Num	16629	16636	8	FEMALE PSNS IN LF 16 YRS+
2086	EM80009 Num	16637	16644	8	FEMALE PSNS IN CVL LF 16 YRS+
2087	EM80010 Num	16645	16652	8	TOTAL PSNS 16 YRS+ IN ARMED FORCES
2088	EM80011 Num	16653	16660	8	TOTAL PSNS 16 YRS+ IN CVL LF: EMPLOYED
2089	EM80012 Num	16661	16668	8	TOTAL PSNS 16 YRS+ IN CVL LF: UNEMPLOYED
2090	EM80013 Num	16669	16676	8	TOTAL PSNS 16 YRS+ NOT IN LF
2091	EM80014 Num	16677	16684	8	MALE PSNS 16 YRS+: ARMED FORCES
2092	EM80015 Num	16685	16692	8	MALE PSNS 16 YRS+ IN CVL LF: EMPLOYED
2093	EM80016 Num	16693	16700	8	MALE PSNS 16 YRS+ IN CVL LF: UNEMPLOYED
2094	EM80017 Num	16701	16708	8	MALE PSNS 16 YRS+ NOT IN LF
2095	EM80018 Num	16709	16716	8	FEMALE PSNS 16 YRS+ IN ARMED FORCES
2096	EM80019 Num	16717	16724	8	FEMALE PSNS 16 YRS+ IN CVL LF: EMPLOYED
2097	EM80020 Num	16725	16732	8	FEMALE PSNS 16 YRS+ IN CVL LF:UNEMPLOYED
2098	EM80021 Num	16733	16740	8	FEMALE PSNS 16 YRS+ NOT IN LF
2099	EM80022 Num	16741	16748	8	WHT PSNS 16 YRS+ IN ARMED FORCES
2100	EM80023 Num	16749	16756	8	WHT PSNS 16 YRS+ IN CVL LF: EMPLOYED
2101	EM80024 Num	16757	16764	8	WHT PSNS 16 YRS+ IN CVL LF: UNEMPLOYED
2102	EM80025 Num	16765	16772	8	WHT PSNS 16 YRS+ NOT IN LF
2103	EM80026 Num	16773	16780	8	WHT MALE PSNS 16 YRS+ IN ARMED FORCES

2104	EM80027 Num	16781	16788	8	WHT MALE PSNS 16 YRS+ IN CVL LF:EMPLOYED
2105	EM80028 Num	16789	16796	8	WHT MALE PSNS 16 YRS+ IN CVL LF:UNEMPLYD
2106	EM80029 Num	16797	16804	8	WHT MALE PSNS 16 YRS+ NOT IN LF
2107	EM80030 Num	16805	16812	8	WHT FEMALE PSNS 16 YRS+ IN ARMED FORCES
2108	EM80031 Num	16813	16820	8	WHT FEM PSNS 16 YRS+ IN CVL LF: EMPLOYED
2109	EM80032 Num	16821	16828	8	WHT FEM PSNS 16 YRS+ IN CVL LF: UNEMPLYD
2110	EM80033 Num	16829	16836	8	WHT FEMALE PSNS 16 YRS+ NOT IN LF
2111	EM80034 Num	16837	16844	8	BLK PSNS 16 YRS+ IN ARMED FORCES
2112	EM80035 Num	16845	16852	8	BLK PSNS 16 YRS+ IN CVL LF: EMPLOYED
2113	EM80036 Num	16853	16860	8	BLK PSNS 16 YRS+ IN CVL LF: UNEMPLOYED
2114	EM80037 Num	16861	16868	8	BLK PSNS 16 YRS+ NOT IN LF
2115	EM80038 Num	16869	16876	8	BLK MALE PSNS 16 YRS+ IN ARMED FORCES
2116	EM80039 Num	16877	16884	8	BLK MALE PSNS 16 YRS+ IN CVL LF: MPLOYED
2117	EM80040 Num	16885	16892	8	BLK MALE PSNS 16 YRS+ IN CVL LF:UNEMPLYD
2118	EM80041 Num	16893	16900	8	BLK MALE PSNS 16 YRS+ NOT IN LF
2119	EM80042 Num	16901	16908	8	BLK FEMALE PSNS 16 YRS+ IN ARMED FORCES
2120	EM80043 Num	16909	16916	8	BLK FEM PSNS 16 YRS+ IN CVL LF: EMPLOYED
2121	EM80044 Num	16917	16924	8	BLK FEM PSNS 16 YRS+ IN CVL LF: UNEMPLYD
2122	EM80045 Num	16925	16932	8	BLK FEMALE PSNS 16 YRS+ NOT IN LF
2123	EM80046 Num	16933	16940	8	HISP PSNS 16 YRS+ IN ARMED FORCES
2124	EM80047 Num	16941	16948	8	HISP PSNS 16 YRS+ IN CVL LF: EMPLOYED
2125	EM80048 Num	16949	16956	8	HISP PSNS 16 YRS+ IN CVL LF: UNEMPLYD
2126	EM80049 Num	16957	16964	8	HISP PSNS 16 YRS+ NOT IN LF
2127	EM80050 Num	16965	16972	8	HISP MALE PSNS 16 YRS+ IN ARMED FORCES
2128	EM80051 Num	16973	16980	8	HISP MALE PSNS 16 YRS+ IN CVL LF:EMPLOYD
2129	EM80052 Num	16981	16988	8	HISP MALE PSNS 16YRS+ IN CVL LF:UNEMPLYD
2130	EM80053 Num	16989	16996	8	HISP MALE PSNS 16 YRS+ NOT IN LF
2131	EM80054 Num	16997	17004	8	HISP FEMALE PSNS 16 YRS+ IN ARMED FORCES
2132	EM80055 Num	17005	17012	8	HISP FEM PSNS 16 YRS+ IN CVL LF:EMPLOYED
2133	EM80056 Num	17013	17020	8	HISP FEM PSNS 16 YRS+ IN CVL LF:UNEMPLYD
2134	EM80057 Num	17021	17028	8	HISP FEMALE PSNS 16 YRS+ NOT IN LF
2135	EM80058 Num	17029	17036	8	CLASS (EMP PSNS 16+): WAGE/SALARY WORKER
2136	EM80059 Num	17037	17044	8	CLASS (EMP PSNS 16+): FEDERAL GOVT WORKE
2137	EM80060 Num	17045	17052	8	CLASS (EMP PSNS 16+): STATE GOVT WORKER
2138	EM80061 Num	17053	17060	8	CLASS (EMP PSNS 16+): LOCAL GOVT WORKER
2139	EM80062 Num	17061	17068	8	CLASS (EMP PSNS 16+): SELF-EMP WORKER
2140	EM80063 Num	17069	17076	8	CLASS (EMP PSNS 16+): UNPAID FAM WORKER
2141	EM80064 Num	17077	17084	8	OCCUP (EMP PSNS 16+): EXEC/ADMI/MANAG
2142	EM80065 Num	17085	17092	8	OCCUP (EMP PSNS 16+): PROFESSIONAL
2143	EM80066 Num	17093	17100	8	OCCUP (EMP PSNS 16+): TECHNI/RLTD SUPPRT
2144	EM80067 Num	17101	17108	8	OCCUP (EMP PSNS 16+): SALES

2145	EM80068	Num	17109	17116	8	OCCUP (EMP PSNS 16+): ADMINI SUPPORT
2146	EM80069	Num	17117	17124	8	OCCUP (EMP PSNS 16+): PRIVT HH SERVICES
2147	EM80070	Num	17125	17132	8	OCCUP (EMP PSNS 16+): PROTECT SERVICES
2148	EM80071	Num	17133	17140	8	OCCUP (EMP PSNS 16+): OTHER SERVICES
2149	EM80072	Num	17141	17148	8	OCCUP (EMP PSNS 16+): FARMING
2150	EM80073	Num	17149	17156	8	OCCUP (EMP PSNS 16+): PROD/CRAFT/REPAIR
2151	EM80074	Num	17157	17164	8	OCCUP (EMP PSNS 16+): MACHINE OPERATOR/ASSEMBLER
2152	EM80075	Num	17165	17172	8	OCCUP (EMP PSNS 16+): TRANSPORT/MATERIAL MOVING
2153	EM80076	Num	17173	17180	8	OCCUP (EMP PSNS 16+): OTHER LABORERS
2154	EM80077	Num	17181	17188	8	IND (EMP PSNS 16+): AGRICULTURE
2155	EM80078	Num	17189	17196	8	IND (EMP PSNS 16+): MINING
2156	EM80079	Num	17197	17204	8	IND (EMP PSNS 16+): CONSTRUCTION
2157	EM80080	Num	17205	17212	8	IND (EMP PSNS 16+): MANUF (NONDURABLE)
2158	EM80081	Num	17213	17220	8	IND (EMP PSNS 16+): MANUF (DURABLE)
2159	EM80082	Num	17221	17228	8	IND (EMP PSNS 16+): TRANSPORTATION
2160	EM80083	Num	17229	17236	8	IND (EMP PSNS 16+): COMMUNI/PUBLIC UTIL
2161	EM80084	Num	17237	17244	8	IND (EMP PSNS 16+): WHOLESALE TRADE
2162	EM80085	Num	17245	17252	8	IND (EMP PSNS 16+): RETAIL TRADE
2163	EM80086	Num	17253	17260	8	IND (EMP PSNS 16+): FINANCE/INSURANCE/REAL ESTATE
2164	EM80087	Num	17261	17268	8	IND (EMP PSNS 16+): BUSINESS/REPAIR SERVICES
2165	EM80088	Num	17269	17276	8	IND (EMP PSNS 16+): PERSONL/ENTERTAINMENT SERVICE
2166	EM80089	Num	17277	17284	8	IND (EMP PSNS 16+): PROFESSIONAL SERVICES (HEALTH)
2167	EM80090	Num	17285	17292	8	IND (EMP PSNS 16+): PROFESSIONAL SERVICES (EDUCAT)
2168	EM80091	Num	17293	17300	8	IND (EMP PSNS 16+): PROFESSIONAL SERVICES (OTHERS)
2169	EM80092	Num	17301	17308	8	IND (EMP PSNS 16+): PUB ADMINISTRATION
2170	EM90001	Num	17309	17316	8	TOTAL PSNS 16 YRS+
2171	EM90002	Num	17317	17324	8	TOTAL PSNS IN LF 16 YRS+
2172	EM90003	Num	17325	17332	8	TOTAL PSNS IN CVL LF 16 YRS+
2173	EM90004	Num	17333	17340	8	MALE PSNS 16 YRS+
2174	EM90005	Num	17341	17348	8	MALE PSNS IN LF 16 YRS+
2175	EM90006	Num	17349	17356	8	MALE PSNS IN CVL LF 16 YRS+
2176	EM90007	Num	17357	17364	8	FEMALE PSNS 16 YRS+
2177	EM90008	Num	17365	17372	8	FEMALE PSNS IN LF 16 YRS+
2178	EM90009	Num	17373	17380	8	FEMALE PSNS IN CVL LF 16 YRS+
2179	EM90010	Num	17381	17388	8	TOTAL PSNS 16 YRS+ IN ARMED FORCES
2180	EM90011	Num	17389	17396	8	TOTAL PSNS 16 YRS+ IN CVL LF: EMPLOYED
2181	EM90012	Num	17397	17404	8	TOTAL PSNS 16 YRS+ IN CVL LF: UNEMPLOYED
2182	EM90013	Num	17405	17412	8	TOTAL PSNS 16 YRS+ NOT IN LF
2183	EM90014	Num	17413	17420	8	MALE PSNS 16 YRS+ IN ARMED FORCES
2184	EM90015	Num	17421	17428	8	MALE PSNS 16 YRS+ IN CVL LF: EMPLOYED

2185	EM90016	Num	17429	17436	8	MALE PSNS 16 YRS+ IN CVL LF: UNEMPLOYED
2186	EM90017	Num	17437	17444	8	MALE PSNS 16 YRS+ NOT IN LABOR FORCE
2187	EM90018	Num	17445	17452	8	FEMALE PSNS 16 YRS+ IN ARMED FORCES
2188	EM90019	Num	17453	17460	8	FEMALE PSNS 16 YRS+ IN CVL LF: EMPLOYED
2189	EM90020	Num	17461	17468	8	FEMALE PSNS 16 YRS+ IN CVL LF:UNEMPLOYED
2190	EM90021	Num	17469	17476	8	FEMALE PSNS 16 YRS+ NOT IN LF
2191	EM90022	Num	17477	17484	8	WHT PSNS 16 YRS+ IN ARMED FORCES
2192	EM90023	Num	17485	17492	8	WHT PSNS 16 YRS+ IN CVL LF: EMPLOYED
2193	EM90024	Num	17493	17500	8	WHT PSNS 16 YRS+ IN CVL LF: UNEMPLOYD
2194	EM90025	Num	17501	17508	8	WHT PSNS 16 YRS+ NOT IN LF
2195	EM90026	Num	17509	17516	8	WHT MALE PSNS 16 YRS+ IN ARMED FORCES
2196	EM90027	Num	17517	17524	8	WHT MALE PSNS 16 YRS+ IN CVL LF:EMPLOYED
2197	EM90028	Num	17525	17532	8	WHT MALE PSNS 16 YRS+ IN CVL LF:UNEMPLYD
2198	EM90029	Num	17533	17540	8	WHT MALE PSNS 16 YRS+ NOT IN LF
2199	EM90030	Num	17541	17548	8	WHT FEMALE PSNS 16 YRS+ IN ARMED FORCES
2200	EM90031	Num	17549	17556	8	WHT FEM PSNS 16 YRS+ IN CVL LF:EMPLOYED
2201	EM90032	Num	17557	17564	8	WHT FEM PSNS 16 YRS+ IN CVL LF: UNEMPLYD
2202	EM90033	Num	17565	17572	8	WHT FEMALE PSNS 16 YRS+ NOT IN LF
2203	EM90034	Num	17573	17580	8	BLK PSNS 16 YRS+ IN ARMED FORCES
2204	EM90035	Num	17581	17588	8	BLK PSNS 16 YRS+ IN CVL LF: EMPLOYED
2205	EM90036	Num	17589	17596	8	BLK PSNS 16 YRS+ IN CVL LF: UNEMPLOYD
2206	EM90037	Num	17597	17604	8	BLK PSNS 16 YRS+ NOT IN LF
2207	EM90038	Num	17605	17612	8	BLK MALE PSNS 16 YRS+ IN ARMED FORCES
2208	EM90039	Num	17613	17620	8	BLK MALE PSNS 16 YRS+ IN CVL LF:EMPLOYED
2209	EM90040	Num	17621	17628	8	BLK MALE PSNS 16 YRS+ IN CVL LF:UNEMPLYD
2210	EM90041	Num	17629	17636	8	BLK MALE PSNS 16 YRS+ NOT IN LF
2211	EM90042	Num	17637	17644	8	BLK FEMALE PSNS 16 YRS+ IN ARMED FORCES
2212	EM90043	Num	17645	17652	8	BLK FEM PSNS 16 YRS+ IN CVL LF:EMPLOYED
2213	EM90044	Num	17653	17660	8	BLK FEM PSNS 16 YRS+ IN CVL LF:UNEMPLOYD
2214	EM90045	Num	17661	17668	8	BLK FEMALE PSNS 16 YRS+ NOT IN LF
2215	EM90046	Num	17669	17676	8	HISP TOTAL PSNS 16 YRS+ IN ARMED FORCES
2216	EM90047	Num	17677	17684	8	HISP PSNS 16 YRS+ IN CVL LF: EMPLOYED
2217	EM90048	Num	17685	17692	8	HISP PSNS 16 YRS+ IN CVL LF: UNEMPLOYED
2218	EM90049	Num	17693	17700	8	HISP TOTAL PSNS 16 YRS+ NOT IN LF
2219	EM90050	Num	17701	17708	8	HISP MALE PSNS 16 YRS+ IN ARMED FORCES
2220	EM90051	Num	17709	17716	8	HISP MALE PSNS 16 YRS+ IN CVL LF:EMPLOYD
2221	EM90052	Num	17717	17724	8	HISP MALE PSNS 16YRS+ IN CVL LF:UNEMPLYD
2222	EM90053	Num	17725	17732	8	HISP MALE PSNS 16 YRS+ NOT IN LF
2223	EM90054	Num	17733	17740	8	HISP FEMALE PSNS 16 YRS+ IN ARMED FORCES
2224	EM90055	Num	17741	17748	8	HISP FEM PSNS 16 YRS+ IN CVL LF:EMPLOYED
2225	EM90056	Num	17749	17756	8	HISP FEM PSNS 16 YRS+ IN CVL LF:UNEMPLYD

2226	EM90057	Num	17757	17764	8	HISP FEMALE PSNS 16 YRS+ NOT IN LF
2227	EM90058	Num	17765	17772	8	CLASS (EMP PSNS 16+): WAGE/SAL-PROFT
2228	EM90059	Num	17773	17780	8	CLASS (EMP PSNS 16+): WAGE/SAL-NON PROFT
2229	EM90060	Num	17781	17788	8	CLASS (EMP PSNS 16+): LOCAL GOVT WORKER
2230	EM90061	Num	17789	17796	8	CLASS (EMP PSNS 16+): STATE GOVT WORKER
2231	EM90062	Num	17797	17804	8	CLASS (EMP PSNS 16+): FEDERAL GOVT WORKE
2232	EM90063	Num	17805	17812	8	CLASS (EMP PSNS 16+): SELF-EMPLD WORKER
2233	EM90064	Num	17813	17820	8	CLASS (EMP PSNS 16+): UNPAID FAM WORKER
2234	EM90065	Num	17821	17828	8	OCCUP (EMP PSNS 16+): EXEC/ADMIN/MANAGE
2235	EM90066	Num	17829	17836	8	OCCUP (EMP PSNS 16+): PROFESSIONAL
2236	EM90067	Num	17837	17844	8	OCCUP (EMP PSNS 16+): TECHNI/RLTD SUPPRT
2237	EM90068	Num	17845	17852	8	OCCUP (EMP PSNS 16+): SALES
2238	EM90069	Num	17853	17860	8	OCCUP (EMP PSNS 16+): ADMINI SUPPORT
2239	EM90070	Num	17861	17868	8	OCCUP (EMP PSNS 16+): PRIVT HH SERVICES
2240	EM90071	Num	17869	17876	8	OCCUP (EMP PSNS 16+): PROTECT SERVICES
2241	EM90072	Num	17877	17884	8	OCCUP (EMP PSNS 16+): OTHER SERVICES
2242	EM90073	Num	17885	17892	8	OCCUP (EMP PSNS 16+): FARMING
2243	EM90074	Num	17893	17900	8	OCCUP (EMP PSNS 16+): PROD/CRAFT/REPAIR
2244	EM90075	Num	17901	17908	8	OCCUP (EMP PSNS 16+): MACHINE OPERATOR/ASSEMBLER
2245	EM90076	Num	17909	17916	8	OCCUP (EMP PSNS 16+): TRANSPORT/MATERIAL MOVING
2246	EM90077	Num	17917	17924	8	OCCUP (EMP PSNS 16+): OTHER LABORERS
2247	EM90078	Num	17925	17932	8	IND (EMP PSNS 16+): AGRICULTURE
2248	EM90079	Num	17933	17940	8	IND (EMP PSNS 16+): MINING
2249	EM90080	Num	17941	17948	8	IND (EMP PSNS 16+): CONSTRUCTION
2250	EM90081	Num	17949	17956	8	IND (EMP PSNS 16+): MANUF (NONDURABLE)
2251	EM90082	Num	17957	17964	8	IND (EMP PSNS 16+): MANUF (DURABLE)
2252	EM90083	Num	17965	17972	8	IND (EMP PSNS 16+): TRANSPORTATION
2253	EM90084	Num	17973	17980	8	IND (EMP PSNS 16+): COMMUNI/PUBLIC UTIL
2254	EM90085	Num	17981	17988	8	IND (EMP PSNS 16+): WHOLESALE TRADE
2255	EM90086	Num	17989	17996	8	IND (EMP PSNS 16+): RETAIL TRADE
2256	EM90087	Num	17997	18004	8	IND (EMP PSNS 16+): FINANCE/INSURANCE/REAL ESTATE
2257	EM90088	Num	18005	18012	8	IND (EMP PSNS 16+): BUSINESS/REPAIR SERVICES
2258	EM90089	Num	18013	18020	8	IND (EMP PSNS 16+): PERSONAL SERVICES
2259	EM90090	Num	18021	18028	8	IND (EMP PSNS 16+): ENTERTAINMNT/RECREATION SERVICES
2260	EM90091	Num	18029	18036	8	IND (EMP PSNS 16+): PROFESSIONAL SERVICES (HEALTH)
2261	EM90092	Num	18037	18044	8	IND (EMP PSNS 16+): PROFESSIONAL SERVICES (EDUCAT)
2262	EM90093	Num	18045	18052	8	IND (EMP PSNS 16+): PROFESSIONAL SERVICES (OTHERS)
2263	EM90094	Num	18053	18060	8	IND (EMP PSNS 16+): PUB ADMINISTRATION
2264	CLASS40	Char	18061	18061	1	OIL DEPENDENCY 1940
2265	CLASS50	Char	18062	18062	1	OIL DEPENDENCY 1950
2266	CLASS60	Char	18063	18063	1	OIL DEPENDENCY 1960

2267	CLASS70	Char	18064	18064	1	OIL DEPENDENCY 1970
2268	CLASS80	Char	18065	18065	1	OIL DEPENDENCY 1980
2269	CLASS90	Char	18066	18066	1	OIL DEPENDENCY 1990
2270	MIN01	Num	18067	18074	8	MINING (EMP PSNS 14+) 1940 (%)
2271	MIN02	Num	18075	18082	8	MINING (EMP PSNS 14+) 1950 (%)
2272	MIN03	Num	18083	18090	8	MINING (EMP PSNS 14+) 1960 (%)
2273	MIN04	Num	18091	18098	8	MINING (EMP PSNS 16+) 1970 (%)
2274	MIN05	Num	18099	18106	8	MINING (EMP PSNS 16+) 1980 (%)
2275	MIN06	Num	18107	18114	8	MINING (EMP PSNS 16+) 1990 (%)
2276	MIN07	Num	18115	18122	8	MINING (PSNS 16+ EVER WKD BW 1975-80%)
2277	MIN08	Num	18123	18130	8	MINING (PSNS 16+ EVER WKD BW 1985-90%)
2278	MIN09	Num	18131	18138	8	OIL/GAS (PSNS 16+ EVER WKD BW 1975-80%)
2279	MIN10	Num	18139	18146	8	OIL/GAS (PSNS 16+ EVER WKD BW 1985-90%)
2280	MIN11	Num	18147	18154	8	MINING-LOCATION QUOTIENT 1940
2281	MIN12	Num	18155	18162	8	MINING-LOCATION QUOTIENT 1950
2282	MIN13	Num	18163	18170	8	MINING-LOCATION QUOTIENT 1960
2283	MIN14	Num	18171	18178	8	MINING-LOCATION QUOTIENT 1970
2284	MIN15	Num	18179	18186	8	MINING-LOCATION QUOTIENT 1980
2285	MIN16	Num	18187	18194	8	MINING-LOCATION QUOTIENT 1990
2286	MIN17	Num	18195	18202	8	MINING-LOCATION QUOTIENT 1980[2]
2287	MIN18	Num	18203	18210	8	MINING-LOCATION QUOTIENT 1990[3]
2288	MIN19	Num	18211	18218	8	OIL/GAS-LOCATION QUOTIENT 1980
2289	MIN20	Num	18219	18226	8	OIL/GAS-LOCATION QUOTIENT 1990
2290	MIN21	Num	18227	18234	8	EMPLOYED PSNS 14+ IN MINING: 1940
2291	MIN22	Num	18235	18242	8	EMPLOYED PSNS 14+ IN MINING: 1950
2292	MIN23	Num	18243	18250	8	EMPLOYED PSNS 14+ IN MINING: 1960
2293	MIN24	Num	18251	18258	8	EMPLOYED PSNS 16+ IN MINING: 1970
2294	MIN25	Num	18259	18266	8	EMPLOYED PSNS 16+ IN MINING: 1980
2295	MIN26	Num	18267	18274	8	EMPLOYED PSNS 16+ IN MINING: 1990
2296	MIN27	Num	18275	18282	8	TOTAL EMPLOYED PSNS 14+: 1940
2297	MIN28	Num	18283	18290	8	TOTAL EMPLOYED PSNS 14+: 1950
2298	MIN29	Num	18291	18298	8	TOTAL EMPLOYED PSNS 14+: 1960
2299	MIN30	Num	18299	18306	8	TOTAL EMPLOYED PSNS 16+: 1970
2300	MIN31	Num	18307	18314	8	TOTAL EMPLOYED PSNS 16+: 1980
2301	MIN32	Num	18315	18322	8	TOTAL EMPLOYED PSNS 16+: 1990
2302	MIN33	Num	18323	18330	8	TOTAL PSNS 16+ EVER WKD BW 1975-80
2303	MIN34	Num	18331	18338	8	MIN-TOTAL (PSNS 16+ EVER WKD BW 1975-80)

---

[2] MIN25 are based on persons 16 years and over ever workerd between 1975-80.

[3] MIN26 are based on persons 16 years and over ever workerd between 1985-90.

2304	MIN35	Num	18339	18346	8	MIN-METAL (PSNS 16+ EVER WKD BW 1975-80)
2305	MIN36	Num	18347	18354	8	MIN-COAL (PSNS 16+ EVER WKD BW 1975-80)
2306	MIN37	Num	18355	18362	8	MIN-OIL/GAS (PSNS 16+ EVER WKD 1975-80)
2307	MIN38	Num	18363	18370	8	MIN-OTHER (PSNS 16+ EVER WKD BW 1975-80)
2308	MIN39	Num	18371	18378	8	TOTAL PSNS 16+ EVER WKD BW 1985-90
2309	MIN40	Num	18379	18386	8	MIN-TOTAL (PSNS 16+ EVER WKD BW 1985-90)
2310	MIN41	Num	18387	18394	8	MIN-METAL (PSNS 16+ EVER WKD BW 1985-90)
2311	MIN42	Num	18395	18402	8	MIN-COAL (PSNS 16+ EVER WKD BW 1985-90)
2312	MIN43	Num	18403	18410	8	MIN-OIL/GAS (PSNS 16+ EVER WKD 1985-90)
2313	MIN44	Num	18411	18418	8	MIN-OTHER (PSNS 16+ EVER WKD BW 1985-90)
2314	MIN45	Num	18419	18426	8	TOTAL EMP PSNS 14+: 1940 (STATE)
2315	MIN46	Num	18427	18434	8	TOTAL EMP PSNS 14+: 1950 (STATE)
2316	MIN47	Num	18435	18442	8	TOTAL EMP PSNS 14+: 1960 (STATE)
2317	MIN48	Num	18443	18450	8	TOTAL EMP PSNS 16+: 1970 (STATE)
2318	MIN49	Num	18451	18458	8	TOTAL EMP PSNS 16+: 1980 (STATE)
2319	MIN50	Num	18459	18466	8	TOTAL EMP PSNS 16+: 1990 (STATE)
2320	MIN51	Num	18467	18474	8	EMP PSNS 14+ IN MINING: 1940 (STATE)
2321	MIN52	Num	18475	18482	8	EMP PSNS 14+ IN MINING: 1950 (STATE)
2322	MIN53	Num	18483	18490	8	EMP PSNS 14+ IN MINING: 1960 (STATE)
2323	MIN54	Num	18491	18498	8	EMP PSNS 16+ IN MINING: 1970 (STATE)
2324	MIN55	Num	18499	18506	8	EMP PSNS 16+ IN MINING: 1980 (STATE)
2325	MIN56	Num	18507	18514	8	EMP PSNS 16+ IN MINING: 1990 (STATE)
2326	MIN57	Num	18515	18522	8	TOT PSNS 16+ EVER WKD BW 75-80 (STATE)
2327	MIN58	Num	18523	18530	8	MIN-TOTAL (PSNS 16+ EV WKD 75-80: STATE)
2328	MIN59	Num	18531	18538	8	MIN-METAL (PSNS 16+ EV WKD 75-80: STATE)
2329	MIN60	Num	18539	18546	8	MIN-COAL (PSNS 16+ EV WKD 75-80: STATE)
2330	MIN61	Num	18547	18554	8	MIN-OIL/GAS (PSNS16+ EV WKD 75-80:STATE)
2331	MIN62	Num	18555	18562	8	MIN-OTHER (PSNS 16+ EV WK 75-80: STATE)
2332	MIN63	Num	18563	18570	8	TOT PSNS 16+ EVER WKD BW 85-90 (STATE)
2333	MIN64	Num	18571	18578	8	MIN-TOTAL (PSNS 16+ EV WKD 85-90: STATE)
2334	MIN65	Num	18579	18586	8	MIN-METAL (PSNS 16+ EV WKD 85-90: STATE)
2335	MIN66	Num	18587	18594	8	MIN-COAL (PSNS 16+ EV WKD 85-90: STATE)
2336	MIN67	Num	18595	18602	8	MIN-OIL/GAS (PSNS16+ EV WKD 85-90:STATE)
2337	MIN68	Num	18603	18610	8	MIN-OTHER (PSNS 16+ EV WKD 85-90: STATE)
2338	IN50001	Num	18611	18618	8	MEDIAN FAMILY INCOME 1950 $
2339	IN50002	Num	18619	18626	8	FAM.PCT.W INC LT $2000 1950
2340	IN50003	Num	18627	18634	8	FAM.PCT.W INC $5000 OR > 1950
2341	IN60001	Num	18635	18642	8	MEDIAN FAMILY INCOME 1960 $
2342	IN60002	Num	18643	18650	8	PER CAPITA INCOME: TOTAL $
2343	IN60003	Num	18651	18658	8	FAM.PCT.W INC LT $3000 1960

2344	IN60004 Num	18659	18666	8	FAM.PCT.W INC $10000 & > 1960
2345	IN60005 Num	18667	18674	8	NUMBER OF RECIPIENTS IN 1960
2346	IN60006 Num	18675	18682	8	PER CAP INCOME OF RECIPIENTS IN 1960 $
2347	IN70001 Num	18683	18690	8	MEDIAN FAMILY INCOME: TOTAL 1970 $
2348	IN70002 Num	18691	18698	8	MEDIAN FAMILY INCOME: WHITE 1970 $
2349	IN70003 Num	18699	18706	8	MEDIAN FAMILY INCOME: BLACK 1970 $
2350	IN70004 Num	18707	18714	8	MEAN FAMILY INCOME: TOTAL $
2351	IN70005 Num	18715	18722	8	MEAN FAMILY INCOME: WHITE $
2352	IN70006 Num	18723	18730	8	MEAN FAMILY INCOME: BLACK $
2353	IN70007 Num	18731	18738	8	MEAN FAMILY INCOME: HISPANIC $
2354	IN70008 Num	18739	18746	8	PER CAPITA INCOME: TOTAL (USA CNTY 94) $[4]
2355	IN70009 Num	18747	18754	8	PER CAPITA INCOME: TOTAL (1970 CENSUS) $[5]
2356	IN70010 Num	18755	18762	8	PER CAPITA INCOME: WHT PSNS $
2357	IN70011 Num	18763	18770	8	PER CAPITA INCOME: BLK PSNS $
2358	IN70012 Num	18771	18778	8	PER CAPITA INCOME: HISP PSNS $
2359	IN70013 Num	18779	18786	8	FAMILY INCOME: UNDER $1,000
2360	IN70014 Num	18787	18794	8	FAMILY INCOME: $1,000-$1,999
2361	IN70015 Num	18795	18802	8	FAMILY INCOME: $2,000-$2,999
2362	IN70016 Num	18803	18810	8	FAMILY INCOME: $3,000-$3,999
2363	IN70017 Num	18811	18818	8	FAMILY INCOME: $4,000-$4,999
2364	IN70018 Num	18819	18826	8	FAMILY INCOME: $5,000-$5,999
2365	IN70019 Num	18827	18834	8	FAMILY INCOME: $6,000-$6,999
2366	IN70020 Num	18835	18842	8	FAMILY INCOME: $7,000-$7,999
2367	IN70021 Num	18843	18850	8	FAMILY INCOME: $8,000-$8,999
2368	IN70022 Num	18851	18858	8	FAMILY INCOME: $9,000-$9,999
2369	IN70023 Num	18859	18866	8	FAMILY INCOME: $10,000-$11,999
2370	IN70024 Num	18867	18874	8	FAMILY INCOME: $12,000-$14,999
2371	IN70025 Num	18875	18882	8	FAMILY INCOME: $15,000-$24,999
2372	IN70026 Num	18883	18890	8	FAMILY INCOME: $25,000-$49,999
2373	IN70027 Num	18891	18898	8	FAMILY INCOME: $50,000 AND OVER
2374	IN70028 Num	18899	18906	8	INCOME-UNREL INDIV: UNDER $1,000
2375	IN70029 Num	18907	18914	8	INCOME-UNREL INDIV: $1,000-$1,999
2376	IN70030 Num	18915	18922	8	INCOME-UNREL INDIV: $2,000-$2,999
2377	IN70031 Num	18923	18930	8	INCOME-UNREL INDIV: $3,000-$3,999
2378	IN70032 Num	18931	18938	8	INCOME-UNREL INDIV: $4,000-$4,999
2379	IN70033 Num	18939	18946	8	INCOME-UNREL INDIV: $5,000-$5,999

[4] Based on USA County 1994 (Bureau of Census, December 1994, CD94-CTY-02).

[5] Based on the result of the 1970 Census.

2380	IN70034 Num	18947	18954	8	INCOME-UNREL INDIV: $6,000-$6,999
2381	IN70035 Num	18955	18962	8	INCOME-UNREL INDIV: $7,000-$7,999
2382	IN70036 Num	18963	18970	8	INCOME-UNREL INDIV: $8,000-$8,999
2383	IN70037 Num	18971	18978	8	INCOME-UNREL INDIV: $9,000-$9,999
2384	IN70038 Num	18979	18986	8	INCOME-UNREL INDIV: $10,000-$11,999
2385	IN70039 Num	18987	18994	8	INCOME-UNREL INDIV: $12,000-$14,999
2386	IN70040 Num	18995	19002	8	INCOME-UNREL INDIV: $15,000-$24,999
2387	IN70041 Num	19003	19010	8	INCOME-UNREL INDIV: $25,000-$49,999
2388	IN70042 Num	19011	19018	8	INCOME-UNREL INDIV: $50,000 AND OVER
2389	IN70043 Num	19019	19026	8	FAMILIES: WAGE & SALARY INCOME
2390	IN70044 Num	19027	19034	8	FAMILIES: NONFARM/SELF-EMP INCOME
2391	IN70045 Num	19035	19042	8	FAMILIES: FARM/SELF-EMP INCOME
2392	IN70046 Num	19043	19050	8	FAMILIES: SOC SECURITY INCOME
2393	IN70047 Num	19051	19058	8	FAMILIES: PUB ASSISTANCE INCOME
2394	IN70048 Num	19059	19066	8	FAMILIES: ALL OTHER INCOME
2395	IN70049 Num	19067	19074	8	FAMILY POVERTY LEVEL: UNDER .50
2396	IN70050 Num	19075	19082	8	FAMILY POVERTY LEVEL: .50-.74
2397	IN70051 Num	19083	19090	8	FAMILY POVERTY LEVEL: .75-.99
2398	IN70052 Num	19091	19098	8	FAMILY POVERTY LEVEL: 1.00-1.24
2399	IN70053 Num	19099	19106	8	FAMILY POVERTY LEVEL: 1.25-1.49
2400	IN70054 Num	19107	19114	8	FAMILY POVERTY LEVEL: 1.50-1.99
2401	IN70055 Num	19115	19122	8	FAMILY POVERTY LEVEL: 2.00-2.99
2402	IN70056 Num	19123	19130	8	FAMILY POVERTY LEVEL: 3.00 OR MORE
2403	IN70057 Num	19131	19138	8	WHT FAMILIES: WAGE & SALARY INCOME
2404	IN70058 Num	19139	19146	8	WHT FAMILIES: NONFARM/SELF-EMP INCOME
2405	IN70059 Num	19147	19154	8	WHT FAMILIES: FARM/SELF-EMP INCOME
2406	IN70060 Num	19155	19162	8	WHT FAMILIES: SOC SECURITY INCOME
2407	IN70061 Num	19163	19170	8	WHT FAMILIES: PUB ASSISTANCE INCOME
2408	IN70062 Num	19171	19178	8	WHT FAMILIES: ALL OTHER INCOME
2409	IN70063 Num	19179	19186	8	WHT FAMILY POVERTY LEVEL: UNDER .50
2410	IN70064 Num	19187	19194	8	WHT FAMILY POVERTY LEVEL: .50-.74
2411	IN70065 Num	19195	19202	8	WHT FAMILY POVERTY LEVEL: .75-.99
2412	IN70066 Num	19203	19210	8	WHT FAMILY POVERTY LEVEL: 1.00-1.24
2413	IN70067 Num	19211	19218	8	WHT FAMILY POVERTY LEVEL: 1.25-1.49
2414	IN70068 Num	19219	19226	8	WHT FAMILY POVERTY LEVEL: 1.50-1.99
2415	IN70069 Num	19227	19234	8	WHT FAMILY POVERTY LEVEL: 2.00-2.99
2416	IN70070 Num	19235	19242	8	WHT FAMILY POVERTY LEVEL: 3.00 OR MORE
2417	IN70071 Num	19243	19250	8	BLK FAMILIES: WAGE & SALARY INCOME
2418	IN70072 Num	19251	19258	8	BLK FAMILIES: NONFARM/SELF-EMP INCOME
2419	IN70073 Num	19259	19266	8	BLK FAMILIES: FARM/SELF-EMP INCOME
2420	IN70074 Num	19267	19274	8	BLK FAMILIES: SOC SECURITY INCOME

2421	IN70075 Num	19275	19282	8	BLK FAMILIES: PUB ASSISTANCE INCOME
2422	IN70076 Num	19283	19290	8	BLK FAMILIES: ALL OTHER INCOME
2423	IN70077 Num	19291	19298	8	BLK FAMILY POVERTY LEVEL: UNDER .50
2424	IN70078 Num	19299	19306	8	BLK FAMILY POVERTY LEVEL: .50-.74
2425	IN70079 Num	19307	19314	8	BLK FAMILY POVERTY LEVEL: .75-.99
2426	IN70080 Num	19315	19322	8	BLK FAMILY POVERTY LEVEL: 1.00-1.24
2427	IN70081 Num	19323	19330	8	BLK FAMILY POVERTY LEVEL: 1.25-1.49
2428	IN70082 Num	19331	19338	8	BLK FAMILY POVERTY LEVEL: 1.50-1.99
2429	IN70083 Num	19339	19346	8	BLK FAMILY POVERTY LEVEL: 2.00-2.99
2430	IN70084 Num	19347	19354	8	BLK FAMILY POVERTY LEVEL: 3.00 OR MORE
2431	IN70085 Num	19355	19362	8	HISP FAMILIES: WAGE & SALARY INCOME
2432	IN70086 Num	19363	19370	8	HISP FAMILIES: NONFARM/SELF-EMP INCOME
2433	IN70087 Num	19371	19378	8	HISP FAMILIES: FARM/SELF-EMP INCOME
2434	IN70088 Num	19379	19386	8	HISP FAMILIES: SOC SECURITY INCOME
2435	IN70089 Num	19387	19394	8	HISP FAMILIES: PUB ASSISTANCE INCOME
2436	IN70090 Num	19395	19402	8	HISP FAMILIES: ALL OTHER INCOME
2437	IN70091 Num	19403	19410	8	HISP FAMILY POVERTY LEVEL: UNDER .50
2438	IN70092 Num	19411	19418	8	HISP FAMILY POVERTY LEVEL: .50-.74
2439	IN70093 Num	19419	19426	8	HISP FAMILY POVERTY LEVEL: .75-.99
2440	IN70094 Num	19427	19434	8	HISP FAMILY POVERTY LEVEL: 1.00-1.24
2441	IN70095 Num	19435	19442	8	HISP FAMILY POVERTY LEVEL: 1.25-1.49
2442	IN70096 Num	19443	19450	8	HISP FAMILY POVERTY LEVEL: 1.50-1.99
2443	IN70097 Num	19451	19458	8	HISP FAMILY POVERTY LEVEL: 2.00-2.99
2444	IN70098 Num	19459	19466	8	HISP FAMILY POVERTY LEVEL: 3.00 OR MORE
2445	IN70099 Num	19467	19474	8	PSNS WITH INCOME ABOVE POVERTY LEVEL[6]
2446	IN70100 Num	19475	19482	8	PSNS WITH INCOME BELOW POVERTY LEVEL
2447	IN70101 Num	19483	19490	8	WHT PSNS WITH INCOME ABOVE POVERTY LEVEL
2448	IN70102 Num	19491	19498	8	WHT PSNS WITH INCOME BELOW POVERTY LEVEL
2449	IN70103 Num	19499	19506	8	BLK PSNS WITH INCOME ABOVE POVERTY LEVEL
2450	IN70104 Num	19507	19514	8	BLK PSNS WITH INCOME BELOW POVERTY LEVEL
2451	IN70105 Num	19515	19522	8	HISP PSNS WITH INCOME ABOVE POVERTY LEVEL
2452	IN70106 Num	19523	19530	8	HISP PSNS WITH INCOME BELOW POVERTY LEVEL
2453	IN80001 Num	19531	19538	8	MEDIAN FAMILY INCOME: ALL FAMILIES $
2454	IN80002 Num	19539	19546	8	MEDIAN HH INCOME, 1979 $
2455	IN80003 Num	19547	19554	8	MEAN FAMILY INCOME: TOTAL $

---

[6] Tallies concerning the "poverty level" (for total persons and by races) generally exclude inmates of institutions, members of the Armed Forces living in barracks, college students living in dormitories, and unrelated individuals under 14 years old. The persons below the poverty level follow this definition. However, the persons above the poverty level are derived by subtracting the persons below the poverty level from the total county (parish) population which include these populations that would need to be excluded. Consequently, the figures given here for the number of persons above the pover level are slightly overstated. For that reason, the poverty rates derived from the persons above and below the poverty line will be slightly underestimated (normally less than 1%) in comparison with the published poverty rates in the 1970 Census.

2456	IN80004 Num	19555	19562	8	MEAN FAMILY INCOME: WHT $
2457	IN80005 Num	19563	19570	8	MEAN FAMILY INCOME: BLK $
2458	IN80006 Num	19571	19578	8	MEAN FAMILY INCOME: HISP
2459	IN80007 Num	19579	19586	8	PER CAPITA INCOME $
2460	IN80008 Num	19587	19594	8	HH INCOME: UNER $2,500
2461	IN80009 Num	19595	19602	8	HH INCOME: $2,500-4,999
2462	IN80010 Num	19603	19610	8	HH INCOME: $5,000-7,499
2463	IN80011 Num	19611	19618	8	HH INCOME: $7,500-9,999
2464	IN80012 Num	19619	19626	8	HH INCOME:$10,000-12,499
2465	IN80013 Num	19627	19634	8	HH INCOME:$12,500-14,999
2466	IN80014 Num	19635	19642	8	HH INCOME:$15,000-17,499
2467	IN80015 Num	19643	19650	8	HH INCOME:$17,500-19,999
2468	IN80016 Num	19651	19658	8	HH INCOME:$20,000-22,499
2469	IN80017 Num	19659	19666	8	HH INCOME:$22,500-24,999
2470	IN80018 Num	19667	19674	8	HH INCOME:$25,000-27,499
2471	IN80019 Num	19675	19682	8	HH INCOME:$27,500-29,999
2472	IN80020 Num	19683	19690	8	HH INCOME:$30,000-34,999
2473	IN80021 Num	19691	19698	8	HH INCOME:$35,000-39,999
2474	IN80022 Num	19699	19706	8	HH INCOME:$40,000-49,999
2475	IN80023 Num	19707	19714	8	HH INCOME:$50,000-74,999
2476	IN80024 Num	19715	19722	8	HH INCOME:$75,000 OR MORE
2477	IN80025 Num	19723	19730	8	HH: WITH EARNINGS
2478	IN80026 Num	19731	19738	8	HH: WAGE/SALARY INCOME
2479	IN80027 Num	19739	19746	8	HH: NON-FARM SELF-EMPL INCOME
2480	IN80028 Num	19747	19754	8	HH: FARM SELF-EMPL INCOME
2481	IN80029 Num	19755	19762	8	HH: INTEREST,DIV.,OR NET RENTAL INCOME
2482	IN80030 Num	19763	19770	8	HH: SOCIAL SECURITY INCOME
2483	IN80031 Num	19771	19778	8	HH: PUBLIC ASSISTANCE INCOME
2484	IN80032 Num	19779	19786	8	HH: ALL OTHER INCOME
2485	IN80033 Num	19787	19794	8	FAMILY INCOME: UNER $2,500
2486	IN80034 Num	19795	19802	8	FAMILY INCOME: $2,500-4,999
2487	IN80035 Num	19803	19810	8	FAMILY INCOME: $5,000-7,499
2488	IN80036 Num	19811	19818	8	FAMILY INCOME: $7,500-9,999
2489	IN80037 Num	19819	19826	8	FAMILY INCOME:$10,000-12,499
2490	IN80038 Num	19827	19834	8	FAMILY INCOME:$12,500-14,999
2491	IN80039 Num	19835	19842	8	FAMILY INCOME:$15,000-17,499
2492	IN80040 Num	19843	19850	8	FAMILY INCOME:$17,500-19,999
2493	IN80041 Num	19851	19858	8	FAMILY INCOME:$20,000-22,499
2494	IN80042 Num	19859	19866	8	FAMILY INCOME:$22,500-24,999
2495	IN80043 Num	19867	19874	8	FAMILY INCOME:$25,000-27,499
2496	IN80044 Num	19875	19882	8	FAMILY INCOME:$27,500-29,999

2497	IN80045	Num	19883	19890	8	FAMILY INCOME:$30,000-34,999
2498	IN80046	Num	19891	19898	8	FAMILY INCOME:$35,000-39,999
2499	IN80047	Num	19899	19906	8	FAMILY INCOME:$40,000-49,999
2500	IN80048	Num	19907	19914	8	FAMILY INCOME:$50,000-74,999
2501	IN80049	Num	19915	19922	8	FAMILY INCOME:$75,000 OR MORE
2502	IN80050	Num	19923	19930	8	FAMILIES BELOW POVERTY LEVEL IN 1979
2503	IN80051	Num	19931	19938	8	PSNS WITH INC ABV POVERTY LEVEL
2504	IN80052	Num	19939	19946	8	PSNS WITH INC BLW POVERTY LEVEL
2505	IN80053	Num	19947	19954	8	WHT PSNS WITH INC ABV POVERTY
2506	IN80054	Num	19955	19962	8	WHT PSNS WITH INC BLW POVERTY
2507	IN80055	Num	19963	19970	8	BLK PSNS WITH INC ABV POVERTY
2508	IN80056	Num	19971	19978	8	BLK PSNS WITH INC BLW POVERTY
2509	IN80057	Num	19979	19986	8	HISP PSNS WITH INC ABV POVERTY
2510	IN80058	Num	19987	19994	8	HISP PSNS WITH INC BLW POVERTY
2511	IN80059	Num	19995	20002	8	PSNS WITH INC < 75% POVERTY LEVEL
2512	IN80060	Num	20003	20010	8	PSNS WITH INC 75-124% POVERTY LEVEL
2513	IN80061	Num	20011	20018	8	PSNS WITH INC 125-149% POVERTY LEVEL
2514	IN80062	Num	20019	20026	8	PSNS WITH INC 150-199% POVERTY LEVEL
2515	IN80063	Num	20027	20034	8	PSNS WITH INC > 200% POVERTY LEVEL
2516	IN90001	Num	20035	20042	8	MEDIAN HOUSEHOLD INCOME $
2517	IN90002	Num	20043	20050	8	MEDIAN FAMILY INCOME $
2518	IN90003	Num	20051	20058	8	MEAN HH INCOME: TOTAL $
2519	IN90004	Num	20059	20066	8	MEAN HH INCOME: WHT $
2520	IN90005	Num	20067	20074	8	MEAN HH INCOME: BLK $
2521	IN90006	Num	20075	20082	8	MEAN HH INCOME: HISP $
2522	IN90007	Num	20083	20090	8	PER CAPITA INCOME: TOTAL $
2523	IN90008	Num	20091	20098	8	PER CAPITA INCOME: WHT $
2524	IN90009	Num	20099	20106	8	PER CAPITA INCOME: BLK $
2525	IN90010	Num	20107	20114	8	PER CAPITA INCOME: HISP $
2526	IN90011	Num	20115	20122	8	HH INCOME: UNDER $5,000
2527	IN90012	Num	20123	20130	8	HH INCOME: $5,000-9,999
2528	IN90013	Num	20131	20138	8	HH INCOME: $10,000-12,499
2529	IN90014	Num	20139	20146	8	HH INCOME: $12,500-14,999
2530	IN90015	Num	20147	20154	8	HH INCOME: $15,000-17,499
2531	IN90016	Num	20155	20162	8	HH INCOME: $17,500-19,999
2532	IN90017	Num	20163	20170	8	HH INCOME: $20,000-22,499
2533	IN90018	Num	20171	20178	8	HH INCOME: $22,500-24,999
2534	IN90019	Num	20179	20186	8	HH INCOME: $25,000-27,499
2535	IN90020	Num	20187	20194	8	HH INCOME: $27,500-29,999
2536	IN90021	Num	20195	20202	8	HH INCOME: $30,000-32,499

2537	IN90022 Num	20203	20210	8	HH INCOME: $32,500-34,999
2538	IN90023 Num	20211	20218	8	HH INCOME: $35,000-37,499
2539	IN90024 Num	20219	20226	8	HH INCOME: $37,500-39,999
2540	IN90025 Num	20227	20234	8	HH INCOME: $40,000-42,499
2541	IN90026 Num	20235	20242	8	HH INCOME: $42,500-44,999
2542	IN90027 Num	20243	20250	8	HH INCOME: $45,000-47,499
2543	IN90028 Num	20251	20258	8	HH INCOME: $47,500-49,999
2544	IN90029 Num	20259	20266	8	HH INCOME: $50,000-54,999
2545	IN90030 Num	20267	20274	8	HH INCOME: $55,000-59,999
2546	IN90031 Num	20275	20282	8	HH INCOME: $60,000-74,999
2547	IN90032 Num	20283	20290	8	HH INCOME: $75,000-99,999
2548	IN90033 Num	20291	20298	8	HH INCOME: $100,000-124,999
2549	IN90034 Num	20299	20306	8	HH INCOME: $125,000-149,999
2550	IN90035 Num	20307	20314	8	HH INCOME: $150,000 OR MORE
2551	IN90036 Num	20315	20322	8	HH: WAGE OR SALARY INCOME
2552	IN90037 Num	20323	20330	8	HH: NONFARM SELF-EMPLOYMENT INCOME
2553	IN90038 Num	20331	20338	8	HH: FARM SELF-EMPLOYMENT INCOME
2554	IN90039 Num	20339	20346	8	HH: INTEREST, DIVIDEND, OR NET RENTAL
2555	IN90040 Num	20347	20354	8	HH: SOCIAL SECURITY INCOME
2556	IN90041 Num	20355	20362	8	HH: PUBLIC ASSISTANCE INCOME
2557	IN90042 Num	20363	20370	8	HH: RETIREMENT INCOME
2558	IN90043 Num	20371	20378	8	HH: OTHER INCOME
2559	IN90044 Num	20379	20386	8	FAMILY INCOME: UNDER $5,000
2560	IN90045 Num	20387	20394	8	FAMILY INCOME: $5,000-9,999
2561	IN90046 Num	20395	20402	8	FAMILY INCOME: $10,000-12,499
2562	IN90047 Num	20403	20410	8	FAMILY INCOME: $12,500-14,999
2563	IN90048 Num	20411	20418	8	FAMILY INCOME: $15,000-17,499
2564	IN90049 Num	20419	20426	8	FAMILY INCOME: $17,500-19,999
2565	IN90050 Num	20427	20434	8	FAMILY INCOME: $20,000-22,499
2566	IN90051 Num	20435	20442	8	FAMILY INCOME: $22,500-24,999
2567	IN90052 Num	20443	20450	8	FAMILY INCOME: $25,000-27,499
2568	IN90053 Num	20451	20458	8	FAMILY INCOME: $27,500-29,999
2569	IN90054 Num	20459	20466	8	FAMILY INCOME: $30,000-32,499
2570	IN90055 Num	20467	20474	8	FAMILY INCOME: $32,500-34,999
2571	IN90056 Num	20475	20482	8	FAMILY INCOME: $35,000-37,499
2572	IN90057 Num	20483	20490	8	FAMILY INCOME: $37,500-39,999
2573	IN90058 Num	20491	20498	8	FAMILY INCOME: $40,000-42,499
2574	IN90059 Num	20499	20506	8	FAMILY INCOME: $42,500-44,999
2575	IN90060 Num	20507	20514	8	FAMILY INCOME: $45,000-47,499
2576	IN90061 Num	20515	20522	8	FAMILY INCOME: $47,500-49,999
2577	IN90062 Num	20523	20530	8	FAMILY INCOME: $50,000-54,999

2578	IN90063 Num	20531	20538	8	FAMILY INCOME: $55,000-59,999
2579	IN90064 Num	20539	20546	8	FAMILY INCOME: $60,000-74,999
2580	IN90065 Num	20547	20554	8	FAMILY INCOME: $75,000-99,999
2581	IN90066 Num	20555	20562	8	FAMILY INCOME: $100,000-124,999
2582	IN90067 Num	20563	20570	8	FAMILY INCOME: $125,000-149,999
2583	IN90068 Num	20571	20578	8	FAMILY INCOME: $150,000 OR MORE
2584	IN90069 Num	20579	20586	8	PSNS BELOW POVERTY LEVEL IN 1989
2585	IN90070 Num	20587	20594	8	PSNS ABOVE POVERTY LEVEL IN 1989
2586	IN90071 Num	20595	20602	8	WHT PSNS BELOW POVERTY LEVEL IN 1989
2587	IN90072 Num	20603	20610	8	WHT PSNS ABOVE POVERTY LEVEL IN 1989
2588	IN90073 Num	20611	20618	8	BLK PSNS BELOW POVERTY LEVEL IN 1989
2589	IN90074 Num	20619	20626	8	BLK PSNS ABOVE POVERTY LEVEL IN 1989
2590	IN90075 Num	20627	20634	8	HISP PSNS BELOW POVERTY LEVEL IN 1989
2591	IN90076 Num	20635	20642	8	HISP PSNS ABOVE POVERTY LEVEL IN 1989
2592	IN90077 Num	20643	20650	8	FAMILIES BELOW POVERTY LEVEL IN 1989
2593	PIN69 Num	20651	20658	8	PER CAPITA PERSONAL INCOME (BEA) 1969 $
2594	PIN70 Num	20659	20666	8	PER CAPITA PERSONAL INCOME (BEA) 1970 $
2595	PIN71 Num	20667	20674	8	PER CAPITA PERSONAL INCOME (BEA) 1971 $
2596	PIN72 Num	20675	20682	8	PER CAPITA PERSONAL INCOME (BEA) 1972 $
2597	PIN73 Num	20683	20690	8	PER CAPITA PERSONAL INCOME (BEA) 1973 $
2598	PIN74 Num	20691	20698	8	PER CAPITA PERSONAL INCOME (BEA) 1974 $
2599	PIN75 Num	20699	20706	8	PER CAPITA PERSONAL INCOME (BEA) 1975 $
2600	PIN76 Num	20707	20714	8	PER CAPITA PERSONAL INCOME (BEA) 1976 $
2601	PIN77 Num	20715	20722	8	PER CAPITA PERSONAL INCOME (BEA) 1977 $
2602	PIN78 Num	20723	20730	8	PER CAPITA PERSONAL INCOME (BEA) 1978 $
2603	PIN79 Num	20731	20738	8	PER CAPITA PERSONAL INCOME (BEA) 1979 $
2604	PIN80 Num	20739	20746	8	PER CAPITA PERSONAL INCOME (BEA) 1980 $
2605	PIN81 Num	20747	20754	8	PER CAPITA PERSONAL INCOME (BEA) 1981 $
2606	PIN82 Num	20755	20762	8	PER CAPITA PERSONAL INCOME (BEA) 1982 $
2607	PIN83 Num	20763	20770	8	PER CAPITA PERSONAL INCOME (BEA) 1983 $
2608	PIN84 Num	20771	20778	8	PER CAPITA PERSONAL INCOME (BEA) 1984 $
2609	PIN85 Num	20779	20786	8	PER CAPITA PERSONAL INCOME (BEA) 1985 $
2610	PIN86 Num	20787	20794	8	PER CAPITA PERSONAL INCOME (BEA) 1986 $
2611	PIN87 Num	20795	20802	8	PER CAPITA PERSONAL INCOME (BEA) 1987 $
2612	PIN88 Num	20803	20810	8	PER CAPITA PERSONAL INCOME (BEA) 1988 $
2613	PIN89 Num	20811	20818	8	PER CAPITA PERSONAL INCOME (BEA) 1989 $
2614	PIN90 Num	20819	20826	8	PER CAPITA PERSONAL INCOME (BEA) 1990 $
2615	ES0139A Num	20827	20834	8	MANUF ESTAB 1939 {47.065}[7]

---

[7] From County and City Data Book 1947, column 65.

2616	ES0139B	Num	20835	20842	8	MANUF ESTAB 1939 {49.045}[8]
2617	ES0147	Num	20843	20850	8	MANUF ESTAB 1947
2618	ES0150	Num	20851	20858	8	MANUF ESTAB 1950
2619	ES0154	Num	20859	20866	8	MANUF ESTAB 1954
2620	ES0158	Num	20867	20874	8	MANUF ESTAB 1958
2621	ES0163	Num	20875	20882	8	MANUF ESTAB 1963
2622	ES0167	Num	20883	20890	8	MANUF ESTAB 1967
2623	ES0172	Num	20891	20898	8	MANUF ESTAB 1972
2624	ES0177	Num	20899	20906	8	MANUF ESTAB 1977
2625	ES0182	Num	20907	20914	8	MANUF ESTAB 1982
2626	ES0187	Num	20915	20922	8	MANUF ESTAB 1987
2627	ES0247A	Num	20923	20930	8	MANUF ESTAB EMPLOYEES 1947 {49.036}[9]
2628	ES0247B	Num	20931	20938	8	MANUF ESTAB EMPLOYEES 1947 {56.078}[10]
2629	ES0249	Num	20939	20946	8	MANUF ESTAB EMPLOYEES 1949
2630	ES0250	Num	20947	20954	8	MANUF ESTAB EMPLOYEES 1950
2631	ES0254	Num	20955	20962	8	MANUF ESTAB EMPLOYEES 1954
2632	ES0258	Num	20963	20970	8	MANUF ESTAB EMPLOYEES 1958
2633	ES0263	Num	20971	20978	8	MANUF ESTAB EMPLOYEES 1963
2634	ES0267	Num	20979	20986	8	MANUF ESTAB EMPLOYEES 1967
2635	ES0272	Num	20987	20994	8	MANUF ESTAB EMPLOYEES 1972
2636	ES0277	Num	20995	21002	8	MANUF ESTAB EMPLOYEES 1977
2637	ES0282	Num	21003	21010	8	MANUF ESTAB EMPLOYEES 1982
2638	ES0287	Num	21011	21018	8	MANUF ESTAB EMPLOYEES 1987
2639	ES0347A	Num	21019	21026	8	MANUF ESTAB WITH 20-49 EMPLOYEES 1947
2640	ES0347B	Num	21027	21034	8	MANUF ESTAB WITH 50-99 EMPLOYEES 1947
2641	ES0350A	Num	21035	21042	8	MANUF ESTAB WITH 20-49 EMPLOYEES 1950
2642	ES0350B	Num	21043	21050	8	MANUF ESTAB WITH 50-99 EMPLOYEES 1950
2643	ES0354	Num	21051	21058	8	MANUF ESTAB WITH 20-99 EMPLOYEES 1954
2644	ES0358	Num	21059	21066	8	MANUF ESTAB WITH 20-99 EMPLOYEES 1958
2645	ES0363	Num	21067	21074	8	MANUF ESTAB WITH 20-99 EMPLOYEES 1963
2646	ES0367	Num	21075	21082	8	MANUF ESTAB WITH 20-99 EMPLOYEES 1967(%)
2647	ES0372	Num	21083	21090	8	MANUF ESTAB WITH 20-99 EMPLOYEES 1972(%)
2648	ES0377	Num	21091	21098	8	MANUF ESTAB WITH 20-99 EMPLOYEES 1977
2649	ES0382	Num	21099	21106	8	MANUF ESTAB WITH 20-99 EMPLOYEES 1982
2650	ES0387	Num	21107	21114	8	MANUF ESTAB WITH 20-99 EMPLOYEES 1987
2651	ES0454	Num	21115	21122	8	MANUF ESTAB WITH 100- EMPLOYEES 1954

---

[8] From County and City Data Book 1949, column 45.

[9] From County and City Data Book 1949, column 36.

[10] From County and City Data Book 1956, column 78.

2652	ES0458	Num	21123	21130	8	MANUF ESTAB WITH 100- EMPLOYEES 1958
2653	ES0463	Num	21131	21138	8	MANUF ESTAB WITH 100- EMPLOYEES 1963
2654	ES0467	Num	21139	21146	8	MANUF ESTAB WITH 100- EMPLOYEES 1967(%)
2655	ES0472	Num	21147	21154	8	MANUF ESTAB WITH 100- EMPLOYEES 1972(%)
2656	ES0477	Num	21155	21162	8	MANUF ESTAB WITH 100- EMPLOYEES 1977
2657	ES0482	Num	21163	21170	8	MANUF ESTAB WITH 100- EMPLOYEES 1982
2658	ES0487	Num	21171	21178	8	MANUF ESTAB WITH 100- EMPLOYEES 1987
2659	ES0539	Num	21179	21186	8	RETAIL TRADE ESTAB 1939
2660	ES0548A	Num	21187	21194	8	RETAIL TRADE ESTAB 1948 {49.001}[11]
2661	ES0548B	Num	21195	21202	8	RETAIL TRADE ESTAB 1948 {56.048}[12]
2662	ES0554	Num	21203	21210	8	RETAIL TRADE ESTAB 1954
2663	ES0558	Num	21211	21218	8	RETAIL TRADE ESTAB 1958
2664	ES0563	Num	21219	21226	8	RETAIL TRADE ESTAB 1963
2665	ES0567	Num	21227	21234	8	RETAIL TRADE ESTAB 1967
2666	ES0572	Num	21235	21242	8	RETAIL TRADE ESTAB 1972
2667	ES0577	Num	21243	21250	8	RETAIL TRADE ESTAB 1977
2668	ES0582	Num	21251	21258	8	RETAIL TRADE ESTAB 1982
2669	ES0587	Num	21259	21266	8	RETAIL TRADE ESTAB 1987
2670	ES0639	Num	21267	21274	8	UNINC RETAIL TRADE ESTAB 1939
2671	ES0648	Num	21275	21282	8	UNINC RETAIL TRADE ESTAB 1948
2672	ES0654	Num	21283	21290	8	UNINC RETAIL TRADE ESTAB 1954
2673	ES0658	Num	21291	21298	8	UNINC RETAIL TRADE ESTAB 1958
2674	ES0663	Num	21299	21306	8	UNINC RETAIL TRADE ESTAB 1963
2675	ES0667	Num	21307	21314	8	UNINC RETAIL TRADE ESTAB 1967
2676	ES0672	Num	21315	21322	8	UNINC RETAIL TRADE ESTAB 1972
2677	ES0677	Num	21323	21330	8	UNINC RETAIL TRADE ESTAB 1977
2678	ES0682	Num	21331	21338	8	UNINC RETAIL TRADE ESTAB 1982
2679	ES0687	Num	21339	21346	8	UNINC RETAIL TRADE ESTAB W/ PAYROLL 1987
2680	ES0739	Num	21347	21354	8	RETAIL TRADE ESTAB PAID EMPLOYEES 1939
2681	ES0748	Num	21355	21362	8	RETAIL TRADE ESTAB PAID EMPLOYEES 1948
2682	ES0754	Num	21363	21370	8	RETAIL TRADE ESTAB PAID EMPLOYEES 1954
2683	ES0758	Num	21371	21378	8	RETAIL TRADE ESTAB PAID EMPLOYEES 1958
2684	ES0763	Num	21379	21386	8	RETAIL TRADE ESTAB PAID EMPLOYEES 1963
2685	ES0767	Num	21387	21394	8	RETAIL TRADE ESTAB PAID EMPLOYEES 1967
2686	ES0772	Num	21395	21402	8	RETAIL TRADE ESTAB PAID EMPLOYEES 1972
2687	ES0777	Num	21403	21410	8	RETAIL TRADE ESTAB PAID EMPLOYEES 1977
2688	ES0782	Num	21411	21418	8	RETAIL TRADE ESTAB PAID EMPLOYEES 1982

---

[11] From County and City Data Book 1949, column 1.

[12] From County and City Data Book 1956, column 48.

2689	ES0787	Num	21419	21426	8	RETAIL TRADE ESTAB PAID EMPLOYEES 1987
2690	ES0854	Num	21427	21434	8	RETAIL TRADE: GEN MERCH 1954
2691	ES0858	Num	21435	21442	8	RETAIL TRADE: GEN MERCH 1958
2692	ES0863	Num	21443	21450	8	RETAIL TRADE: GEN MERCH 1963
2693	ES0872	Num	21451	21458	8	RETAIL TRADE: GEN MERCH 1972
2694	ES0877	Num	21459	21466	8	RETAIL TRADE: GEN MERCH 1977
2695	ES0882	Num	21467	21474	8	RETAIL TRADE: GEN MERCH W/ PAYROLL 1982
2696	ES0887	Num	21475	21482	8	RETAIL TRADE: GEN MERCH W/ PAYROLL 1987
2697	ES0948	Num	21483	21490	8	RETAIL TRADE: FOOD STORES 1948
2698	ES0954	Num	21491	21498	8	RETAIL TRADE: FOOD STORES 1954
2699	ES0958	Num	21499	21506	8	RETAIL TRADE: FOOD STORES 1958
2700	ES0963	Num	21507	21514	8	RETAIL TRADE: FOOD STORES 1963
2701	ES0972	Num	21515	21522	8	RETAIL TRADE: FOOD STORES 1972
2702	ES0977	Num	21523	21530	8	RETAIL TRADE: FOOD STORES 1977
2703	ES0982	Num	21531	21538	8	RETAIL TRADE: FOOD STORES 1982
2704	ES0987	Num	21539	21546	8	RETAIL TRADE: FOOD STORES 1987
2705	ES1054	Num	21547	21554	8	RETAIL TRADE: AUTOMOTIVE DEALERS 1954
2706	ES1058	Num	21555	21562	8	RETAIL TRADE: AUTOMOTIVE DEALERS 1958
2707	ES1063	Num	21563	21570	8	RETAIL TRADE: AUTOMOTIVE DEALERS 1963
2708	ES1072	Num	21571	21578	8	RETAIL TRADE: AUTOMOTIVE DEALERS 1972
2709	ES1077	Num	21579	21586	8	RETAIL TRADE: AUTOMOTIVE DEALERS 1977
2710	ES1082	Num	21587	21594	8	RETAIL TRADE: AUTOMOTIVE DEALERS 1982
2711	ES1087	Num	21595	21602	8	RETAIL TRADE: AUTOMOTIVE DEALERS 1987
2712	ES1148	Num	21603	21610	8	RETAIL TRADE: EATING AND DRINKING 1948
2713	ES1154	Num	21611	21618	8	RETAIL TRADE: EATING AND DRINKING 1954
2714	ES1172	Num	21619	21626	8	RETAIL TRADE: EATING AND DRINKING 1972
2715	ES1177	Num	21627	21634	8	RETAIL TRADE: EATING AND DRINKING 1977
2716	ES1182	Num	21635	21642	8	RETAIL TRADE: EATING AND DRINKING 1982
2717	ES1187	Num	21643	21650	8	RETAIL TRADE: EATING AND DRINKING 1987
2718	ES1254	Num	21651	21658	8	RETAIL TRADE: GAS SERVICE STATIONS 1954
2719	ES1272	Num	21659	21666	8	RETAIL TRADE: GAS SERVICE STATIONS 1972
2720	ES1277	Num	21667	21674	8	RETAIL TRADE: GAS SERVICE STATIONS 1977
2721	ES1282	Num	21675	21682	8	RETAIL TRADE: GAS SERVICE STATIONS 1982
2722	ES1287	Num	21683	21690	8	RETAIL TRADE: GAS SERVICE STATIONS 1987
2723	ES1354	Num	21691	21698	8	RETAIL TRADE: HOME FURNISHINGS 1954
2724	ES1372	Num	21699	21706	8	RETAIL TRADE: HOME FURNISHINGS 1972
2725	ES1377	Num	21707	21714	8	RETAIL TRADE: HOME FURNISHINGS 1977
2726	ES1382	Num	21715	21722	8	RETAIL TRADE: HOME FURNISHINGS 1982
2727	ES1387	Num	21723	21730	8	RETAIL TRADE: HOME FURNISHINGS 1987
2728	ES1448	Num	21731	21738	8	RETAIL TRADE: APPAREL 1948
2729	ES1454	Num	21739	21746	8	RETAIL TRADE: APPAREL 1954

2730	ES1477	Num	21747	21754	8	RETAIL TRADE: APPAREL 1977
2731	ES1482	Num	21755	21762	8	RETAIL TRADE: APPAREL 1982
2732	ES1487	Num	21763	21770	8	RETAIL TRADE: APPAREL 1987
2733	ES1539	Num	21771	21778	8	SERVICE ESTAB 1939
2734	ES1554	Num	21779	21786	8	SERVICE ESTAB 1954
2735	ES1558	Num	21787	21794	8	SERVICE ESTAB 1958
2736	ES1563	Num	21795	21802	8	SERVICE ESTAB 1963
2737	ES1567	Num	21803	21810	8	SERVICE ESTAB 1967
2738	ES1572	Num	21811	21818	8	SERVICE ESTAB 1972
2739	ES1577	Num	21819	21826	8	SERVICE ESTAB 1977
2740	ES1658	Num	21827	21834	8	SERVICE ESTAB WITH PAYROLL 1958
2741	ES1663	Num	21835	21842	8	SERVICE ESTAB WITH PAYROLL 1963
2742	ES1677	Num	21843	21850	8	SERVICE ESTAB WITH PAYROLL 1977
2743	ES1682	Num	21851	21858	8	SERVICE ESTAB WITH PAYROLL 1982
2744	ES1687	Num	21859	21866	8	SERVICE ESTAB WITH PAYROLL 1987
2745	ES1739	Num	21867	21874	8	SERVICE ESTAB - PAID EMPLOYEES 1939
2746	ES1754	Num	21875	21882	8	SERVICE ESTAB - PAID EMPLOYEES 1954
2747	ES1758	Num	21883	21890	8	SERVICE ESTAB - PAID EMPLOYEES 1958
2748	ES1763	Num	21891	21898	8	SERVICE ESTAB - PAID EMPLOYEES 1963
2749	ES1767	Num	21899	21906	8	SERVICE ESTAB - PAID EMPLOYEES 1967
2750	ES1772	Num	21907	21914	8	SERVICE ESTAB - PAID EMPLOYEES 1972
2751	ES1777	Num	21915	21922	8	SERVICE ESTAB - PAID EMPLOYEES 1977
2752	ES1782	Num	21923	21930	8	SERVICE ESTAB - PAID EMPLOYEES 1982
2753	ES1787	Num	21931	21938	8	SERVICE ESTAB - PAID EMPLOYEES 1987
2754	ES1839	Num	21939	21946	8	WHOLESALE TRADE ESTAB 1939
2755	ES1848	Num	21947	21954	8	WHOLESALE TRADE ESTAB 1948
2756	ES1854	Num	21955	21962	8	WHOLESALE TRADE ESTAB 1954
2757	ES1858	Num	21963	21970	8	WHOLESALE TRADE ESTAB 1958
2758	ES1863	Num	21971	21978	8	WHOLESALE TRADE ESTAB 1963
2759	ES1867	Num	21979	21986	8	WHOLESALE TRADE ESTAB 1967
2760	ES1872	Num	21987	21994	8	WHOLESALE TRADE ESTAB 1972
2761	ES1877	Num	21995	22002	8	WHOLESALE TRADE ESTAB 1977
2762	ES1882	Num	22003	22010	8	WHOLESALE TRADE ESTAB 1982
2763	ES1887	Num	22011	22018	8	WHOLESALE TRADE ESTAB 1987
2764	ES1948	Num	22019	22026	8	WHOLESALE TRADE - PAID EMPLOYEES 1948
2765	ES1954	Num	22027	22034	8	WHOLESALE TRADE - PAID EMPLOYEES 1954
2766	ES1958	Num	22035	22042	8	WHOLESALE TRADE - PAID EMPLOYEES 1958
2767	ES1963	Num	22043	22050	8	WHOLESALE TRADE - PAID EMPLOYEES 1963
2768	ES1967	Num	22051	22058	8	WHOLESALE TRADE - PAID EMPLOYEES 1967
2769	ES1972	Num	22059	22066	8	WHOLESALE TRADE - PAID EMPLOYEES 1972
2770	ES1977	Num	22067	22074	8	WHOLESALE TRADE - PAID EMPLOYEES 1977

2771	ES1982	Num	22075	22082	8	WHOLESALE TRADE - PAID EMPLOYEES 1982
2772	ES1987	Num	22083	22090	8	WHOLESALE TRADE - PAID EMPLOYEES 1987
2773	ES2040	Num	22091	22098	8	FARMS - NUMBER 1940
2774	ES2045	Num	22099	22106	8	FARMS - NUMBER 1945
2775	ES2050	Num	22107	22114	8	FARMS - NUMBER 1950
2776	ES2054	Num	22115	22122	8	FARMS - NUMBER 1954
2777	ES2059	Num	22123	22130	8	FARMS - NUMBER 1959
2778	ES2064	Num	22131	22138	8	FARMS - NUMBER 1964
2779	ES2069	Num	22139	22146	8	FARMS - NUMBER 1969
2780	ES2074	Num	22147	22154	8	FARMS - NUMBER 1974
2781	ES2078	Num	22155	22162	8	FARMS - NUMBER 1978
2782	ES2082	Num	22163	22170	8	FARMS - NUMBER 1982
2783	ES2087	Num	22171	22178	8	FARMS - NUMBER 1987
2784	ES2145	Num	22179	22186	8	LAND IN FARMS 1000 ACRES 1945
2785	ES2150	Num	22187	22194	8	LAND IN FARMS 1000 ACRES 1950
2786	ES2154	Num	22195	22202	8	LAND IN FARMS 1000 ACRES 1954
2787	ES2159	Num	22203	22210	8	LAND IN FARMS 1000 ACRES 1959
2788	ES2164	Num	22211	22218	8	LAND IN FARMS 1000 ACRES 1964
2789	ES2169	Num	22219	22226	8	LAND IN FARMS 1000 ACRES 1969
2790	ES2174	Num	22227	22234	8	LAND IN FARMS 1000 ACRES 1974
2791	ES2178	Num	22235	22242	8	LAND IN FARMS 1978 (ACRES)
2792	ES2182	Num	22243	22250	8	LAND IN FARMS 1982 (ACRES)
2793	ES2187	Num	22251	22258	8	LAND IN FARMS 1987 (ACRES)
2794	ES2254	Num	22259	22266	8	AVERAGE SIZE OF FARM 1954 (ACRES)
2795	ES2259	Num	22267	22274	8	AVERAGE SIZE OF FARM 1959 (ACRES)
2796	ES2264	Num	22275	22282	8	AVERAGE SIZE OF FARM 1964 (ACRES)
2797	ES2269	Num	22283	22290	8	AVERAGE SIZE OF FARM 1969 (ACRES)
2798	ES2274	Num	22291	22298	8	AVERAGE SIZE OF FARM 1974 (ACRES)
2799	ES2278	Num	22299	22306	8	AVERAGE SIZE OF FARM 1978 (ACRES)
2800	ES2282	Num	22307	22314	8	AVERAGE SIZE OF FARM 1982 (ACRES)
2801	ES2287	Num	22315	22322	8	AVERAGE SIZE OF FARM 1987 (ACRES)
2802	ES2354	Num	22323	22330	8	FARMS BY SIZE - UNDER 10 ACRES 1954
2803	ES2359	Num	22331	22338	8	FARMS BY SIZE - UNDER 10 ACRES 1959
2804	ES2364	Num	22339	22346	8	FARMS BY SIZE - UNDER 10 ACRES 1964
2805	ES2369	Num	22347	22354	8	FARMS BY SIZE - UNDER 10 ACRES 1969
2806	ES2374	Num	22355	22362	8	FARMS BY SIZE - UNDER 10 ACRES 1974
2807	ES2378	Num	22363	22370	8	FARMS BY SIZE - UNDER 10 ACRES 1978
2808	ES2382	Num	22371	22378	8	FARMS BY SIZE - UNDER 10 ACRES 1982
2809	ES2387	Num	22379	22386	8	FARMS BY SIZE - UNDER 10 ACRES 1987
2810	ES2450	Num	22387	22394	8	VALUE OF FARM PROD SOLD $1000 1950
2811	ES2454	Num	22395	22402	8	VALUE OF FARM PROD SOLD $1000 1954

2812	ES2459 Num	22403	22410	8	VALUE OF FARM PROD SOLD $1000 1959
2813	ES2464 Num	22411	22418	8	VALUE OF FARM PROD SOLD $1000 1964
2814	ES2478 Num	22419	22426	8	VALUE OF FARM PROD SOLD 1978
2815	ES2482 Num	22427	22434	8	VALUE OF FARM PROD SOLD 1982
2816	ES2487 Num	22435	22442	8	VALUE OF FARM PROD SOLD 1987
2817	GF57002 Num	22443	22450	8	REV: TOTAL REV $1000
2818	GF57003 Num	22451	22458	8	REV: TOTAL GENERAL REV $1000
2819	GF57004 Num	22459	22466	8	REV: TOTAL INT GOVT REV $1000
2820	GF57006 Num	22467	22474	8	REV: INT GOVT REV: STATE $1000
2821	GF57007 Num	22475	22482	8	REV: TOT GEN. REV FROM OWN SOURCES $1000
2822	GF57008 Num	22483	22490	8	REV: TOTAL TAXES $1000
2823	GF57009 Num	22491	22498	8	REV: PROPERTY TAXES $1000
2824	GF57010 Num	22499	22506	8	REV: TOTAL CHARGES AND MISC $1000
2825	GF57012 Num	22507	22514	8	REV: UTILITY $1000
2826	GF57013 Num	22515	22522	8	REV: INSUR TRUST REV $1000
2827	GF57014 Num	22523	22530	8	EXP: TOTAL EXP $1000
2828	GF57015 Num	22531	22538	8	EXP: INTER GOV EXP $1000
2829	GF57016 Num	22539	22546	8	EXP: TOTAL DIRECT EXP $1000
2830	GF57017 Num	22547	22554	8	EXP: TOTAL DIRECT GENERAL EXP $1000
2831	GF57019 Num	22555	22562	8	EXP: EDUCATION $1000
2832	GF57021 Num	22563	22570	8	EXP: PUBLIC WELFARE $1000
2833	GF57022 Num	22571	22578	8	EXP: HOSPITALS $1000
2834	GF57023 Num	22579	22586	8	EXP: HEALTH OTHER THAN HOSPITALS $1000
2835	GF57024 Num	22587	22594	8	EXP: HIGHWAYS $1000
2836	GF57026 Num	22595	22602	8	EXP: POLICE PROTECTION $1000
2837	GF57027 Num	22603	22610	8	EXP: FIRE PROTECTION $1000
2838	GF57029 Num	22611	22618	8	EXP: PROTECTIVE INSPECTION $1000
2839	GF57030 Num	22619	22626	8	EXP: NATURAL RESSOURCES $1000
2840	GF57031 Num	22627	22634	8	EXP: PARKS & RECREATION $1000
2841	GF57033 Num	22635	22642	8	EXP: SEWERAGE $1000
2842	GF57034 Num	22643	22650	8	EXP:SANITATION OTHER THAN SEWERAGE $1000
2843	GF57037 Num	22651	22658	8	EXP: INTEREST ON GENERAL DEBT $1000
2844	GF57038 Num	22659	22666	8	EXP: OTHER GENERAL EXP $1000
2845	GF57039 Num	22667	22674	8	EXP: UTILITY
2846	GF57040 Num	22675	22682	8	EXP: INSUR TRUST EXP $1000
2847	GF57041 Num	22683	22690	8	TOTAL DEBT $1000
2848	GF57042 Num	22691	22698	8	TOTAL LONG-TERM DEBT $1000
2849	GF57045 Num	22699	22706	8	CASH & SECURITIES $1000
2850	GF62003 Num	22707	22714	8	REV: TOTAL GENERAL REV $1000
2851	GF62004 Num	22715	22722	8	REV: TOTAL INT GOVT REV $1000

2852	GF62006 Num	22723	22730	8	REV: INT GOVT REV: STATE $1000
2853	GF62007 Num	22731	22738	8	REV: TOT GEN. REV FROM OWN SOURCES $1000
2854	GF62008 Num	22739	22746	8	REV: TOTAL TAXES $1000
2855	GF62009 Num	22747	22754	8	REV: PROPERTY TAXES $1000
2856	GF62010 Num	22755	22762	8	REV: TOTAL CHARGES AND MISC $1000
2857	GF62012 Num	22763	22770	8	REV: UTILITY (WATER ONLY) $1000
2858	GF62017 Num	22771	22778	8	EXP: TOTAL DIRECT GENERAL EXP $1000
2859	GF62019 Num	22779	22786	8	EXP: EDUCATION $1000
2860	GF62020 Num	22787	22794	8	EXP: LIBRARIES $1000
2861	GF62021 Num	22795	22802	8	EXP: PUBLIC WELFARE $1000
2862	GF62022 Num	22803	22810	8	EXP: HOSPITALS & HEALTH $1000
2863	GF62024 Num	22811	22818	8	EXP: HIGHWAYS $1000
2864	GF62026 Num	22819	22826	8	EXP: POLICE PROTECTION $1000
2865	GF62027 Num	22827	22834	8	EXP: FIRE PROTECTION $1000
2866	GF62028 Num	22835	22842	8	EXP: CORRECTION $1000
2867	GF62029 Num	22843	22850	8	EXP: PROTECTIVE INSPECTION $1000
2868	GF62030 Num	22851	22858	8	EXP: NATURAL RESSOURCES $1000
2869	GF62031 Num	22859	22866	8	EXP: PARKS & RECREATION $1000
2870	GF62032 Num	22867	22874	8	EXP: HOUSING & URBAN RENEWAL $1000
2871	GF62033 Num	22875	22882	8	EXP: SEWERAGE $1000
2872	GF62034 Num	22883	22890	8	EXP:SANITATION OTHER THAN SEWERAGE $1000
2873	GF62035 Num	22891	22898	8	EXP: FINANCIL ADMINISTRATION $1000
2874	GF62036 Num	22899	22906	8	EXP: OTHER GOVT ADMINI $1000
2875	GF62037 Num	22907	22914	8	EXP: INTEREST ON GENERAL DEBT $1000
2876	GF62038 Num	22915	22922	8	EXP: OTHER GENERAL EXP $1000
2877	GF62039 Num	22923	22930	8	EXP: UTILITY (WATER ONLY) $1000
2878	GF62041 Num	22931	22938	8	TOTAL DEBT $1000
2879	GF62042 Num	22939	22946	8	TOTAL LONG-TERM DEBT $1000
2880	GF62043 Num	22947	22954	8	TOTAL LONG-TERM DEBT-EDUCATION $1000
2881	GF72002 Num	22955	22962	8	REV: TOTAL REV $1000
2882	GF72003 Num	22963	22970	8	REV: TOTAL GENERAL REV $1000
2883	GF72004 Num	22971	22978	8	REV: TOTAL INT GOVT REV $1000
2884	GF72005 Num	22979	22986	8	REV: INT GOVT REV: FED GOVT $1000
2885	GF72006 Num	22987	22994	8	REV: INT GOVT REV: STATE $1000
2886	GF72007 Num	22995	23002	8	REV: TOT GEN. REV FROM OWN SOURCES $1000
2887	GF72008 Num	23003	23010	8	REV: TOTAL TAXES $1000
2888	GF72009 Num	23011	23018	8	REV: PROPERTY TAXES $1000
2889	GF72010 Num	23019	23026	8	REV: TOTAL CHARGES AND MISC $1000
2890	GF72011 Num	23027	23034	8	REV: CURRENT CHARGES $1000
2891	GF72012 Num	23035	23042	8	REV: UTILITY $1000

2892	GF72013 Num	23043	23050	8	REV: LIQUOR & INSUR TRUST REV $1000
2893	GF72014 Num	23051	23058	8	EXP: TOTAL EXP $1000
2894	GF72015 Num	23059	23066	8	EXP: INTER GOV EXP $1000
2895	GF72016 Num	23067	23074	8	EXP: TOTAL DIRECT EXP $1000
2896	GF72017 Num	23075	23082	8	EXP: TOTAL DIRECT GENERAL EXP $1000
2897	GF72019 Num	23083	23090	8	EXP: EDUCATION $1000
2898	GF72020 Num	23091	23098	8	EXP: LIBRARIES $1000
2899	GF72021 Num	23099	23106	8	EXP: PUBLIC WELFARE $1000
2900	GF72022 Num	23107	23114	8	EXP: HOSPITALS $1000
2901	GF72023 Num	23115	23122	8	EXP: HEALTH OTHER THAN HOSPITALS $1000
2902	GF72024 Num	23123	23130	8	EXP: HIGHWAYS $1000
2903	GF72025 Num	23131	23138	8	EXP: OTHER TRANSPORTATION $1000
2904	GF72026 Num	23139	23146	8	EXP: POLICE PROTECTION $1000
2905	GF72027 Num	23147	23154	8	EXP: FIRE PROTECTION $1000
2906	GF72028 Num	23155	23162	8	EXP: CORRECTION $1000
2907	GF72029 Num	23163	23170	8	EXP: PROTECTIVE INSPECTION $1000
2908	GF72030 Num	23171	23178	8	EXP: NATURAL RESSOURCES $1000
2909	GF72031 Num	23179	23186	8	EXP: PARKS & RECREATION $1000
2910	GF72032 Num	23187	23194	8	EXP: HOUSING & URBAN RENEWAL $1000
2911	GF72033 Num	23195	23202	8	EXP: SEWERAGE $1000
2912	GF72034 Num	23203	23210	8	EXP:SANITATION OTHER THAN SEWERAGE $1000
2913	GF72035 Num	23211	23218	8	EXP: FINANCIL ADMINISTRATION $1000
2914	GF72036 Num	23219	23226	8	EXP: OTHER GOVT ADMINI $1000
2915	GF72037 Num	23227	23234	8	EXP: INTEREST ON GENERAL DEBT $1000
2916	GF72038 Num	23235	23242	8	EXP: OTHER GENERAL EXP $1000
2917	GF72039 Num	23243	23250	8	EXP: UTILITY $1000
2918	GF72040 Num	23251	23258	8	EXP: LIQUOR & INSUR TRUST EXP $1000
2919	GF72041 Num	23259	23266	8	TOTAL DEBT $1000
2920	GF72042 Num	23267	23274	8	TOTAL LONG-TERM DEBT $1000
2921	GF72043 Num	23275	23282	8	TOTAL LONG-TERM DEBT-EDUCATION $1000
2922	GF77002 Num	23283	23290	8	REV: TOTAL REV $1000
2923	GF77003 Num	23291	23298	8	REV: TOTAL GENERAL REV $1000
2924	GF77004 Num	23299	23306	8	REV: TOTAL INT GOVT REV $1000
2925	GF77005 Num	23307	23314	8	REV: INT GOVT REV: FED GOVT $1000
2926	GF77006 Num	23315	23322	8	REV: INT GOVT REV: STATE $1000
2927	GF77007 Num	23323	23330	8	REV: TOT GEN. REV FROM OWN SOURCES $1000
2928	GF77008 Num	23331	23338	8	REV: TOTAL TAXES $1000
2929	GF77009 Num	23339	23346	8	REV: PROPERTY TAXES $1000
2930	GF77010 Num	23347	23354	8	REV: TOTAL CHARGES AND MISC $1000
2931	GF77011 Num	23355	23362	8	REV: CURRENT CHARGES $1000

2932	GF77012 Num	23363	23370	8	REV: UTILITY $1000
2933	GF77013 Num	23371	23378	8	REV: LIQUOR & INSUR TRUST REV $1000
2934	GF77014 Num	23379	23386	8	EXP: TOTAL EXP $1000
2935	GF77015 Num	23387	23394	8	EXP: INTER GOV EXP $1000
2936	GF77016 Num	23395	23402	8	EXP: TOTAL DIRECT EXP $1000
2937	GF77017 Num	23403	23410	8	EXP: TOTAL DIRECT GENERAL EXP $1000
2938	GF77019 Num	23411	23418	8	EXP: EDUCATION $1000
2939	GF77020 Num	23419	23426	8	EXP: LIBRARIES $1000
2940	GF77021 Num	23427	23434	8	EXP: PUBLIC WELFARE $1000
2941	GF77022 Num	23435	23442	8	EXP: HOSPITALS $1000
2942	GF77023 Num	23443	23450	8	EXP: HEALTH OTHER THAN HOSPITALS $1000
2943	GF77024 Num	23451	23458	8	EXP: HIGHWAYS $1000
2944	GF77025 Num	23459	23466	8	EXP: OTHER TRANSPORTATION $1000
2945	GF77026 Num	23467	23474	8	EXP: POLICE PROTECTION $1000
2946	GF77027 Num	23475	23482	8	EXP: FIRE PROTECTION $1000
2947	GF77028 Num	23483	23490	8	EXP: CORRECTION $1000
2948	GF77030 Num	23491	23498	8	EXP: NATURAL RESSOURCES $1000
2949	GF77031 Num	23499	23506	8	EXP: PARKS & RECREATION $1000
2950	GF77032 Num	23507	23514	8	EXP: HOUSING & URBAN RENEWAL $1000
2951	GF77033 Num	23515	23522	8	EXP: SEWERAGE $1000
2952	GF77034 Num	23523	23530	8	EXP:SANITATION OTHER THAN SEWERAGE $1000
2953	GF77035 Num	23531	23538	8	EXP: FINANCIL ADMINISTRATION $1000
2954	GF77036 Num	23539	23546	8	EXP: OTHER GOVT ADMINI $1000
2955	GF77037 Num	23547	23554	8	EXP: INTEREST ON GENERAL DEBT $1000
2956	GF77038 Num	23555	23562	8	EXP:OTHR GEN EXP (INCL PROTEC INSP)$1000
2957	GF77039 Num	23563	23570	8	EXP: UTILITY $1000
2958	GF77040 Num	23571	23578	8	EXP: LIQUOR & INSUR TRUST EXP $1000
2959	GF77041 Num	23579	23586	8	TOTAL DEBT $1000
2960	GF77042 Num	23587	23594	8	TOTAL LONG-TERM DEBT $1000
2961	GF77043 Num	23595	23602	8	TOTAL LONG-TERM DEBT-EDUCATION $1000
2962	GF82002 Num	23603	23610	8	REV: TOTAL REV $1000
2963	GF82003 Num	23611	23618	8	REV: TOTAL GENERAL REV $1000
2964	GF82004 Num	23619	23626	8	REV: TOTAL INT GOVT REV $1000
2965	GF82005 Num	23627	23634	8	REV: INT GOVT REV: FED GOVT $1000
2966	GF82006 Num	23635	23642	8	REV: INT GOVT REV: STATE $1000
2967	GF82007 Num	23643	23650	8	REV: TOT GEN. REV FROM OWN SOURCES $1000
2968	GF82008 Num	23651	23658	8	REV: TOTAL TAXES $1000
2969	GF82009 Num	23659	23666	8	REV: PROPERTY TAXES $1000
2970	GF82010 Num	23667	23674	8	REV: TOTAL CHARGES AND MISC $1000
2971	GF82011 Num	23675	23682	8	REV: CURRENT CHARGES $1000

2972	GF82012 Num	23683	23690	8	REV: UTILITY $1000
2973	GF82013 Num	23691	23698	8	REV: LIQUOR & INSUR TRUST REV $1000
2974	GF82014 Num	23699	23706	8	EXP: TOTAL EXP $1000
2975	GF82015 Num	23707	23714	8	EXP: INTER GOV EXP $1000
2976	GF82016 Num	23715	23722	8	EXP: TOTAL DIRECT EXP $1000
2977	GF82017 Num	23723	23730	8	EXP: TOTAL DIRECT GENERAL EXP $1000
2978	GF82019 Num	23731	23738	8	EXP: EDUCATION $1000
2979	GF82020 Num	23739	23746	8	EXP: LIBRARIES $1000
2980	GF82021 Num	23747	23754	8	EXP: PUBLIC WELFARE $1000
2981	GF82022 Num	23755	23762	8	EXP: HOSPITALS $1000
2982	GF82023 Num	23763	23770	8	EXP: HEALTH OTHER THAN HOSPITALS $1000
2983	GF82024 Num	23771	23778	8	EXP: HIGHWAYS $1000
2984	GF82025 Num	23779	23786	8	EXP: OTHER TRANSPORTATION $1000
2985	GF82026 Num	23787	23794	8	EXP: POLICE PROTECTION $1000
2986	GF82027 Num	23795	23802	8	EXP: FIRE PROTECTION $1000
2987	GF82028 Num	23803	23810	8	EXP: CORRECTION $1000
2988	GF82030 Num	23811	23818	8	EXP: NATURAL RESSOURCES $1000
2989	GF82031 Num	23819	23826	8	EXP: PARKS & RECREATION $1000
2990	GF82032 Num	23827	23834	8	EXP: HOUSING & URBAN RENEWAL $1000
2991	GF82033 Num	23835	23842	8	EXP: SEWERAGE $1000
2992	GF82034 Num	23843	23850	8	EXP:SANITATION OTHER THAN SEWERAGE $1000
2993	GF82035 Num	23851	23858	8	EXP: FINANCIL ADMINISTRATION $1000
2994	GF82036 Num	23859	23866	8	EXP: OTHER GOVT ADMINI $1000
2995	GF82037 Num	23867	23874	8	EXP: INTEREST ON GENERAL DEBT $1000
2996	GF82038 Num	23875	23882	8	EXP: OTHER GENERAL EXP $1000
2997	GF82039 Num	23883	23890	8	EXP: UTILITY $1000
2998	GF82040 Num	23891	23898	8	EXP: LIQUOR & INSUR TRUST EXP $1000
2999	GF82041 Num	23899	23906	8	TOTAL DEBT $1000
3000	GF82042 Num	23907	23914	8	TOTAL LONG-TERM DEBT $1000
3001	GF82043 Num	23915	23922	8	TOTAL LONG-TERM DEBT-EDUCATION $1000
3002	GF82044 Num	23923	23930	8	TOTAL LONG-TERM DEBT-UTILITY $1000
3003	GF82045 Num	23931	23938	8	CASH & SECURITIES $1000
3004	GF87001 Num	23939	23946	8	POPULATION
3005	GF87002 Num	23947	23954	8	REV: TOTAL REV $1000
3006	GF87003 Num	23955	23962	8	REV: TOTAL GENERAL REV $1000
3007	GF87004 Num	23963	23970	8	REV: TOTAL INT GOVT REV $1000
3008	GF87005 Num	23971	23978	8	REV: INT GOVT REV: FED GOVT $1000
3009	GF87006 Num	23979	23986	8	REV: INT GOVT REV: STATE $1000
3010	GF87007 Num	23987	23994	8	REV: TOT GEN. REV FROM OWN SOURCES $1000
3011	GF87008 Num	23995	24002	8	REV: TOTAL TAXES $1000

3012	GF87009	Num	24003	24010	8	REV: TOTAL TAXES: PROPERTY $1000
3013	GF87010	Num	24011	24018	8	REV: TOTAL CHARGES AND MISC $1000
3014	GF87011	Num	24019	24026	8	REV: CURRENT CHARGES $1000
3015	GF87012	Num	24027	24034	8	REV: UTILITY $1000
3016	GF87013	Num	24035	24042	8	REV: LIQUOR & INSUR TRUST REV $1000
3017	GF87014	Num	24043	24050	8	EXP: TOTAL EXP $1000
3018	GF87015	Num	24051	24058	8	EXP: INTER GOV EXP $1000
3019	GF87016	Num	24059	24066	8	EXP: TOTAL DIRECT EXP $1000
3020	GF87017	Num	24067	24074	8	EXP: TOTAL DIRECT GENERAL EXP $1000
3021	GF87019	Num	24075	24082	8	EXP: EDUCATION $1000
3022	GF87020	Num	24083	24090	8	EXP: LIBRARIES $1000
3023	GF87021	Num	24091	24098	8	EXP: PUBLIC WELFARE $1000
3024	GF87022	Num	24099	24106	8	EXP: HOSPITALS $1000
3025	GF87023	Num	24107	24114	8	EXP: HEALTH OTHER THAN HOSPITALS $1000
3026	GF87024	Num	24115	24122	8	EXP: HIGHWAYS $1000
3027	GF87025	Num	24123	24130	8	EXP: OTHER TRANSPORTATION $1000
3028	GF87026	Num	24131	24138	8	EXP: POLICE PROTECTION $1000
3029	GF87027	Num	24139	24146	8	EXP: FIRE PROTECTION $1000
3030	GF87028	Num	24147	24154	8	EXP: CORRECTION $1000
3031	GF87029	Num	24155	24162	8	EXP: PROTECTIVE INSPECTION $1000
3032	GF87030	Num	24163	24170	8	EXP: NATURAL RESSOURCES $1000
3033	GF87031	Num	24171	24178	8	EXP: PARKS & RECREATION $1000
3034	GF87032	Num	24179	24186	8	EXP: HOUSING & URBAN RENEWAL $1000
3035	GF87033	Num	24187	24194	8	EXP: SEWERAGE $1000
3036	GF87034	Num	24195	24202	8	EXP:SANITATION OTHER THAN SEWERAGE $1000
3037	GF87035	Num	24203	24210	8	EXP: FINANCIL ADMINISTRATION $1000
3038	GF87036	Num	24211	24218	8	EXP: OTHER GOVT ADMINI $1000
3039	GF87037	Num	24219	24226	8	EXP: INTEREST ON GENERAL DEBT $1000
3040	GF87038	Num	24227	24234	8	EXP: OTHER GENERAL EXP $1000
3041	GF87039	Num	24235	24242	8	EXP: UTILITY $1000
3042	GF87040	Num	24243	24250	8	EXP: LIQUOR & INSUR TRUST EXP $1000
3043	GF87041	Num	24251	24258	8	TOTAL DEBT $1000
3044	GF87042	Num	24259	24266	8	TOTAL LONG-TERM DEBT $1000
3045	GF87043	Num	24267	24274	8	TOTAL LONG-TERM DEBT-EDUCATION $1000
3046	GF87044	Num	24275	24282	8	TOTAL LONG-TERM DEBT-UTILITY $1000
3047	GF87045	Num	24283	24290	8	CASH & SECURITIES $1000
3048	GE57001	Num	24291	24298	8	TOTALS: F.T.EMP
3049	GE57002	Num	24299	24306	8	TOTALS: P.T.EMP
3050	GE57003	Num	24307	24314	8	TOTALS: F.T.EQV
3051	GE57005	Num	24315	24322	8	EDUCATION INSTRUCTIONAL: F.T.ONLY

3052	GE62001 Num	24323	24330	8	TOTALS: F.T.EMP
3053	GE62002 Num	24331	24338	8	TOTALS: P.T.EMP
3054	GE62003 Num	24339	24346	8	TOTALS: F.T.EQV
3055	GE62004 Num	24347	24354	8	EDUCATION TOTAL: F.T.EQV
3056	GE62005 Num	24355	24362	8	EDUCATION INSTRUCTIONAL ONLY: F.T.EQV
3057	GE62008 Num	24363	24370	8	HOSPITALS & HEALTH: F.T.EQV
3058	GE62010 Num	24371	24378	8	HIGHWAYS & OTHER TRANSP: F.T.EQV
3059	GE62011 Num	24379	24386	8	POLICE PROTECTION: F.T.EQV
3060	GE62012 Num	24387	24394	8	FIRE PROTECTION: F.T.EQV
3061	GE62020 Num	24395	24402	8	FINANCE & OTHER ADMINISTRATION: F.T.EQV
3062	GE62021 Num	24403	24410	8	UTILITY: F.T.EQV
3063	GE62022 Num	24411	24418	8	OTHER & UNALLOCABLE: F.T.EQV
3064	GE72001 Num	24419	24426	8	TOTALS: F.T.EMP
3065	GE72002 Num	24427	24434	8	TOTALS: P.T.EMP
3066	GE72003 Num	24435	24442	8	TOTALS: F.T.EQV
3067	GE72004 Num	24443	24450	8	EDUCATION TOTAL: F.T.EQV
3068	GE72005 Num	24451	24458	8	EDUCATION INSTRUCTIONAL ONLY: F.T.EQV
3069	GE72006 Num	24459	24466	8	LIBRARIES: F.T.EQV
3070	GE72007 Num	24467	24474	8	PUBLIC WELFARE: F.T.EQV
3071	GE72008 Num	24475	24482	8	HOSPITALS: F.T.EQV
3072	GE72009 Num	24483	24490	8	HEALTH OTHER THAN HOSPITALS: F.T.EQV
3073	GE72010 Num	24491	24498	8	HIGHWAYS & OTHER TRANSP: F.T.EQV
3074	GE72011 Num	24499	24506	8	POLICE PROTECTION: F.T.EQV
3075	GE72012 Num	24507	24514	8	FIRE PROTECTION: F.T.EQV
3076	GE72013 Num	24515	24522	8	NATURAL RESOURCES: F.T.EQV
3077	GE72014 Num	24523	24530	8	PARKS & RECREATION: F.T.EQV
3078	GE72015 Num	24531	24538	8	HOUSING & URBAN RENEWAL: F.T.EQV
3079	GE72016 Num	24539	24546	8	SEWERAGE: F.T.EQV
3080	GE72017 Num	24547	24554	8	SANITATION OTHER THAN SEWERAGE: F.T.EQV
3081	GE72019 Num	24555	24562	8	CORRECTION: F.T.EQV
3082	GE72020 Num	24563	24570	8	FINANCE & OTHER ADMINISTRATION: F.T.EQV
3083	GE72021 Num	24571	24578	8	UTILITY: F.T.EQV
3084	GE72022 Num	24579	24586	8	OTHER & UNALLOCABLE: F.T.EQV
3085	GE77001 Num	24587	24594	8	TOTALS: F.T.EMP
3086	GE77002 Num	24595	24602	8	TOTALS: P.T.EMP
3087	GE77003 Num	24603	24610	8	TOTALS: F.T.EQV
3088	GE77004 Num	24611	24618	8	EDUCATION TOTAL: F.T.EQV
3089	GE77005 Num	24619	24626	8	EDUCATION INSTRUCTIONAL ONLY: F.T.EQV
3090	GE77006 Num	24627	24634	8	LIBRARIES: F.T.EQV

3091	GE77007 Num	24635	24642	8	PUBLIC WELFARE: F.T.EQV
3092	GE77008 Num	24643	24650	8	HOSPITALS: F.T.EQV
3093	GE77009 Num	24651	24658	8	HEALTH OTHER THAN HOSPITALS: F.T.EQV
3094	GE77010 Num	24659	24666	8	HIGHWAYS & OTHER TRANSP: F.T.EQV
3095	GE77011 Num	24667	24674	8	POLICE PROTECTION: F.T.EQV
3096	GE77012 Num	24675	24682	8	FIRE PROTECTION: F.T.EQV
3097	GE77013 Num	24683	24690	8	NATURAL RESOURCES: F.T.EQV
3098	GE77014 Num	24691	24698	8	PARKS & RECREATION: F.T.EQV
3099	GE77015 Num	24699	24706	8	HOUSING & URBAN RENEWAL: F.T.EQV
3100	GE77016 Num	24707	24714	8	SEWERAGE: F.T.EQV
3101	GE77017 Num	24715	24722	8	SANITATION OTHER THAN SEWERAGE: F.T.EQV
3102	GE77019 Num	24723	24730	8	CORRECTION: F.T.EQV
3103	GE77020 Num	24731	24738	8	FINANCE & OTHER ADMINISTRATION: F.T.EQV
3104	GE77021 Num	24739	24746	8	UTILITY: F.T.EQV
3105	GE77022 Num	24747	24754	8	OTHER & UNALLOCABLE: F.T.EQV
3106	GE82001 Num	24755	24762	8	TOTALS: F.T.EMP
3107	GE82002 Num	24763	24770	8	TOTALS: P.T.EMP
3108	GE82003 Num	24771	24778	8	TOTALS: F.T.EQV
3109	GE82004 Num	24779	24786	8	EDUCATION TOTAL: F.T.EQV
3110	GE82005 Num	24787	24794	8	EDUCATION INSTRUCTIONAL ONLY: F.T.EQV
3111	GE82006 Num	24795	24802	8	LIBRARIES: F.T.EQV
3112	GE82007 Num	24803	24810	8	PUBLIC WELFARE: F.T.EQV
3113	GE82008 Num	24811	24818	8	HOSPITALS: F.T.EQV
3114	GE82009 Num	24819	24826	8	HEALTH OTHER THAN HOSPITALS: F.T.EQV
3115	GE82010 Num	24827	24834	8	HIGHWAYS & OTHER TRANSP: F.T.EQV
3116	GE82011 Num	24835	24842	8	POLICE PROTECTION: F.T.EQV
3117	GE82012 Num	24843	24850	8	FIRE PROTECTION: F.T.EQV
3118	GE82013 Num	24851	24858	8	NATURAL RESOURCES: F.T.EQV
3119	GE82014 Num	24859	24866	8	PARKS & RECREATION: F.T.EQV
3120	GE82015 Num	24867	24874	8	HOUSING & URBAN RENEWAL: F.T.EQV
3121	GE82016 Num	24875	24882	8	SEWERAGE: F.T.EQV
3122	GE82017 Num	24883	24890	8	SANITATION OTHER THAN SEWERAGE: F.T.EQV
3123	GE82018 Num	24891	24898	8	JUDICIAL & LEGAL: F.T.EQV
3124	GE82019 Num	24899	24906	8	CORRECTION: F.T.EQV
3125	GE82020 Num	24907	24914	8	FINANCE & OTHER ADMINISTRATION: F.T.EQV
3126	GE82021 Num	24915	24922	8	UTILITY: F.T.EQV
3127	GE82022 Num	24923	24930	8	OTHER & UNALLOCABLE: F.T.EQV
3128	GE87001 Num	24931	24938	8	TOTALS: F.T.EMP
3129	GE87002 Num	24939	24946	8	TOTALS: P.T.EMP

3130	GE87003 Num	24947	24954	8	TOTALS: F.T.EQV
3131	GE87004 Num	24955	24962	8	EDUCATION TOTAL: F.T.EQV
3132	GE87005 Num	24963	24970	8	EDUCATION INSTRUCTIONAL ONLY: F.T.EQV
3133	GE87006 Num	24971	24978	8	LIBRARIES: F.T.EQV
3134	GE87007 Num	24979	24986	8	PUBLIC WELFARE: F.T.EQV
3135	GE87008 Num	24987	24994	8	HOSPITALS: F.T.EQV
3136	GE87009 Num	24995	25002	8	HEALTH OTHER THAN HOSPITALS: F.T.EQV
3137	GE87010 Num	25003	25010	8	HIGHWAYS & OTHER TRANSP: F.T.EQV
3138	GE87011 Num	25011	25018	8	POLICE PROTECTION: F.T.EQV
3139	GE87012 Num	25019	25026	8	FIRE PROTECTION: F.T.EQV
3140	GE87013 Num	25027	25034	8	NATURAL RESOURCES: F.T.EQV
3141	GE87014 Num	25035	25042	8	PARKS & RECREATION: F.T.EQV
3142	GE87015 Num	25043	25050	8	HOUSING & URBAN RENEWAL: F.T.EQV
3143	GE87016 Num	25051	25058	8	SEWERAGE: F.T.EQV
3144	GE87017 Num	25059	25066	8	SANITATION OTHER THAN SEWERAGE: F.T.EQV
3145	GE87018 Num	25067	25074	8	JUDICIAL & LEGAL: F.T.EQV
3146	GE87019 Num	25075	25082	8	CORRECTION: F.T.EQV
3147	GE87020 Num	25083	25090	8	FINANCE & OTHER ADMINISTRATION: F.T.EQV
3148	GE87021 Num	25091	25098	8	UTILITY: F.T.EQV
3149	GE87022 Num	25099	25106	8	OTHER & UNALLOCABLE: F.T.EQV

APPENDIX B

FIPS STATE/COUNTY CODES

FIPS	County
Alabama	
01001	Autauga
01003	Baldwin
01005	Barbour
01007	Bibb
01009	Blount
01011	Bullock
01013	Butler
01015	Calhoun
01017	Chambers
01019	Cherokee
01021	Chilton
01023	Choctaw
01025	Clarke
01027	Clay
01029	Cleburne
01031	Coffee
01033	Colbert
01035	Conecuh
01037	Coosa
01039	Covington
01041	Crenshaw
01043	Cullman
01045	Dale
01047	Dallas
01049	De Kalb
01051	Elmore
01053	Escambia

01055	Etowah
01057	Fayette
01059	Franklin
01061	Geneva
01063	Greene
01065	Hale
01067	Henry
01069	Houston
01071	Jackson
01073	Jefferson
01075	Lamar
01077	Lauderdale
01079	Lawrence
01081	Lee
01083	Limestone
01085	Lowndes
01087	Macon
01089	Madison
01091	Marengo
01093	Marion
01095	Marshall
01097	Mobile
01099	Monroe
01101	Montgomery
01103	Morgan
01105	Perry
01107	Pickens
01109	Pike
01111	Randolph
01113	Russell
01115	St. Clair
01117	Shelby
01119	Sumter
01121	Talladega
01123	Tallapoosa

01125	Tuscaloosa
01127	Walker
01129	Washington
01131	Wilcox
01133	Winston

Florida

12001	Alachua
12003	Baker
12005	Bay
12007	Bradford
12009	Brevard
12011	Broward
12013	Calhoun
12015	Charlotte
12017	Citrus
12019	Clay
12021	Collier
12023	Columbia
12025	Dade
12027	De Soto
12029	Dixie
12031	Duval
12033	Escambia
12035	Flagler
12037	Franklin
12039	Gadsden
12041	Gilchrist
12043	Glades
12045	Gulf
12047	Hamilton
12049	Hardee
12051	Hendry
12053	Hernando
12055	Highlands

12057	Hillsborough
12059	Holmes
12061	Indian River
12063	Jackson
12065	Jefferson
12067	Lafayette
12069	Lake
12071	Lee
12073	Leon
12075	Levy
12077	Liberty
12079	Madison
12081	Manatee
12083	Marion
12085	Martin
12087	Monroe
12089	Nassau
12091	Okaloosa
12093	Okeechobee
12095	Orange
12097	Osceola
12099	Palm Beach
12101	Pasco
12103	Pinellas
12105	Polk
12107	Putnam
12109	St. Johns
12111	St. Lucie
12113	Santa Rosa
12115	Sarasota
12117	Seminole
12119	Sumter
12121	Suwannee
12123	Taylor
12125	Union

12127	Volusia
12129	Wakulla
12131	Walton
12133	Washington

Louisiana

22001	Acadia
22003	Allen
22005	Ascension
22007	Assumption
22009	Avoyelles
22011	Beauregard
22013	Bienville
22015	Bossier
22017	Caddo
22019	Calcasieu
22021	Caldwell
22023	Cameron
22025	Catahoula
22027	Claiborne
22029	Concordia
22031	De Soto
22033	East Baton Rouge
22035	East Carroll
22037	East Feliciana
22039	Evangeline
22041	Franklin
22043	Grant
22045	Iberia
22047	Iberville
22049	Jackson
22051	Jefferson
22053	Jefferson Davis
22055	Lafayette
22057	Lafourche

22059	La Salle
22061	Lincoln
22063	Livingston
22065	Madison
22067	Morehouse
22069	Natchitoches
22071	Orleans
22073	Ouachita
22075	Plaquemines
22077	Pointe Coupee
22079	Rapides
22081	Red River
22083	Richland
22085	Sabine
22087	St. Bernard
22089	St. Charles
22091	St. Helena
22093	St. James
22095	St. John the Baptist
22097	St. Landry
22099	St. Martin
22101	St. Mary
22103	St. Tammany
22105	Tangipahoa
22107	Tensas
22109	Terrebonne
22111	Union
22113	Vermilion
22115	Vernon
22117	Washington
22119	Webster
22121	West Baton Rouge
22123	West Carroll
22125	West Feliciana
22127	Winn

Mississippi

28001	Adams
28003	Alcorn
28005	Amite
28007	Attala
28009	Benton
28011	Bolivar
28013	Calhoun
28015	Carroll
28017	Chickasaw
28019	Choctaw
28021	Claiborne
28023	Clarke
28025	Clay
28027	Coahoma
28029	Copiah
28031	Covington
28033	De Soto
28035	Forrest
28037	Franklin
28039	George
28041	Greene
28043	Grenada
28045	Hancock
28047	Harrison
28049	Hinds
28051	Holmes
28053	Humphreys
28055	Issaquena
28057	Itawamba
28059	Jackson
28061	Jasper
28063	Jefferson
28065	Jefferson Davis

28067	Jones
28069	Kemper
28071	Lafayette
28073	Lamar
28075	Lauderdale
28077	Lawrence
28079	Leake
28081	Lee
28083	Leflore
28085	Lincoln
28087	Lowndes
28089	Madison
28091	Marion
28093	Marshall
28095	Monroe
28097	Montgomery
28099	Neshoba
28101	Newton
28103	Noxubee
28105	Oktibbeha
28107	Panola
28109	Pearl River
28111	Perry
28113	Pike
28115	Pontotoc
28117	Prentiss
28119	Quitman
28121	Rankin
28123	Scott
28125	Sharkey
28127	Simpson
28129	Smith
28131	Stone
28133	Sunflower
28135	Tallahatchie

28137	Tate
28139	Tippah
28141	Tishomingo
28143	Tunica
28145	Union
28147	Walthall
28149	Warren
28151	Washington
28153	Wayne
28155	Webster
28157	Wilkinson
28159	Winston
28161	Yalobusha
28163	Yazoo

Texas

48001	Anderson
48003	Andrews
48005	Angelina
48007	Aransas
48009	Archer
48011	Armstrong
48013	Atascosa
48015	Austin
48017	Bailey
48019	Bandera
48021	Bastrop
48023	Baylor
48025	Bee
48027	Bell
48029	Bexar
48031	Blanco
48033	Borden
48035	Bosque
48037	Bowie

48039	Brazoria
48041	Brazos
48043	Brewster
48045	Briscoe
48047	Brooks
48049	Brown
48051	Burleson
48053	Burnet
48055	Caldwell
48057	Calhoun
48059	Callahan
48061	Cameron
48063	Camp
48065	Carson
48067	Cass
48069	Castro
48071	Chambers
48073	Cherokee
48075	Childress
48077	Clay
48079	Cochran
48081	Coke
48083	Coleman
48085	Collin
48087	Collingsworth
48089	Colorado
48091	Comal
48093	Comanche
48095	Concho
48097	Cooke
48099	Coryell
48101	Cottle
48103	Crane
48105	Crockett
48107	Crosby

48109	Culberson
48111	Dallam
48113	Dallas
48115	Dawson
48117	Deaf Smith
48119	Delta
48121	Denton
48123	De Witt
48125	Dickens
48127	Dimmit
48129	Donley
48131	Duval
48133	Eastland
48135	Ector
48137	Edwards
48139	Ellis
48141	El Paso
48143	Erath
48145	Falls
48147	Fannin
48149	Fayette
48151	Fisher
48153	Floyd
48155	Foard
48157	Fort Bend
48159	Franklin
48161	Freestone
48163	Frio
48165	Gaines
48167	Galveston
48169	Garza
48171	Gillespie
48173	Glasscock
48175	Goliad
48177	Gonzales

48179	Gray
48181	Grayson
48183	Gregg
48185	Grimes
48187	Guadalupe
48189	Hale
48191	Hall
48193	Hamilton
48195	Hansford
48197	Hardeman
48199	Hardin
48201	Harris
48203	Harrison
48205	Hartley
48207	Haskell
48209	Hays
48211	Hemphill
48213	Henderson
48215	Hidalgo
48217	Hill
48219	Hockley
48221	Hood
48223	Hopkins
48225	Houston
48227	Howard
48229	Hudspeth
48231	Hunt
48233	Hutchinson
48235	Irion
48237	Jack
48239	Jackson
48241	Jasper
48243	Jeff Davis
48245	Jefferson
48247	Jim Hogg

48249	Jim Wells
48251	Johnson
48253	Jones
48255	Karnes
48257	Kaufman
48259	Kendall
48261	Kenedy
48263	Kent
48265	Kerr
48267	Kimble
48269	King
48271	Kinney
48273	Kleberg
48275	Knox
48277	Lamar
48279	Lamb
48281	Lampasas
48283	La Salle
48285	Lavaca
48287	Lee
48289	Leon
48291	Liberty
48293	Limestone
48295	Lipscomb
48297	Live Oak
48299	Llano
48301	Loving
48303	Lubbock
48305	Lynn
48307	McCulloch
48309	McLennan
48311	McMullen
48313	Madison
48315	Marion
48317	Martin

48319	Mason
48321	Matagorda
48323	Maverick
48325	Medina
48327	Menard
48329	Midland
48331	Milam
48333	Mills
48335	Mitchell
48337	Montague
48339	Montgomery
48341	Moore
48343	Morris
48345	Motley
48347	Nacogdoches
48349	Navarro
48351	Newton
48353	Nolan
48355	Nueces
48357	Ochiltree
48359	Oldham
48361	Orange
48363	Palo Pinto
48365	Panola
48367	Parker
48369	Parmer
48371	Pecos
48373	Polk
48375	Potter
48377	Presidio
48379	Rains
48381	Randall
48383	Reagan
48385	Real
48387	Red River

48389	Reeves
48391	Refugio
48393	Roberts
48395	Robertson
48397	Rockwall
48399	Runnels
48401	Rusk
48403	Sabine
48405	San Augustine
48407	San Jacinto
48409	San Patricio
48411	San Saba
48413	Schleicher
48415	Scurry
48417	Shackelford
48419	Shelby
48421	Sherman
48423	Smith
48425	Somervell
48427	Starr
48429	Stephens
48431	Sterling
48433	Stonewall
48435	Sutton
48437	Swisher
48439	Tarrant
48441	Taylor
48443	Terrell
48445	Terry
48447	Throckmorton
48449	Titus
48451	Tom Green
48453	Travis
48455	Trinity
48457	Tyler

48459	Upshur
48461	Upton
48463	Uvalde
48465	Val Verde
48467	Van Zandt
48469	Victoria
48471	Walker
48473	Waller
48475	Ward
48477	Washington
48479	Webb
48481	Wharton
48483	Wheeler
48485	Wichita
48487	Wilbarger
48489	Willacy
48491	Williamson
48493	Wilson
48495	Winkler
48497	Wise
48499	Wood
48501	Yoakum
48503	Young
48505	Zapata
48507	Zavala

The Department of the Interior Mission

As the Nation's principal conservation agency, the Department of the Interior has responsibility for most of our nationally owned public lands and natural resources. This includes fostering sound use of our land and water resources; protecting our fish, wildlife, and biological diversity; preserving the environmental and cultural values of our national parks and historical places; and providing for the enjoyment of life through outdoor recreation. The Department assesses our energy and mineral resources and works to ensure that their development is in the best interests of all our people by encouraging stewardship and citizen participation in their care. The Department also has a major responsibility for American Indian reservation communities and for people who live in island territories under U.S. administration.

The Minerals Management Service Mission

As a bureau of the Department of the Interior, the Minerals Management Service's (MMS) primary responsibilities are to manage the mineral resources located on the Nation's Outer Continental Shelf (OCS), collect revenue from the Federal OCS and onshore Federal and Indian lands, and distribute those revenues.

Moreover, in working to meet its responsibilities, the **Offshore Minerals Management Program** administers the OCS competitive leasing program and oversees the safe and environmentally sound exploration and production of our Nation's offshore natural gas, oil and other mineral resources. The MMS **Minerals Revenue Management** meets its responsibilities by ensuring the efficient, timely and accurate collection and disbursement of revenue from mineral leasing and production due to Indian tribes and allottees, States and the U.S. Treasury.

The MMS strives to fulfill its responsibilities through the general guiding principles of: (1) being responsive to the public's concerns and interests by maintaining a dialogue with all potentially affected parties and (2) carrying out its programs with an emphasis on working to enhance the quality of life for all Americans by lending MMS assistance and expertise to economic development and environmental protection.

www.ingramcontent.com/pod-product-compliance
Lightning Source LLC
Chambersburg PA
CBHW051958280526
45793CB00005B/772